Why Man Takes Chances

Contributors

Jessie Bernard, Ph.D.
Research Scholar *honoris causa,* Pennsylvania State University

Kenneth D. Burke
Professor Emeritus of Literary Criticism, Bennington College

David Brion Davis, Ph.D.
Professor of History, Cornell University

Richard A. Falk, J.S.D.
Professor of International Law, Woodrow Wilson School of Public and International Affairs, Princeton University

Charles S. Houston, M.D.
Professor of Community Medicine, College of Medicine, The University of Vermont

Samuel Z. Klausner, Ed.D., Ph.D.
Associate Professor of Sociology, University of Pennsylvania

Samuel L. A. Marshall
Brigadier General, USAR (Ret.)

Elton B. McNeil, Ph.D.
Professor of Psychology, The University of Michigan

E. Paul Torrance, Ph.D.
Professor of Educational Psychology, The University of Georgia

Why Man Takes Chances

STUDIES IN STRESS-SEEKING

EDITED, WITH A FOREWORD, BY

Samuel Z. Klausner

ANCHOR BOOKS
DOUBLEDAY & COMPANY, INC.
GARDEN CITY, NEW YORK
1968

The Anchor Books edition is
the first publication of *Why Man Takes Chances*

Anchor Books edition: 1968

Foreword

Some men are peaceable, but not many among our companions. Meditative souls are lost among the passionate and activist in our society. This striving, with its conflictual and competitive accompaniments, is said to be our response to stress, our way of coping with the world. Stress, anxiety, and fear are considered unwanted states imposed by a cruel environment—by our corrupt fellows, by a harsh natural world, and by a devilish internal legacy of our formative years.

The assumption is that man, left to himself, would prefer not to strive. Individuals who in times of tranquillity seek adventure, "look for trouble," "spoil for a fight," or go through life with "chips on their shoulders" are colloquially recognized as "deviant" types. The businessman who admits to enjoying the risks concomitant to competitive struggle is accepted but is pitied or feared. Only in play and sports can an individual who creates artificial obstacles, pursues contests, and tempts fear achieve full toleration. A sportsman who values the prize above the thrill of contest is held to distort the meaning of the game.

Scientific theory adumbrates these colloquial attitudes. The scientific investigator's empathy is with the man who rationally weighs his goals and rationally selects means appropriate to them, risking himself only as required for their achievement. Affectual and traditional action, to use Max Weber's categories—action in which the calculation of costs is not central—are treated as variants of the ideal rational type. One quickly infers that the "advance" of civilization consists in the displacement of nonrational by rational action. From this vantage, some behavioral theorists associate stress acceptance with the seeking of an ulterior goal. Games are played for the enhancement of victory. Wars are fought to assure markets or living space. Business is pursued for profits. Crime is a shortcut to economic fruits. These goals or motives are, of course, incontrovertible. Yet, they only partially account for a loser's interest in continuing the game, the United States' entry into the Spanish-American War, haggling in an oriental bazaar, the persistence of business despite a government curb on profits, or the young criminal's destruction rather than consumption of illegitimately obtained booty.

Such observations suggest that some individuals seek danger and search for problems resistant to solution, and even seek the stress, fear, or anxiety engendered by such encounters. In this activity, these negative emotions seem swept up in excitement, adventure, or challenge. Individuals and groups promote stress through the play conflict of sports and through the "real" social conflict of business, war, and crime; through engaging the challenge of the natural environment in changing the landscape or exploring land that resists exploration; or in creating an aesthetic entity out of an undirected shape; through changing the mental and physical self by learning; or by mastering behavior against the contrary press of emotion. The individual's reflexive struggle encompasses his struggles with other men and with nature. Commitment to an engagement presupposes that the social or the natural protagonists and antagonists have been internalized.

What types of men, what types of societies are more prone to seek stress by pitting themselves against a resistance? Under what conditions are they apt to do so? What societal arrangements are made for promoting, facilitating, and controlling stress-seeking behavior? When does this tendency ally itself with hostile emotions and eventuate in aggression, and when does it ally itself with a "moral equivalent of war" and advance the creative development of the individual or of his society?

The phenomenon of stress-seeking has been examined under many guises. Charles Darwin documented a pervasive struggle in the biotic world. Struggle was immanent in life and determined by conditions external to the struggling species. Late epigones have read natural selection as purposeful evolutionary development. Sigmund Freud wrote of *eros,* a life instinct, a need for stimulation in constant tension with *thanatos,* a death instinct, a need to reduce the level of tension. Otto Fenichel analyzed the counterphobic attitude of seeking fear-provoking situations so that, by mastering them, more basic anxieties could be fended off. Erik Erikson traces growth stages emerging from successive resolutions of developmental conflicts. The type of resolution at each stage affects the nature of the succeeding stage of growth. By failing to engage the conflict typical of a given stage, the individual fails to progress properly to the next stage. Gregory Bateson and Anton Boisen have understood schizophrenia as one manifestation of an inner struggle over alternative ultimate values. Students of sensory deprivation have observed a need for stimulation—perhaps to compensate for its lack but also to expel frightening imagery released by the cessation of external stimulation. D. E. Berlyne wrote of "epistemic curiosity" driving individuals to explore and to change themselves in the process.

Stress-seeking also has its social outcomes. David McClelland described an achievement need which emerges when there is a gap between a person's aspiration and his perception of his present condition. Where there is an achievement need there may be a risk-taker—an individual who enjoys a challenge. A good population of risk-takers, particularly as economic entrepreneurs, enhances the probability of economic development of society. Arnold Toynbee traced conditions under which some societies successfully respond to challenge as well as those under which they do not, in accounting for the rise and fall of civilizations. Lewis Coser described "struggle groups" in pursuit of particular goals. Achievement of the original goal may spark interest in finding new bases for conflict; in this way, conflict may become functionally autonomous. According to Georg Simmel, conflict and cooperation are interwoven forms of sociation alternating in priority to produce a war-peace rhythm.

The term "tropism," coming to us from an earlier biology, recalls unconscious or instinctual aspects of the stress-seeking behavior of both individuals and societies. Stress-seeking is a kind of voluntary tropistic behavior.

On November 11 and 12, 1966, the editor met with the eight other contributors to this volume. The goal of the conference was to draw together psychological, sociological, anthropological, and literary materials related to voluntary stress-seeking or tropistic behavior in man—methods of studying it, a description of some situations in which it occurs, personality and social conditions that favor and channel it—to integrate the concept of stress-seeking in a broader theory of human behavior. The conferees had read the vague description of stress-seeking essentially as given above. They had been asked to analyze stress-seeking behavior from the perspective of their own work.

Each author blended this initial vague image of stress-seeking with his own experience. As a result, the papers were not consistent in assigning priority to a single type of stress-seeker. To focus on a single type would have had obvious advantages for exploration of the concept in depth. Alternatively, to crystallize the image at this stage could be counterproductive. The most fruitful direction of inquiry might well be inspired by the imagery of some contributor other than the editor.

The nine papers comprising this volume are revisions of those presented at the conference. Three quite different "real-life" pictures of stress-seekers are drawn in the first part of this volume. Jessie Bernard's stress-seeker is Dionysian, heroic, ecstatic, and above all, irrational. Charles Houston's image is of a rational planner, exposing himself to controlled risks, plodding, pulling, and stretching toward self-fulfillment. Samuel L. A. Marshall argues that the difference between the dramatic stress of the soldier and the simple stresses of everyday life is only one of degree. Whether explosive or controlled, planned or irrational, Marshall reminds us that what is stressful pioneering effort for one may be an easy, well-trod path for another.

The second part of the volume shifts from these real-life stress-seekers to the images of the novelist. In evolving the interplay of protagonists and antagonists, he reaches for an understanding of the stress-seeker and through the literary medium attempts to transmit this understanding to others. Kenneth Burke's stress-seeker is the product of a divided self, "homeopathically" calming his troubled imaginings by creating actual troubles and then throwing himself into them. David B. Davis tries to understand the stress-seeking American through the image projected in his literature. Davis' stress-seeker lives like a tightrope walker balanced between the death of conformity on the one side and the death of excessive stress on the other. He may be a ruthless and daring strong man who reverts to the wild to regenerate his self.

The third part of this volume supplements these literary insights into the motivation of stress-seekers with three fragments of empirically based theories. Samuel Z. Klausner turns to the apparent paradox of individuals drawn to painful situations and argues that pleasure and pain are alternative appraisals of the same underlying excitement. He explains the rationality and egocentricity of some stress-seekers by applying concepts from ego psychology. Elton B. McNeil compares stress-seekers who attain political leadership to delinquents—both are impulsive, want power, and suffer from defective egos. E. Paul Torrance classifies stress-seekers according to whether their behavior is a response to inner forces, to outer challenges, or to threats, and then examines the influence of culture in producing one or another of these types.

The concluding paper by Richard A. Falk takes society as the stress-seeker. He posits a competition for dominance, correlated with stress-seeking, persisting in relations between states. A rule of law is needed to provide a framework for this competition lest it escalate into destructiveness.

The conference on Stress-seeking in Man, upon which this volume is based, was supported by the Office of Scientific Research of the United States Air Force under Contract AF 49(638)–1510 with the Bureau of Social Science Research, Inc.

Samuel Z. Klausner

Washington, D.C.
April 14, 1967

Be strong and courageous—
Joshua 1:6

—exercise good manners.
Rashi's comment

Contents

PART IV: STRESS-SEEKING AND THE LEGAL ORDER

PART I

Stress-seekers in Everyday Life

Jessie Bernard

The impact of social institutions on human relationships has been a persistent theme in Jessie Bernard's research. In 1939 she published, together with her then associates in the Department of Labor, A. D. H. Kaplan and F. M. Williams, a volume entitled *Family Income and Expenditure in the Southeastern Region, 1935–1936.** Three intellectual seeds that would germinate during the succeeding years were discernible in this study: concern with the family as a social institution; with the relation of the family to other, particularly economic, institutions; and an interest in family life in the American Southeast. Her interest in a quantitative-empirical approach to family sociology had been reflected in a study employing demographic data in the study of the family and reported in 1934 in the article "Factors in the Distribution of Success in Marriage." "Differential Influence of the Business Cycle on the Number of Marriages in Several Age Groupings," published in 1940, applied quantitative methods in studying an interinstitutional relation.

The role of social norms in regulating family relationships provided the conceptual underpinning for *American Family Behavior*, published in 1942. A mass of statistical material is presented in this work showing the economic condition and the social position of the contemporary American family. She asked, "Is the American family, as it exists today, fulfilling its functions of providing protection for its members and of socializing children?" What happens when there is an "aberration of affections" in a family? A chapter on family "conflict" harbingered later work, and one on the "Theory of Love" scientifically illuminated individualistic romantic love in America.

Just seven years later, *American Community Behavior* was a popular sociology text. Jessie Bernard's in-

---

* Bibliographic information about writings mentioned in this and the following introductions may be found in the listing, Selected Works of the Contributors, after the last article in this volume.

terest turned toward relations among the ethnic, religious, and racial groups that constitute the community. Conflicts between labor and management and between the consumer and the marketer were pointed up as focal community processes. By emphasizing the role of institutional norms in mediating these conflicts, Jessie Bernard was staking a claim for sociology in an area dominated by psychologists. Intergroup conflicts tended to be examined more in the light of sociological than of cultural or personality variables. The discussion of family conflict in the previous work was here extended to include consideration of community violence. Violence is ubiquitous in human culture but should be examined in terms of what she would now call its "eufunctions" as well as its "dysfunctions."

During the past fifteen years, Jessie Bernard has returned to analyze adjustments in family life, again giving priority to social norms over psychological factors. Previous work tended to attribute marital failure to personality factors. *Remarriage* reported on 2009 people who had been involved in more than one marriage. By observing the same individuals in more than one relationship she could analyze the viability of specific matings.

Jessie Bernard has observed that women holding the doctorate tend to be more intelligent, as measured by tests, than men holding that degree; yet, during their subsequent academic life, the doctoral women tend to be less productive than the doctoral men. In *Academic Women* she attempts to explain this anomaly. Women scholars tend to gravitate to the type of academic positions that are less conducive to productivity. This book documents the decrease from 30 per cent to 20 per cent in college teaching positions held by women between the First World War and the present.

She has now returned to the study of conflict. In 1950 she had asked, "Where is the Modern Sociology of Conflict?" Her question was catalytic. In 1965 she was able to respond to it in an article entitled "Some Current Conceptualizations in the Field of Conflict."

The southeastern United States is again a focus of her most recent work, *Marriage and the Family Among Negroes*. From the time of emancipation until the First World War, the proportion of Negro children born out of wedlock each year was decreasing. From then to the present day this proportion has been increasing. This trend is analyzed in terms of the impact of social institutions on individual behavior—here, the effect of urbanization and the depression on the behavior of both Negro men and Negro women.

Jessie Bernard's paper on stress-seeking is rooted in her studies of conflict. Her stress-seeker is a combatant, expressing his "primal strength," and consuming energy and generating energy in the process. He is fierce and frenzied, possessed of a "happy spirit"—a eudaemonist. Doubtless, such eudaemonic citizens exist in the nooks and crannies of all societies. They may become a ruling elite. Eudaemonists may war against others or against nature. The vicarious eustress of the drama and the simulated eustress of mock combat are enjoyable to them.

Why does eudaemonism take the form it does in a particular society and culture? Social-science theory, even the theory of conflict, has not always faced this question. Sociologists have found it difficult to assimilate nonrational behavior to their models, preferring theories of exchange resting upon computed advantages and disadvantages. Jessie Bernard explores a number of social factors accounting for eudaemonistic stress-seeking. Eudaemonistic behavior is youthful behavior; the upper classes contribute to its prestige by honoring militancy. Some cultures are active and others meditative, but there is little evidence on how they become so. Puritanism fought the eudaemonic hero-warrior pleasuring himself with the world and converted him into a capitalist risk-taker, a keeper of rational accounts. Women can be as eudaemonistic as men, though with a difference—"Minerva's wars were defensive, Mars' offensive." A Puritan society has been slow to recognize sexually eudaemonic women, though it recognizes the role of women in inciting men to war.

THE EUDAEMONISTS

And, you all know, security
Is mortals' chiefest enemy.

(*Hecate in "Macbeth"*
Act III, Scene 5)

SOME PRELIMINARY COMMENTS

The prospectus for this conference invited us to explore, under the general umbrella rubric "stress-seeking," such variegated phenomena as the active and voluntary seeking of danger; the searching for problems resistant to solution; the seeking out of excitement, adventure, challenge; the participation in individual and team sports; social conflict in business, war, and crime; exploration, artistic creativity, achievement, struggle with men and with nature; and personal commitment and learning which demand hard effort.

Rational stress-seeking in the sense of stresses "acceptable only as an unavoidable concomitant to the attainment of an ulterior goal," that is, as part of the means toward an end, is not relevant for our purposes. Difficult as it may be to understand, explain, or interpret the goals of some individuals and societies, once they are given, it is not necessarily difficult to explain the stresses people are willing to endure to achieve them. Indeed, a great deal of modern theory of conflict is designed for precisely this type of rationalistic model, a model in which parties balance the costs and the gains to be expected from different courses of action and behave in a manner to minimize one and maximize the other. A considerable literature on the nature of rationality undergirds this kind of theory, for, in general, it is almost by definition rational in the means-end sense.[1]

[1] ". . defining 'rational,' 'consistent,' or 'non-contradictory' for

But, Dr. Klausner reminds us, some people "may seek danger and its attendant stress, fear, or anxiety . . . in the form of excitement, adventure, or challenge," not as the accepted means toward ends, but regardless of them. How do they fit into our theoretical constructs? What provision do our theories make for them? "What types of men are more prone to seek tension and conflict? Under what conditions are they apt to do so? What societal arrangements are made for promoting, facilitating, and controlling tension and conflict?" To flesh out our understanding of these phenomena is our assignment here.

From out of this array of problems, my own thinking has been directed by Dr. Klausner toward the relevance of social conflict. I am not asked to explain or interpret the individual psychological mechanisms, normal or pathological, that lead people to stress-seeking. The sadist or the compulsive can be ignored. Dr. Klausner has himself summarized some of the efforts by psychologists, psychoanalysts, and anthropologists—Freud, Fenichel, Erikson, Bateson, Boisen, Berlyne, and McClelland—in this direction. "If," he says, "we start by saying that [for whatever reason] people look for trouble, or that societies in Toynbee-like manner seek their challenges, then we could try to identify mechanisms that promote and control this process." I am to begin, then, with givens—that is, with acceptance of the fact that people do, indeed, seek stress in the forms of adventure, excitement, challenge, opponents worthy of their steel. What, then, do societies do to promote and control this activity?

A SEMANTIC DISTINCTION: DYS- AND EUSTRESS

We are somewhat handicapped in our discussion because there is by no means consensus with respect to the use of terms. Since the work of Freud and Hans Selye, stress has been viewed as essentially a pathogenic factor and—beyond

---

interdependent decisions is . . . part of the business of game theory." T. C. Schelling, "What is Game Theory?" (mimeographed; June 1966), p. 5.

the necessary stress involved in the socialization process—
something to be minimized, if not wholly avoided. This
view rests on a homeostatic conception of the human
body, one that sees it as admirably equipped to give apt
responses to threats from the outside and thus to preserve
normal functioning; but, this view states, if—as occurs frequently in this day and age—the body's responses are inept,
illnesses rather than balanced functioning result. Research
has tended to emphasize this aspect of stress.[2] There has
been relatively little attention to any other kind, especially
to the kind we are examining here.

It may be useful to apply different terms to different
kinds of stress. The unpleasant, even painful, kind of stress
studied by Selye and his followers may be referred to as
dys-stress; the pleasant kind, which Dr. Klausner asks us to
explore here, as eustress. Both may be voluntary. Voluntary
dys-stress is the kind associated with the assumption of
activities and responsibilities beyond the call of duty; no
one is forcing the unmarried woman, let us say, to support
her ill brother's family, but she assumes this disagreeable
responsibility voluntarily. This too, in a way, is stress-
seeking. Such dys-stress is difficult, sometimes depressing.
It is associated with the Protestant Ethic, with Puritanism,
with bluenoses. Eustress, contrariwise, is associated with
excitement, adventure, thrilling experiences. It is fun, it enhances vital sensations, it "turns people on," it releases
energy. Indeed, one of the reasons for studying stress-
seeking, as Dr. Klausner notes, lies in the key it may supply for unlocking the "motivational reservoir for social
action."[3] If we can learn how to make activities eustressful,

[2] Some writers distinguish between the outside factor which threatens the organism and the organism's response. Thus Langner's study
of mental health in midtown Manhattan referred to the outside factors as stresses and the internal responses as strains. See Thomas S.
Langner and Stanley T. Michael, *Life Stress and Mental Health* (New
York: The Free Press, 1963), pp. 6–7. See also Jessie Bernard, *Social
Problems at Midcentury* (New York: Holt, Rinehart & Winston, Inc.,
1957), Chapter 4.

[3] The practice of labeling social action "crusades," with overtones
of warlike excitement, reflects intuitive recognition of Dr. Klausner's
point by popular leaders.

we may find ways to motivate at least some people to engage in them.[4]

EUDAEMONISM

Both rational and non-, even antirational, behavior have long been recognized as intrinsic to human beings. Sometimes one kind is emphasized, sometimes another:

> The intellectual climate of the West seems to show oscillations between strong emphasis on the rationalistic aspects of human nature and strong emphasis on the nonrationalistic aspects. The late eighteenth century has come to be known as the Age of Reason because man was viewed as essentially rational. Both economics and political theory reflected this view. The rational man maximized his gains, minimized his losses. When or if all men behaved this way, the result was an efficient economy. In the nineteenth century there was a swing away from the emphasis on reason toward emphasis on emotions. The Romantic Movement in literature played up feeling rather than reason. In psychology, instinct came to overshadow reason in the interpretation of human behavior. In sociology, Sumner, who emphasized the non-rational, overshadowed Ward, who emphasized the rational. The apotheosis of the nonrationalistic came with Freud, who revealed such—from the rationalistic point of view—irrational behavior as masochism and the death instinct.[5]

The contrasting nature of these two views was a major preoccupation of thinkers in the nineteenth century. The antithesis provided "great fun for critics and philosophers for generations. Herder, Schiller, Hegel have played with it; Spengler [took] it up. . . ."[6] But its most dramatic statement was that of Nietzsche in the form of "Dionysianism" versus "Apollonianism." He became the great apolo-

---

[4] It is alleged that total lack of eustress in schoolwork contributes to dropouts. Pupils are bored, suffer dys-stress. If learning can be made exciting, it may be more appealing to eustress-seekers.

[5] Jessie Bernard, "Some Current Conceptualizations in the Field of Conflict," *American Journal of Sociology*, Vol. 70 (January 1965), pp. 442–43.

[6] Crane Brinton, *Nietzsche* (Cambridge: Harvard University Press, 1941), p. 39.

gist and advocate of Dionysianism. For him it was the natural, the spontaneous, the untrammeled, even the wild. Crane Brinton has summarized Nietzsche's statement of the great antithesis as follows:

> The Birth of Tragedy from the Spirit of Music . . . was . . . a brief, lively, and literary defense of an old thesis in philosophy, an old folk-belief among German intellectuals. According to Nietzsche, art—and therefore, of course, everything in human life—has two poles, the Dionysian and the Apollonian. The Dionysian is A Good Thing: it is God's and Nature's primal strength, the unending turbulent lust and longing in men which drives them to conquest, to drunkenness, to mystic ecstasy, to love-deaths. The Apollonian is A Bad Thing—though not unattractive in its proper place: it is man's attempt to stop this unending struggle, to find peace, harmony, balance, to restrain the brute in himself. But the brute is life, and cannot be long restrained.[7]

Max Weber spoke of "eudaemonism,"[8] which, I take it, refers essentially to what Nietzsche meant by Dionysianism. And I will use it as a shortcut term for the kind of eustress-seeking under exploration here. Eudaemonism, then, is in the Nietzschean sense A Good Thing, an unending struggle, an expression of primal strength, a "lust for life" that cannot be long restrained. Actually, even Nietzsche recognized that it does become restrained;[9] no society could maintain any kind of order with unrestrained eudaemonism. It is not a matter of eliminating eudaemonism but one of finding suitable expressions for it. Even Christianity, which Nietzsche hated because it seemed to him to repress eustress-seeking, found acceptable ways for eudaemonic expression in crusades, revivals, cults. Eudaemonism is not here viewed as intrinsically good in the Nietzschean sense or as intrinsically bad in the Apollonian sense. It is the form it takes that invites judgment.

---

[7] Brinton, *op. cit.*, p. 39.

[8] Max Weber, *The Protestant Ethic and The Spirit of Capitalism* (New York: Charles Scribner's Sons, 1948), p. 78.

[9] Nietzsche himself noted that the Apollonian ethos won with Socrates and Euripides, and Greek culture became, in Brinton's words, "restrained, harmonious, gentlemanly, reasonable, beautiful—and dead" (Brinton, *op. cit.*, p. 39).

HUMAN ENERGY AS AN ARTICLE OF CONSUMPTION

John Dewey reminded us that we err if we approach human behavior as though activity were the thing that required explanation, as though passivity were the natural state of the organism, which required a stimulus to set it in motion, to respond. Activity, he noted, except among the sick and old who have to conserve energy, is the natural state of man. The social scientist can begin with activity as given, leaving to the physiologist and the biochemist the explanations of it. What needs explanation by the social scientist is not the activity of the organism but the form or direction it takes.

We are accustomed to thinking of human physical energy, along with other forms of energy, as a factor of economic production. In the form of labor it is invested in work of different kinds. But human physical energy may also be viewed as an item of consumption. Human physical energy may be consumed in many ways besides work; eustress-seeking is one. Among the most basic considerations for such use, therefore, must be the amount of human physical energy available. The form that eudaemonism takes can be expected to be related to the physical resources available.[10]

Dr. Klausner has shown that stress-seeking in the form of sport parachuting is related to individual differences in physical energy; "thrilled" jumpers differ from "tempered"

[10] Samuel Z. Klausner, "The Transformation of Fear" (mimeographed; Washington, D.C.: Bureau of Social Science Research, Inc., 1966). Dr. Klausner points out that eustress is not necessarily energy-consuming, that it may be energy-productive or energy-mobilizing. In fact, he is of the opinion that eustress-seeking may release energy for constructive social activities. It is, indeed, true that most people have great untapped energy resources that they are themselves unaware of. People often surprise themselves in an emergency when they find themselves undertaking feats they never felt themselves capable of. Still, there is a strong energy component in active forms of eustress-seeking. In some cases, in fact, the eustress-seeking is precisely a test of the eudaemonist's endurance, as Dr. Houston's paper on mountain climbing in this volume illustrates.

jumpers in several energy-related ways. They are more energetic, less accident-prone, and feel less endangered than the "tempered"; the adaptation to fear is more active among the "thrilled," more passive among the "tempered"; the attitudes toward women differ among the two types also.[11]

These findings suggest that in times and places where hunger was a constant threat, if not an actuality, we would expect relatively little active stress-seeking. Nor would we expect much active stress-seeking in a society suffering from malnutrition.[12] Energy-conserving rather than energy-consuming forms of eudaemonism would be expectable. If there is a human need for stress-seeking, it would have to be satisfied with forms that did not make large demands on limited physiological resources. Drug- or vision-induced mystical experience, for example. Or vicarious forms.

---

[11] If the individual differences found by Dr. Klausner among skydivers are so great, then the differences in energy available to them and to those who find more sedentary, even vicarious, forms enough to satisfy them must be much greater.

[12] We are reminded of the alleged German control of occupied territories by means of planned nutritional deficiencies designed to prevent dangerous resistance activities in the underground. Alvin Schorr has also noted the possibly functional apathy of the slum-dweller who, because of nutritional inadequacy, must conserve his energies. We are told that missionaries to China used to report that Chinese children did not have the "play instinct," as Western children did. But when better agricultural methods produced adequate nutrition, these children, like children everywhere, began to play. T. B. Veblen believed that savages were peaceable; when they passed to a predatory life, "aggression becomes the accredited form of action." This change came, he believed, with technological advances (*Theory of the Leisure Class*, New York: The Macmillan Co., 1917, pp. 17, 20). Veblen did not deny that conflict occurred at the pre-predatory stages of development. What changed was the attitude toward it. The predatory phase was reached "when the fight has become the dominant note . . . when the common-sense appreciation of men and things has come to be an appreciation with a view to combat" (p. 19). A more adequate food supply may be inferred. Historians of the French Revolution long ago noted that it was not among the poorest and the hungriest that it was fomented but among the more prosperous. For a statement of the converse theory, namely that affluence had a depressing effect on stress-seeking, that therefore affluence had to be counteracted or it would lead to effeteness, see the paper by David Brion Davis in this volume.

VICARIOUS AND SIMULATED EUSTRESS-SEEKING

It appears that one of the characterizing aspects of eustress is its relatively limited duration. The kinds of stresses people seek seem to be the kinds associated with a proximate climax and resolution. They tend to occur in a context of crisis, a context that is the antithesis of routine, stability, fixity, boredom, ennui. Hope deferred makes the heart grow faint, we are told. If the battle drags on endlessly, morale sags.[13] If there is no confrontation, excitement subsides. Almost by definition, eustress is episodic and relatively transient in nature. In addition to the "real" forms that eustress-seeking may take, there are also vicarious and simulated forms that may be provided by a society, either as a sop or as a method of controlling the real forms.[14]

VICARIOUS EUSTRESS-SEEKING

Drama is, *par excellence,* a vehicle for vicarious eustress. Or, conversely, eustress tends to occur in a dramatic structure. Whether expressed in folk and fairy tales, novels, or theater, the dramatic form makes provision for vicarious eustress. The listener, reader, or viewer shares the dangers of the young prince who goes forth to slay the dragon. Children and the naïve sometimes find even these vicarious

[13] "Give us some successes!" was the plea Dr. Martin Luther King made when rioting broke out on the streets of the Negro ghetto of Chicago on July 16, 1966. The endless procession of days that promised no climactic success provided no occasion for eustress. The sagging of morale with endless dragging-out of the battle seems subject to cultural differences. The Chinese seem to have more patience when confronted with this situation. So also do those with a transcendental orientation and evangelicals.

[14] Nietzschean Dionysianism included drug-induced excitement, especially intoxication. The North American Indians cultivated this form of Dionysianism. Certain cultists today also advocate this form, including lysergic acid "trips." The literature on intoxication as a form of eustress-seeking, especially by way of alcohol, is so extensive that even a cursory bow in its direction would take our discussion far afield. It is therefore not included here.

stresses very painful; they cannot bear suspenseful stories or stories that are too threatening to the hero. But initiated audiences listen with deliciously bated breath and ask for more.

The classic structure of drama has eustress built into it.[15] There is the first phase, in which the two contending forces are introduced (originally the protagonist and the antagonist)[16] and the "stage set." In the second phase there is a mounting tension as the two conflicting parties move toward the climactic confrontation. The third phase shows the crisis of climax itself. And then, finally, there is the last phase or *dénouement,* or untying, which leaves the conflict resolved and the viewer relieved, released, or exalted.[17]

Fairy tales and novels may also take on dramatic form

[15] Greek theater, we are told, "grew directly out of the Dionysian celebrations, out of the rites, the dances, the songs . . . in honor of Dionysus" (Sheldon Cheney, *The Theater,* London: Longmans, Green & Co., 1952, p. xiv). Dionysus was a "god of nature and of wild things, and of all human-divine wild impulses" (*Ibid.,* p. xiii).

[16] An "agon" was basic to both tragedy and comedy. The tragic forces might be summer versus winter, life versus death, the new year versus the old, Daemon versus an enemy, a knightly hero versus malevolent enemies. In comedy, the agon was less profound; it took the form of competition in rudeness, mutual peltings *à la* Punch and Judy, jeering, mocking, scurrilous dialogue (Ivor Brown, *First Player,* London: Gerald Howe, 1927, pp. 80–81). ". . . the 'agon' became an integral and constant part of drama. . . . It is almost certain to be exciting" (*Ibid.,* p. 82). ". . . there is a natural excitability of an audience, which can be touched by the spectacle of any contest as it rises to its climax and decision" (*Ibid.,* p. 84). Aristotle codified the kinds of conflicting forces that were appropriate for tragedy; they had to be terrible but not monstrous; dreadful and lamentable. Minturno, following Aristotle, said that "tragedy . . . introduces persons who act and speak, arousing feelings of pity and terror, and tending to purge the mind of the beholder of similar passions to his delight and profit" (Cheney, *op. cit.,* p. 43). In general, tragedy had protagonists of high and noble birth; comedy, middle-class folk such as farmers, soldiers, and petty merchants; and satirical comedy, humble folk (*Ibid.,* p. 42).

[17] It is interesting, whether or not it is relevant, that the dramatic form parallels the phases of sexual orgasm, as sketched by William H. Masters and Virginia E. Johnson in *Human Sexual Response* (Boston: Little, Brown & Company, 1966), p. 5. Most other body functions have a more even rhythm. Kinsey likens orgasmic response to sneezing and draws a parallel to epileptic seizures (A. C. Kinsey and associates, *Sexual Behavior in the Human Female,* Philadelphia: W. B. Saunders Company, 1953, pp. 631–32).

and provide vicarious eustress. The conflicting forces are introduced, the issues are clarified and lead inevitably to the great confrontation at the climax, and are resolved in a *dénouement*. The eustress at the mounting tension is experienced as a delicious thrill.[18]

[18] In the West there has seemed to be something almost compulsive about dramatic structure. It has pervaded most art forms. Americans especially have tended to be impatient with situations that do not lend themselves to this structural form. A society permeated by this dramatic mentality tends to have a characteristic world view. It looks for a beginning, a middle, and an end. Such a viewpoint is, apparently, not universal. "In the Chinese theater," we are told, "song and pantomime predominate, while the interest in traditional stock types leaves little room for creative dialogue; and as a result the occasional attempts to introduce Chinese plays on the Western stage have proved universally unsuccessful" (Julius Bob, "Theater," in *Encyclopedia of the Social Sciences*, New York: The Macmillan Co., 1931, Vol. 14, p. 599). And, "dramatic poetry . . . has never developed in Japan as a form of national or cultural expression" (*Ibid.*, p. 599). A dramatic mentality apparently leaves its impress on other aspects of a culture also. A society permeated by this dramatic mentality is not, for example, satisfied with chronology; it imposes a dramatic structure on the past which becomes history. Chronology merely relates the events of the past; it conforms to no set form; there is no structure, no highlights; therefore it has little meaning. But a society with a dramatic mentality transforms chronology; its writers select, emphasize, and thus, willy-nilly, interpret. History finds causes and effects, antecedents and consequences; in between are climactic events. It finds decisive battles and turning points. It finds rises and declines, ebb and flow. People with and those without a dramatic mentality approach the present differently also. In war, those with a dramatic mentality must have victories and defeats; in elections there must be clear-cut winners and losers. They want things settled. A conflict that seems to have no foreseeable climax is almost unendurable. There is no eustress in a long-drawn-out contest. In the 1960's, we are told, the Chinese and the North Vietnamese are relying on precisely this characteristic impatience of Western mentality, on its inability to sustain a longtime operation that does not lead to a clearcut victory, to give them success in the long run. With a mentality that calls for decisive climaxes and *dénouements* we are, they believe, incapable of sustaining the dys-stresses of war. And among the greatest disappointments of the twentieth century in the West has been the discovery of how hard it is to change old cultural patterns in modernizing nations. Community-development workers have reported limited success in their efforts to bring even simple technological changes to them. There are, as both sociologists and anthropologists have made abundantly clear, many reasons for this failure. In the Orient this cultural inertia may also be related to a nondramatic mentality, to a mentality that sees the past in terms of an even flow, or all of life in terms of endless nonclimactic cycles. The leaders of modernizing nations sometimes borrow dramatic schemes; they set goals for themselves; they establish five-year plans; presumably the

In addition to vicarious eustress created by words, there are also vicarious eustresses created by body actions, such, for example, as those provided for in spectator sports. Gladiatorial combats, bearbaiting, cockfighting, bullfighting, boxing, automobile racing, competitive sports of all kinds, contests of almost any nature, have supplied and still continue to supply eustress not only to the participants but also to millions of spectators all over the world.[19] That even such vicarious eustress does, in fact, generate enormous amounts of energy is attested to by the difficulty almost universally experienced of keeping fights from breaking out among the spectators during or after such spectacles.

SIMULATED EUSTRESS-SEEKING

In simulated or self-involved eustress-seeking, the subject is not, as in vicarious eustress-seeking, experiencing emotions stimulated by seeing another's emotions; he is actively engaged in producing them himself. Simulated eustress among the Greeks preceded vicarious verbal eustress. Mock combats, we are told, were originally a part of folk dances. Rites, ceremonies, and dance might all simulate genuine agons.

Spectator sports may also become transformed into simulated eustress-seeking when the spectator interjects, let us say, a bet. He has now identified himself with one of the agonists and thus becomes a participant as well as a spectator. When the opposing agonist is chance, luck, or fate, as in casino-type gambling, the eustress-seeking has ceased to be simulated.

Vicarious and simulated eustress-seeking appear to be perennial and universal in one form or another. It would

---

eustress associated with the effort leading to the achievement of these goals, a kind of race with themselves or with time toward a climax, provides the social energy for reaching them. In nations with a nondramatic mentality they have not been notably successful.

[19] Sports that have no intrinsic eustress associated with them, such as, for example, golf, usually have to introduce a competitive element to make them attractive to eustress-seekers. The player competes with "par for the course," or with himself. Noncompetitive sports are usually engaged in primarily for exercise rather than for eustress.

require an almost case-by-case analysis to determine the precise function performed by them at different times and in different places. In some cases they might serve to drain off energies that would otherwise be used in destructive activities, in others, to generate energies that, as Dr. Klausner has suggested, are then available for desired social action. In still others, they might serve both of these functions. All we can say is that both are possible. Or, finally, they might provide for the satisfaction of a simple human need, escape from boredom.

EUDAEMONISM AND SOME RELATED VARIABLES

If we assume that in all societies that do not have to invest all their energies in work or sheer survival there will be energy available for pleasurable consumption, we then have to ask not why people seek eustress but how the forms that eustress-seeking takes are related to such other factors as, for example, class, age, race, culture, and even sex, for clearly it does differ in relation to these variables.

CLASS

One of the most striking characteristics of eudaemonism has been its class-bound nature. Either the lower classes were greatly restricted in opportunities for eustress-seeking, or they were permitted quite different forms from those reserved for the upper classes. In its aggressive, militant form, eudaemonism was the prerogative of nobles, knights, aristocrats, heroes, gentlemen; adventure was their privilege. Serfs and villeins, chained to the daily grind of routine productivity, had to find other outlets. Just as sumptuary laws controlled the consumption of food and clothing in medieval times, so crescive norms controlled the consumption of energy. The upper classes participated in jousting, fighting, tournaments. Lower-class men who wanted this kind of energy-consumption were outlaws, like Robin Hood. Or they might become troubadours, jongleurs, or minstrels. Or, at the lowest level, they might just resort to brawling.

In Germany, duelling clubs remained an aristocratic privilege until yesterday.

Because so much of the energy in the lower classes has had to be invested in the hard work of the world, much of its eustress-seeking has had to be vicarious in form. In the Greek world, we are told, feasts and festivals—sometimes orgiastic in nature—were introduced by the gods to supply eudaemonism for the hardworking lower classes.[20] But even in its vicarious form, there were class differences. Tragedy was appropriate for the upper classes, comedy for the middle classes, and satiric comedy—even slapstick—for the lower classes.[21] Whatever form eudaemonism has taken in the lower classes, it is abundantly clear that in the upper classes it has taken the form of conflict of some kind or other.

Nietzsche defined nobility in terms of eudaemonism. In answer to the question: What is noble? he replied:

> That [is noble] which . . . leaves happiness to the *greatest number*, the happiness which consists of inner peacefulness, of virtue, of comfort, and of Anglo-angelic-back-parlor-smugness, à la Spencer. That one [is noble who] instinctively seeks for heavy responsibilities. That one [is noble who] contradicts the greatest number, not in words at all, but by continually behaving differently from them.[22]

Crane Brinton has summarized Nietzsche's apotheosis of the noble in his description of the Warrior, the eudaemonist *par excellence*, as follows:

> The Warrior is essentially noble. He represents for Nietzsche the "good" and also . . . the "natural." The Warrior is frank and open in his exercise of the Will to Power. He has a strong body, good health, handsome features, noble bearing; he delights in the use of

[20] Antonio Sebastiano Minturno, an Italian scholar, in his "The Art of Poetry" cited Plato to the effect that "the gods took pity on the tedious life of mortals, wearied with never-ending tasks and labors, and that they might not lack recreations and that they take heart again, the gods established festivals, banquets, and games" which evolved into comedy (Barrett H. Clark, *European Theories of the Drama*, New York: Crown Publishers, Inc., 1965, p. 44).

[21] See footnote 16 above.

[22] Friedrich Wilhelm Nietzsche, *The Will to Power*, #947.

his strength in bodily combat, in the indulgence of all
the fine gifts of enjoyment his lusty senses afford him.
He is capable, at his best, of that flashing physical
ecstasy . . . which Nietzsche liked to call "Dionysian."
He is guided by honor, not by interest. . . . He hates as
strongly and as much as he loves—perhaps he hates
rather more than he loves? He has a "loathing of dema-
gogism, of enlightenment, of amiability, and plebian familiarity."[23]

The Warrior's latter-day descendant, the gentleman, retained many of his traits. He was also characteristically an
eudaemonist with Dionysian prerogatives:

> The concepts that may be severally detected in the
> complex of notions embraced under the word gentleman
> belong to all historic times and peoples. The sentiments
> which they express vary in intensity and in their relative
> importance to one another. One fundamental charac-
> teristic nevertheless accompanies them in all times and
> places: they are sentiments of combat; they are concepts
> of social competition. . . . Montesquieu . . . was coura-
> geous enough to contrast the gentleman's morality with
> the plain man's morality and to locate the concept of
> gentility in the sphere of social struggle. . . . Casti-
> glione in particular, but older theorists of the genteel in
> general, stress the exercise of arms and expertness in
> dueling as the characteristic pursuits of the gentleman.
> The ethics of the gentleman are ethics of combat, of
> competition in a struggle for eminence and distinction,
> and are therefore antithetical to humility, self-efface-
> ment, altruism, and abnegation. . . . The gentleman's
> ideal is not virtue but honor. . . . In general, the test of
> the gentleman is his superiority to external controls, es-
> pecially the physical, moral and sentimental limitations
> that determine mediocrity. The ethic of the gentleman in
> all times and places is Nietzschean, not Christian. . . .
> The gentleman may be a hero, but not a martyr.[24]

Dr. Klausner suggests that "societies in Toynbee-like
manner seek their challenges." So far as they seek their
challenges by way of conflict, it is doubtless through this
eudaemonistic elite. A hero like Alexander weeps when

[23] Crane Brinton, *op. cit.*, p. 134.
[24] Arthur Livingston, "Theory of the Gentleman," *Encyclopedia of
the Social Sciences* (New York: The Macmillan Co., 1931), Vol. 6,
pp. 617–20.

there are no more worlds to conquer. The Vikings roam
the world in their eudaemonistic quest. The Crusades are
too complex a phenomenon to reduce to a particularistic
conceptualization, but undoubtedly sheer eudaemonism was
among the forces that produced them. So, too, with the
explorers and discoverers of new worlds in the fifteenth
century. Social scientists will not, of course, let it go at
that. They must find out why the combative eudaemonistic
elites occur now here, now there, and why they seek their
eustress now here, now there. And we must grant them
their professional argument. Still, it is interesting to note
that there seems always to be available, in one society or
another, a supply of eudaemonism to go forth in search
of challenges.[25]

The basis for class differences in the forms of eudaemonism was traced by Veblen to the intrinsic nature of the
division of labor. He differentiated honorific occupations,
which were predatory and exploitative and hence "worthy,
honourable, noble,"[26] from the nonhonorific, which were
humble and productive and hence ignoble and debasing.
"Chief among the honourable employments in any feudal
community is warfare."[27] Nonhonorific were industrial
tasks. Originally, he thought, this distinction was on the
basis of sex. Thus among hunting tribes, women were assigned the industrial work, which was drudgery and required diligence; men were exempt. "War, hunting, sports,
and devout observances" were reserved for them; exploit
and prowess rather than diligence were the required virtues.[28] Later, slavery changed the situation so far as the
sex-based division of labor was concerned; male slaves were
assigned the industrial, nonhonorific work and some women
joined men in the leisure class.

[25] Again it is the form which eustress-seeking takes that is challenging. It is not difficult to see why exploring the earth preceded
exploring space as a form of stress-seeking; where stress-seeking depends on technology, the relationship is not hard to explain. Why
"strenuosity" as a form of stress-seeking at the turn of the century?
This is the kind of question that intrigues me much more. See, for
example, the paper by David Brion Davis in this volume.
[26] T. B. Veblen, *Theory of the Leisure Class*, p. 15.
[27] *Ibid.*, p. 1.
[28] *Ibid.*, pp. 4, 9–10.

> At the earlier stage . . . the all-dominating institution of slavery and status acted resistlessly to discountenance exertion directed to other than naively predatory ends. It was still possible to find some habitual employment for the inclination to action in the way of forcible aggression or repression directed against hostile groups or against the subject classes within the group; and thus served to relieve the pressure and draw off the energy of the leisure class without a resort to actually useful, or even ostensibly useful employment. The practice of hunting also served the same purpose in some degree.[29]

As modern industrialization, essentially a peaceful system, made it harder and harder to find honorific, nonuseful employment, other outlets had to be devised; a system of highly cultivated sports activity was the answer.[30]

Whatever may be the basis for it, class differences in the forms of eudaemonism still remain.[31] It is not now so much in terms of the amount of energy available for consumption in this nonutilitarian form of activity—all classes have time and energy for such consumption—but perhaps in the expenses involved in indulging in it. Polo and regattas—as well as skydiving—are still expensive forms of eudaemonism.

AGE

Eudaemonism, calling, as we have noted, for a considerable investment of physical energy, is almost by definition a prerogative of youth. It implies the availability of energy above the level demanded by the daily routine of living. The roles assigned or available to youth—soldier, for example—often depend on energy. It has been suggested that if young people, especially young men, could somehow or other be quarantined or laid away on ice from ages eighteen to twenty-five, most violence, even traditional crime, could

---

[29] *Ibid.,* pp. 94–95.

[30] *Ibid.,* Chapter 10. It is interesting to note that Veblen was relentlessly consistent in his definition of the leisure class; he included juvenile delinquents, as well as the upper class. Both were bellicose eustress-seekers (pp. 246–50).

[31] Jessie Bernard, *American Community Behavior* (New York: Holt, Rinehart & Winston, Inc., 1962). Chapter 26 deals with one form of eudaemonism, namely violence.

be eliminated. Almost daily our television screens report riots, demonstrations, street-fighting all over the world; some of the faces and bodies are those of children; almost all are young adults; rarely does one see an older face. The eudaemonistic nature of the Watts riot was evident in the intense, almost orgiastic, nonsmiling faces of many of the participants.

RACE

Differences among races in eudaemonism have been alleged, especially in the nineteenth century. Veblen spoke of a bellicose temperament as a race as well as a class trait.[32] And nineteenth-century racists were enamored of the concept of certain eudaemonic races, especially the Nordic race. Some races were made to conquer and to rule, others to serve. Nietzsche, again, celebrated the great blonde beast:

> It is impossible not to recognize at the core of all these aristocratic races the beast of prey; the magnificent blonde brute, avidly rampant for spoil and victory; this hidden core needed an outlet from time to time—the Roman, Arabic, German and Japanese nobility, the Homeric heroes, the Scandinavian Vikings, are all alike in this need. It is the aristocratic races who have left the idea "Barbarian" on all the tracks in which they have marched. . . . The profound, icy mistrust which the German provokes as soon as he arrives at power, even at the present time, is always still an aftermath of that inextinguishable horror with which for whole centuries Europe has regarded the wrath of the blonde Teuton beast.[33]

It is clear that this line of thought is based on a fallacious conception of race, on a conception that confuses cultural characteristics with racial characteristics. If we think in terms of three, four, or five major races, at least two of them—Caucasian and Mongolian—are included among the eudaemonistic races specified by Nietzsche. If we think in

[32] T. B. Veblen, *op. cit.*, p. 252.
[33] F. W. Nietzsche, *Genealogy of Morals,* Part I (11).

terms of subraces, Mediterranean, Alpine, and Nordic are all included.

It would be an act of superarrogation to think it necessary to disprove this theory that race *per se,* race in its correct, genetic conceptualization, plays a part in eudaemonism. All that is called for are illustrations that it does not. We know, for example, that members of even the same subraces at different times behave in different ways with respect to eudaemonism. Young Sabras—Israel-born descendants of early European settlers—are, we are told, horrified and ashamed when they learn how little resistance German and East European Jews put up against their German oppressors. All are members of the same genetic pool.[34] Negroes have been criticized for their submission to slavery; they have also been charged with Dionysianism. We know also that the same race—the American Indians—showed quite different patterns of eudaemonism; some—like the Kwakiutl and the Plains Indians—exalted it above everything else, while others—the Zuñi—allegedly rejected it.[35] We know, finally, that members of different races—Germans and Plains Indians, for example—may be equally eudaemonistic.

Although there would be few today to argue in terms of genetic race as a factor in Dionysianism, there do seem to be serious differences among peoples with respect to their evaluation of eudaemonism. It was not accidental that the glorification of war and the military virtues occurred in Germany at the end of the nineteenth and beginning of the twentieth centuries.[36] But evaluation is a cultural, not a racial, phenomenon.

[34] For many Jews, the migration to Israel was eustress-seeking on the heroic scale.

[35] Ruth Benedict, *Patterns of Culture* (Baltimore: Penguin Books, Inc. [paperback], 1934), pp. 74 ff. See footnote 43 below.

[36] Studies by social psychologists on child-rearing practices, by anthropologists of folklore and tales, by sociologists of family relations, only scratched the surface but gave us enough insight to interpret the course of German history and flesh out the politico-economic interpretations. The work of the school directed by Max Horkheimer, especially on the authoritarian personality, may be cited in this connection.

CULTURE

It was Ruth Benedict who familiarized us with the idea that some cultures were characteristically Dionysian and others Apollonian. She found, for example, that the Kwakiutls of Vancouver Island were "in almost direct antithesis to the Zuñi with their Dionysian preference for individual rivalry and ecstasies."[37] Although Ruth Benedict emphasized especially the cultivation of Dionysian psychological experience in terms of visions, fasting, and drugs among American Indians, she also noted its combative form. Among the Plains Indians, for example, there was "passionate enthusiasm" for guerrilla warfare.

> Their war parties were ordinarily less than a dozen strong, and the individual acted alone in their simple engagements in a way that stands at the other pole from the rigid discipline and subordination of modern warfare. Their war was a game in which each individual amassed counts. These counts were for cutting loose a picketed horse, or touching an enemy, or taking a scalp. The individual, usually by personal dare-deviltry, acquired as many as he could, and used them for joining societies, giving feasts, qualifying as a chief. Without initiative and ability to act alone, an Indian of the plains was not recognized in his society. The testimony of early explorers, the rise of outstanding individuals in their conflicts with the whites, the contrast with the Pueblos, all go to show how their institutions fostered personality, almost in the Nietzschean sense of the superman.[38]

Among the Kwakiutls, Dionysianism—though it also pervaded initiation and ceremonial dances—characteristically took the form of the potlatch, which was a battle in which property was the weapon.[39] "They say, 'We do not fight with weapons. We fight with property.' A man who had given away a copper had overcome his rival as much as if he had overcome him in battle."[40] And, to reassure us

[37] Ruth Benedict, *op. cit.*, unpaged introductory statement.
[38] *Ibid.*, pp. 89–90.
[39] *Ibid.*, p. 168.
[40] *Ibid.*, p. 175.

on the nonrational nature of this kind of battle, Ruth Benedict notes that it had none of the characteristics of normal trade.

Among advanced cultures, the German, according to Nietzsche, tended almost compulsively toward the Dionysian, however deeply buried this tendency might be. He says:

> . . . in some inaccessible abyss the German spirit still rests and dreams, undestroyed, in glorious health, profoundity, and Dionysian strength, like a knight sunk in slumber; from which abyss the Dionysian song rises to our ears to let us know that this German knight even now is dreaming his primitive Dionysian myth in blissfully earnest visions. . . . Someday the German spirit will find itself awake in all the morning freshness following a deep sleep; then it will slay the dragons, destroy the malignant dwarfs, waken Brunhilde—and Wotan's spear itself will be unable to obstruct its course!"[41]

Unfortunately, when this German knight awoke in all the morning freshness, his Dionysianism took a very bureaucratic form: it killed not in Dionysian frenzy or ecstasy, but in cold-blooded efficiency.

If we assume that it is not the existence but the form eudaemonism takes that requires explanation, the question arises as to the form it takes in Apollonian cultures. In Apollonian Greece, we may invoke vicarious stress-seeking. But among the Apollonian Zuñi, Ruth Benedict has carefully and meticulously cut off any possible cultural item that could be interpreted as a form of Dionysianism. One by one she shows how even identical rituals and customs among, let us say, the Plains Indians and among the Zuñi are differently used so that they become Dionysian among the Plains Indians but Apollonian among the Zuñi.[42] The Zuñi have, in fact, become the archetype of the peaceful and peaceable society, relied on by idealists who look to the time when conflict will disappear. Zuñi culture anticipates and forestalls every occasion for eudaemonic self-

[41] W. F. Nietzsche, *The Birth of Tragedy*, Ch. 24.
[42] Ruth Benedict, *op. cit.*, pp. 73–119.

expression.[43] The price paid takes the form of the elimination of individual initiative.

Cultures, in brief, differ in their evaluation of eustress-seeking.[44] It is both encouraged, valued, and promoted on the one hand, and discouraged, repressed, and deplored on the other. It is played up and played down, permitted and forbidden, rewarded and punished, tolerated and exalted. Why these differences among cultures arise and persist is not explained even by Ruth Benedict, despite her detailed descriptions of archetypical eudaemonistic and noneudaemonistic types.

SOCIALIZATION: ROLE SPECIFICATIONS FOR THE EUDAEMONIC HERO

Whatever the reasons might be for playing up or playing down eudaemonism in any given culture, the mechanisms involved are the usual ones of socialization. Admittedly merely naming a process does not explain it nor add much to our understanding. When the statement is made that a certain kind of eudaemonism—one involving conflict or conquest—was an intrinsic aspect of the noble's, gentleman's, aristocrat's, or brave's role, it is not thereby explained. It leaves unexplored the functional contribution of the role on one side and the psychological mechanisms which undergirded it on the other.[45]

[43] Except one. "A wife may fall upon her rival and beat her up publicly. They call each other names and give each other a black eye. It never settles anything, and even in the rare cases when it occurs, it dies down as quickly as it has flared. It is the only recognized fist-fight in Zuñi" (p. 99). There are probably other deviations from the Apollonian pattern. Thus when a man insulted Leo and Quatsia by taking care of their yard, Ruth Benedict plays up their mild forbearance rather than the interloper's insult (p. 98). She doubtless—unwittingly—overlooked other instances that violated her interpretation of Zuñi Apollonianism.

[44] Even within the United States such cultural differences occur among regions. Thus in 1966 a West Coast father was denied custody of his own son by an Iowa court which expressed sober, Apollonian distrust of the eustress-seeking life the father would provide for the child.

[45] Konrad Lorenz in his book *On Aggression* (New York: Harcourt, Brace & World, Inc., 1966) finds at least three functions per-

Still, it is interesting to note, as in the quotations presented above, how insistent the role specifications were for heroes, nobles, gentlemen, braves, and the leisure class. There must have been some men to whom these aggressive role specifications were onerous, men who would have preferred gentler activities; they may have been like the "tempered" skydivers. (King Louis XVI comes to mind; he preferred to work in his locksmith shop. Upper-class men —kings, nobles, aristocrats—who are not dashing, who prefer study to combat, have been reported, but they are viewed as offbeat, out of character.)

Was the predatory nature of the gentleman's role an antecedent or a consequence? Did he achieve—and keep—his position because he was predatory and exploitative, and guarantee it by maintaining a eudaemonic code that kept him in readiness always against challenge, either from peers or underlings? Or is there a "natural" preference for this form of eudaemonism among all men which is permitted as a privilege only to the upper classes? Klausner's suggestion that stress-seeking behavior "provides a motivational reservoir for social action" and that "this may be one of the social functions of competition and conflict" would tend to favor the first alternative.

In any event, the role specifications of the hero have undergone a profound transformation. The eudaemonic hero was destroyed by the spirit of capitalism, a spirit whose most urgent task was "the destruction of spontaneous, impulsive enjoyment."[46]

DEATH OF THE HERO: THE PROTESTANT ETHIC

We are so accustomed to the controls imposed on us by the Protestant Ethic that we take them for granted; they

formed by aggressive behavior in the case of subhuman animals, namely: "balanced distribution of animals of the same species over the available environment, selection of the strongest by rival fights, and defense of the young" (p. 43). It is never safe, however, to translate subhuman behavior into human terms.

[46] Max Weber, *op. cit.*, p. 119. Weber was by no means the first to make this point. Freud had also noted it in his *Civilization and Its Discontents*.

seem not only right but also wholly natural to us. Not until Max Weber analyzed the Protestant Ethic for us did we learn how it operated to tame and control wayward "human nature." For the Protestant Ethic, according to Weber, created the model for a kind of personality that was motivated to act in a way suitable for the capitalistic economy, whether disagreeable or not. By substituting the concept of a calling for traditional—more natural—motivations,[47] it transformed both the top and the bottom of the occupational setup.

> The capitalistic system so needs this devotion to the calling of making money, it is an attitude toward material goods which is so well suited to that system, so intimately bound up with the conditions of survival in the economic struggle for existence, that there can today no longer be any question of a necessary connection of that acquisitive manner of life with any single Weltanschauung.[48]

There had always been pirates, buccaneers, speculators, adventurers, and men who loved to make money as an exciting game, like the chase. Eustress-seekers all. And men who made money as a means to an end. But this was not the Protestant Ethic model. It prescribed making money as a moral duty rather than as eustress-seeking or even as a means to an end. Thus when a retired friend of Jacob Fugger tried to persuade Fugger to retire also, Fugger re-

---

[47] Weber was true to the German Dionysian tradition. To him the concept of a calling that stimulated so much hard work for its own sake was not rational but, rather, irrational from the eudaemonistic point of view: "If you ask . . . [businessmen] what is the meaning of their restless activity, why they are never satisfied with what they have, thus appearing so senseless to any purely worldly view of life, they would perhaps give the answer, if they know any at all: 'to provide for my children and grandchildren.' But more often and, since that motive is not peculiar to them, but was just as effective for the traditionalist, more correctly, simply: that business with its continuous work has become a necessary part of their lives. That is in fact the only possible motivation, but it at the same time expresses what is—seen from the viewpoint of personal happiness—so irrational about this sort of life, where a man exists for the sake of his business, instead of the reverse" (Max Weber, *op. cit.*, p. 70). "He gets nothing out of his wealth for himself, except the irrational sense of having done his job well" (p. 71).

[48] *Ibid.*, p. 72.

plied that such a course was pusillanimous; he wanted to make money as long as he could. Weber contrasts Fugger's "commercial daring" but morally neutral attitude with Benjamin Franklin's utilitarian moral attitudes. The Protestant Ethic had made the difference.

First, at the top of the occupational structure: men who created fortunes, who speculated daringly, who gambled recklessly—economic eudaemonists, in brief—were not the kind of men needed to create the capital for financing the Industrial Revolution. Risk-takers, yes, but takers of calculated risks (which are not nearly so much fun). Not the fine indifference to costs of the warrior, hero, gentleman, but the careful counting of costs of the accountant.[49] Creating this type of model was the work of the Protestant Ethic.

> Capitalistic acquisition as an adventure has been at home in all types of economic society which have known trade with the use of money and which have offered it opportunities. . . . Likewise the inner attitude of the adventurer, which laughs at all ethical limitations, has been universal. Absolute and conscious ruthlessness in acquisition has often stood in the closest connection with the strictest conformity to tradition. Moreover, with the breakdown of tradition and the more or less complete extension of free economic enterprise, even to within the social group, the new thing has not generally been ethically justified and encouraged, but only tolerated as a fact. And this fact has been treated either as ethically indifferent or as reprehensible, but unfortunately unavoidable. . . . Now just this attitude was one of the strongest inner obstacles which the adaptation of men to the conditions of an ordered bourgeois-capitalistic economy has encountered everywhere. The most important opponent with which the spirit of capitalism—in the sense of a definite standard of life claiming ethical sanction—has had to struggle, was that type of attitude and reaction to

[49] The precapitalistic entrepreneur probably counted costs to some extent; Shakespeare's merchants of Venice were undoubtedly aware of the risks they were taking, preferring ships with good bottoms to decaying hulks. Both Dr. Klausner and Dr. Houston in this volume note that stress-seekers do assess risks. We are speaking in terms of relative emphasis. The eustress-seeker will probably take a greater chance than the non-eustress-seeker.

the new situations which we may designate as tradi-
tionalism.[50]

Inherited capital tended to be traditionalistic in the above,
eudaemonistic, sense. The men who controlled capital were
not exponents of the virtues needed to create and accumulate more capital. The new fortunes needed for financing
industrialization in a capitalistic system were created by
parvenus of lower-class origin who practiced the virtues of
the Protestant Ethic and therefore succeeded:

> The old leisurely and comfortable attitude toward life
> gave way to a hard frugality in which some participated
> and came to the top. . . . The question of the motive
> forces in the expansion of modern capitalism, is not in
> the first instance a question of the origin of the capital
> sums which were available for capitalistic uses, but,
> above all, of the development of the spirit of capitalism.
> Where it appears and is able to work itself out, it pro-
> duces its own capital and monetary supplies as the means
> to its ends, but the reverse is not true. Its entry on the
> scene was not generally peaceful. A flood of mistrust,
> sometimes of hatred, above all of moral indignation,
> regularly opposed itself to its first innovator. . . . Along
> with clarity of vision and ability to act, it is only by vir-
> tue of very definite and highly developed ethical qualities
> that it has been possible for him to command the ab-
> solutely indispensable confidence of his customers and
> workmen. Nothing else could have given him the strength
> to overcome the innumerable obstacles, above all the
> infinitely more intensive work which is demanded by the
> modern entrepreneur. But these are ethical qualities of
> quite a different sort from those adapted to the tradi-
> tionalism of the past.
>   And, as a rule, it has been neither dare-devil and un-

---

[50] Max Weber, *op. cit.*, pp. 58–59. T. B. Veblen also found it necessary to explain and interpret the changes from the eudaemonistic
hero to the more pedestrian type characteristic of capitalism. He in-
voked what he called "the instinct of workmanship," which was the
antithesis of the waste required by the leisure class: "A reconcili-
ation between the two conflicting requirements is effected by a resort
to make-believe. Many and intricate polite observances and social
duties of a ceremonial nature are developed; many organisations are
founded, with some specious object of amelioration embodied in
their official style and title; there is much coming and going, and a
deal of talk, to the end that the talkers may not have occasion to reflect on what is the effectual economic value of their traffic . . ."
(Veblen, *op. cit.*, p. 96).

scrupulous speculators, economic adventurers such as
we meet at all periods of economic history, nor simply
great financiers who have carried through this change,
. . . so decisive for the penetration of economic life
with the new spirit. On the contrary, they were men
who had grown up in the hard school of life, calculating
and daring at the same time, above all temperate and
reliable, shrewd and completely devoted to their business,
with strictly bourgeois opinions and principles.[51]

A very far cry, indeed, from the eudaemonistic hero-
warrior. The contrast between this extremely disciplined,
hardworking capitalist and the hero-warrior is spectacular.

At the other end of the occupational ladder the Protestant
Ethic was also at work. Weber paints an almost idyllic picture of the life of workers in precapitalistic days, in which
men worked at a natural pace and sought only enough to
maintain their traditional plane of living.

A man does not "by nature" wish to earn more and
more money, but simply to live as he is accustomed to
live and to earn as much as is necessary for that purpose.
Wherever modern capitalism has begun its work of increasing the productivity of human labour by increasing
its intensity, it has encountered the immensely stubborn
resistance of this leading trait of precapitalistic labour.[52]

And the way this stubborn resistance to work was overcome
was by giving work a religious sanction; the concept of the
calling did precisely that. "This it was which inevitably
gave everyday worldly activity a religious significance."[53]
For, "the only way of living acceptable to God was . . .
solely through the fulfillment of the obligations imposed
upon the individual by his position in the world. That was
his calling."[54] The Protestant Ethic taught the dull virtues:
early to bed, early to rise; a bird in the hand is worth two
in the bush; never put off till tomorrow what you can do
today; waste not, want not; and so on.

The battle of Puritanism against eudaemonism was by no
means easy. Weber presents an interesting illustration:

[51] Max Weber, *op. cit.,* p. 68–69.
[52] *Ibid.,* p. 60.
[53] *Ibid.,* p. 80.
[54] *Ibid.,* p. 80.

Puritan . . . asceticism turned with all its force against one thing: the spontaneous enjoyment of life and all it had to offer. This is perhaps most characteristically brought out in the struggle over the *Book of Sports* which James I and Charles I made into law expressly as a means of counteracting Puritanism, and which the latter ordered to be read from all the pulpits. The fanatical opposition of the Puritans to . . . certain popular amusements[55] . . . was . . . explained [in part] by resentment against the intentional diversion from the ordered life of the saint, which it caused. And, on his side, the King's threats of severe punishment for every attack on the legality of those sports were motivated by his purpose of breaking the anti-authoritarian ascetic tendency of Puritanism, which was so dangerous to the State. . . .

The Puritan aversion to sport . . . was by no means simply one of principle. Sport was accepted if it served a rational purpose, that of recreation necessary for physical efficiency. But as a means for the spontaneous expression of undisciplined impulses, it was under suspicion; and insofar as it became purely a means of enjoyment, or awakened pride, raw instincts or the irrational gambling instinct, it was of course strictly condemned. Impulsive enjoyment of life, which leads away both from work in a calling and from religion, was as such the enemy of rational asceticism, whether in the form of seigneurial sports, or the enjoyment of the dance-hall or the public-house of the common man.[56]

Even when recreation was justified as contributing to physical efficiency, it was limited because it "must not cost anything."[57]

DIONYSUS VERSUS THE COMPUTER: REVENGE OF THE EUDAEMONISTIC HERO

The spirit of capitalism, then, tolled the death knell of the eudaemonistic hero. He had no place on the new in-

---

[55] We are reminded of Lord Macaulay's statement that the Puritans opposed bearbaiting not because it hurt the bear but because the viewers enjoyed it.

[56] Max Weber, *op. cit.*, pp. 167–68.

[57] *Ibid.*, p. 170.

dustrial scene. Risk-takers, yes; but only calculated-risk-takers. (Item: An Air Force training officer has been quoted as saying that he did not want heroes in his outfit; what he wanted was the well-trained technician who minimized risks and always took the lesser risk when he had a choice.) For the spirit of capitalism rests on an exchange-minded man, a cost accountant. Secretary McNamara introduced the so-called cost-effectiveness system in the Defense Department, and since then an increasing number of agencies, governmental and nongovernmental, have been following his lead. Such a system leaves as little as possible to the judgment of the decision-maker, and precious little to the hero. As many decisions as possible—and an increasing number are—are turned over to the computer. Officially, the hero has been outlawed. In characteristically (if not typically) modern fiction—since Hemingway glorified him—he is unknown; his place has been taken by the non-hero, even the antihero, just as the characteristic theater fare is non- or antidrama.

But the eudaemonistic hero is hard to destroy.[58] In the United States he retreated to the legendary West and remains to this day the most popular character in the folk mind everywhere throughout the world where he is permitted to be known. He still reaps adulation in the form of the private eye or the secret agent. A bow is made in the direction of the Protestant Ethic by endowing these current heroes with a calling, for their eustress-seeking must have enough relationship to an approved end to pass its scrutiny. Eustress-seeking for its own sake would not pass muster. Exceptions are made for men who climb mountains simply because the mountains are there, but going to the moon just because it is there is not accepted; we may only go as a means of surpassing our enemies.

Dionysus remains powerful. The eudaemonist cannot be ignored. His seemingly senseless outbursts of violence chal-

---

[58] Charles Wilson, when he was President Eisenhower's Secretary of Defense, contrasted kennel dogs with hunting dogs. Whole generations are castigated for wanting security rather than adventure. Eisenhower himself once—erroneously—associated the security of the welfare state in Scandinavia with a high suicide rate.

lenge our unwilling attention. John Fischer has revived
William James' concept of a moral equivalent for war as
a way of dealing with him. Fischer believes that pugnacity
was bred into the human species by natural selection and
that the hero—as noted above—was a Great Fighter. Within
the last century, the primordial commandment "be a
fighter" has been abrogated in favor of the commandment
to be nonviolent. Almost all channels for the expression
of eudaemonism—war, village donnybrooks, the struggle
against nature—are now blocked, and those that remain—
risky sports—are expensive and available only to the middle
and upper classes. For some, the civil-rights movement or
the Peace Corps are still available. But there still remain
many millions who, having no outlets for inbred aggression
—whether innate or not—turn to crime and senseless violence. Fischer warns us that we must invest a great deal
more ingenuity "in the search for acceptable substitutes
for violence."[59] Dionysus is no mean adversary.

SEX AND STRESS: WOMEN AS STRESS-ALLAYERS, AS STRESS-SEEKERS, AND AS STRESS-EVOKERS

WOMEN AS STRESS-ALLAYERS

Sober laboratory research at the present time eschews
such dramatic concepts as eudaemonism or Dionysian and
Apollonian patterns of response. It has nothing to say of
the principles of Ying and Yang. Still, in its own pedestrian
way it also comes up with its own polarities. Thus, for
example, it has been reported that in task-oriented groups
at least two functions have to be performed if the assigned
task is to be completed. The group must be kept at work,

[59] John Fischer, "Substitutes for Violence," *Harper's Magazine*
(January 1966), p. 24. Fischer is not without hope, however. "Some-
day (I hope and believe) the craving for violence will leach out of
the human system. But the reversal of an evolutionary process takes
a long time. For a good many generations . . . the Old Adam is
likely to linger in our genes; and during that transitional period,
probably the best we can hope for is to keep him reasonably quiet"
(p. 24).

labeled an instrumental function; and it must be kept at peace, labeled an expressive function.[60] The stresses, in brief, which will inevitably be created by the instrumental function (as in all socialization) must also be allayed by the expressive function. Normally there must always be a balance between stress-creating and stress-allaying forces. If there is too little stress, the task will not be pressed or ennui may result.[61] But if there is too much stress, the group will disintegrate.[62] In a successful task-oriented group, as in an equilibrated social system, there is a nice balance between stress-production and stress-reduction.

It is possible for both sexes to perform both roles. There is no necessary relationship between sex and either the instrumental or the expressive function. Still, a study of fifty-six societies around the world found that in forty-six of them the expressive role was assigned to women and the instrumental to men.[63] The archetypical male was supposed to lean in the direction of the instrumental function, and the archetypical female, of the expressive.

Traditionally, therefore, stress-seeking has tended to be a male prerogative.[64] Adventure, excitement, the joys of battle, thrilling experience were for men only. Men might go forth to fight dragons but women should stay home and mind the hearth.[65] Justification for reserving excitement and adventure for men has sometimes rested on the nature

[60] Robert F. Bales, *Interaction Process Analysis: A Method for the Study of Small Groups* (Reading, Mass.: Addison-Wesley Publishing Company, Inc., 1950).

[61] It has been alleged that too much security in a social system is related to suicide; there is no firm evidence for this.

[62] In a stressful situation physical illness may result for the individual, especially psychosomatic illnesses.

[63] Morris Zelditch, "Role Differentiation in the Nuclear Family," in Talcott Parsons and Robert F. Bales, *Family, Socialization, and Interaction Process* (New York: The Free Press, 1955), Chapter 6.

[64] But we cannot ignore the permissiveness among the stress-repressing Zuñi with respect to fighting among women. Women were allowed to fight, but not men. (Ruth Benedict, *op. cit.*, p. 99)

[65] Stress-seeking in the form of self-sacrifice, however, of performance beyond the call of duty, or as auxiliaries to men, has been accepted and even encouraged. Few doctoral dissertations omit the tribute to the wife who bore hardships patiently while the author devoted himself to his work, often a stress-full period of long duration.

of the differences between the sexes.[66] The metabolism of
women is catabolic; that of men, anabolic. Women have
less speed and kinetic strength, qualities often needed in
adventure; they tend to be more passive and submissive, etc.
It is not at all difficult to amass a great deal of data to document sex differences if one wishes to justify the *status quo*
with respect to stress-seeking and sex. One sociologist has
noted that much of the recreational life of men and women
is segregated: that of the men leading in the direction of
hunting, fishing, sports, and other stress-seeking activities,
and that of the women, in the direction of sedentary and
nonexciting pastimes.[67] And women engaging in laboratory
game situations have been reported as tending to solve
competitive problems in a cooperative rather than in an
aggressive manner; the stresses of competition are not the
eustresses for them.[68]

Erik Erikson has reported among boys and girls in our
society a difference between the sexes that tends to support
the almost universal role assignments of the sexes. He found
that "girls and boys used space differently. . . . The girls
emphasized inner and the boys outer space."[69] With the
figures and the blocks at their disposal, girls tended to make
enclosures. "In a number of cases . . . the interior was
intruded by animals or dangerous men . . . [but] the majority of these intrusions have an element of humor."[70]
The boys depicted adventure, castles to be stormed, and

[66] "Why, my wife asks me," John Fischer tells us in connection
with his moral equivalent for war, "is all that necessary? Wouldn't
it be simpler for you men to stop acting like savages? Since you
realize that belligerence is no longer a socially useful trait, why don't
you try to cultivate your gentler and more human instincts?" (*Loc.
cit.,* p. 24).

[67] E. E. LeMasters, *Modern Courtship and Marriage* (New York:
The Macmillan Co., 1957), Chapter 21.

[68] W. E. Vinacke, "Sex Roles in a Three-Person Game," *Sociometry,*
Vol. 22 (December 1959), pp. 343–60; John R. Bond and W. E.
Vinacke, "Coalitions in Mixed Sex Trends," *Ibid.,* Vol. 24 (March
1961), pp. 61–75; T. C. Uesugi and W. E. Vinacke, "Strategy in a
Feminine Game," *Ibid.,* Vol. 26 (March 1963), pp. 75–88.

[69] Erik H. Erikson, "Inner and Outer Space: Reflections on Woman-
hood," in Robert Jay Lifton, ed., *The Woman in America* (Boston:
Houghton Mifflin Company, 1965), p. 9.

[70] *Ibid.,* p. 9.

other stress-providing situations. Both Minerva and Mars, it will be recalled, were gods of war; but Minerva's wars were defensive, Mars', offensive.

The old oriental Ying-Yang concept implied a sexual equilibrium, an interdependent polarity in which, perhaps, one sex provides stress and the other alleviates it. Whether the sexual role assignments reported by Zelditch—giving women a conciliatory function—are based on biology or culture (Kingsley Davis believes they are related to the child-bearing and child-rearing functions[71]), Erikson is of the opinion that men prefer them to remain. "No doubt," he says, "there exists among men an honest sense of wishing to save at whatever cost a sexual polarity, a vital tension and an essential difference which they fear may be lost in too much sameness, equality, and equivalence, or at any rate in too much self-conscious talk."[72]

Whatever may be the almost universal cultural prescriptions for women with respect to stress-seeking—prescriptions requiring them to be conciliatory and peacemakers, stress-damping rather than stress-stimulating—and despite whatever intrinsic sex differences there may be and what male preferences may be, some women do belong to the world of stress-seekers; they are as stress-seeking as men.

WOMEN AS STRESS-SEEKERS

The Amazons, who cut off a breast in order to use their bows better, revealed an image of women who were clearly not stress-allayers. There were archetypical stress-seekers among the pioneer women of the Old West, including not only the wives of the pioneering men but also such characters as Calamity Jane, Cattle Kate, Annie Oakley, among others.

> They all possessed a cold courage whether they were
> using their sex to steal military secrets or holding up a
> stagecoach. Their appetite for life, action, and excitement

[71] Kingsley Davis, *Human Society* (New York: The Macmillan Co., 1949), Chapter 4. "The secret both of woman's physical weakness and of her usual assignment of status is her child-bearing function."
[72] Erik H. Erikson, *op. cit.*, p. 9.

was insatiable. They committed espionage as coolly as they sipped their tea, seduced men in high places for their country and their causes; held their liquor, rode like Comanches, dealt stud poker, packed guns, rustled cattle, and played road agent with great efficiency and picturesqueness.[73]

And Klausner found that 7 per cent of his sample of parachutists were women. In the spring of 1966, a group of girls escaped from a detention home in suburban Washington, not because they were interested in their freedom but because they wanted to prove they could get farther than a group of boys who had broken out the day before. The first question they asked when they were caught was, "Did we do better than the boys?" And when reassured on this score, they returned contentedly to the detention home. Girl auxiliaries to fighting gangs have been reported in most major cities. Tomboys can turn up anywhere. Amelia Earhart was among the first to fly around the world. Babe Diedrickson excelled at all kinds of sports. One psychologist has reported on a type of woman he calls the "James Bond" type. He studied one hundred models with the Strong Blank, an interest inventory, and concluded that "the particular characteristics attributed to pretty girls by the late Ian Fleming may not be terribly inaccurate. As he implied, they are swingers."[74] He found among them what he labeled the "James Bond syndrome," which included: strong aversion to routine; "preference for exciting, adventuresome activities, including those with the abstract feel of danger, . . . the dramatic . . . the unstructured. . . ."[75] This syndrome was spelled out in an advertisement in a well-known periodical in the winter of 1966 under Personnel Wanted:

> Girl Friday. . . . Fierce, sense of humor. Very fierce. $700 month. Unattached. Unemployed. . . . No wall- flowers. None. No nine-to-fivers or captives of conven-

[73] James David Horan, *Desperate Women* (New York: G. P. Putnam's Sons, 1952), p. vii.

[74] David P. Campbell, "The Vocational Interests of Beautiful Women," paper given at the Midwestern Psychological Association, May 1966 (mimeographed), p. 5.

[75] *Ibid.,* pp. 4–6.

tion. Constant contact with the Congress, business, labor, the press, and the professors. No security, much adventure. This is an unequalled opportunity job. . . . No dilettantes. No apron-string worriers. No rote thinkers. . . .[76]

There is, then, no reason to believe that women are naturally any less stress-seeking than men, or even, perhaps, less violent. It is, however, not difficult to see that their bodies are less well equipped than those of men for the successful use of physical force, especially if or when pitted against the bodies of men. Although many women succeed in, let us say, karate or jujitsu, and although scratching and biting are sometimes a match for muscular power, still, for most women, excitement has to be sought in different channels. With fewer outlets for stress-seeking open to them, women have tended to look for excitement, for adventure, and for danger in the area of sex itself. Quite aside from the sober issues in the battle of the sexes, there is a wide front where there are no serious issues but only battle for its own sake.[77] Nothing, as Upton Sinclair once noted, is bleaker to women than the indifference of men at work. Bored or neglected wives, we are told, sometimes find that the only way they can engage the attention of their husbands is to pick a fight with them. Anything is better than being ignored.[78] Women thus seek to divert

---

[76] *Saturday Review of Literature* (December 4, 1965) p. 96, and succeeding weeks.

[77] Among some rodents—notably, for example, the mink—a battle is necessary to stimulate ovulation. Contrariwise, among some other animals, there is an intrinsic conflict between sexuality and aggression. Among the Cichlids, a kind of fish, "if the male has even the slightest fear of his partner, his sexuality is completely extinguished. In the female, there is the same relation between aggression and sexuality; if she is so little in awe of her partner that her aggression is not entirely suppressed, she does not react to him sexually at all. She becomes a Brunhilde and attacks him the more ferociously the more potentially ready she is for sexual reactions, that is, the nearer she is to spawning, in respect of her ovarian and hormonal state" (Konrad Lorenz, *op. cit.*, p. 103).

[78] Several generations ago social workers used to report cases among immigrant women who complained that their husbands did not love them anymore; they never beat them up. Even today wife-spanking is common enough—and enjoyed enough—that discussions of it find an interested audience in a popular magazine like *Playboy*.

men for their own excitement. They sometimes tempt fortune by "leading men on."[79]

WOMEN AS STRESS-EVOKERS: CHERCHEZ LA FEMME

It is not only as a form of feminine stress-seeking that women "lead men on." They are sometimes used by others to stimulate stress-seeking in men. For, if women have been more restricted in stress-seeking—in the form of adventure and excitement—than men, they have been used as stimuli to stress-seeking in men. Klausner reports that his "thrilled" jumpers were more susceptible to women than his "tempered" jumpers.

The folk mind has seen women as stress-provokers. Eve, it will be recalled, was the one who was approached by the serpent, and it was her willingness to try something new that finally persuaded her not only to taste the forbidden fruit but also to get Adam to follow suit. They thereby paid for knowledge with innocence; they exchanged security for stress. (The emphasis on security in Eden and the severe punishment meted out for anything that rocked the boat are noteworthy.) Circe lured adventurous men by her beauty and then turned them into swine when they accepted her challenge. The Lorelei lured men to their death on the Rhine.

A favorite conceit among peace-loving people is that if women were in charge of the world they could stop war forever. The reply sometimes is, in effect, a cynical "Oh, yeah?" and a reminder that women have been great promoters of war, that their admiration of the military hero has been one of the incentives for men to engage in warlike activities, that feminine adulation of the war hero has been a major reward, and so on. In World War I, the women sang, "Oh, we don't want to lose you" but we want you to go; and in the song "Oh, What a Lovely War" they acted in effect as recruiting agents.[80] There is little evidence

---

[79] Eric Berne, *Games People Play* (New York: Grove Press, Inc., 1964), Chapters 7 and 9.

[80] Joan Littlewood, *Oh, What a Lovely War.*

that women have ever been very successful, or even interested, in reining men in. It has become a cliché that one looks for a woman when men have done dangerous, reckless things.

SEX AS STRESS

Sexual excitement is perhaps the prototype or the archetype of most forms of eustress.[81] It is certainly among the most sought-after forms; in fact, censorship is often resorted to in order to restrain the search for this kind of eustress. The figure of speech "wooing danger" or "courting death" is an old one; and the fifth verse of Psalm 19 refers to "a bridegroom coming out of his chamber" who "rejoiceth as a strong man to run a race." Wordsworth's Happy Warrior, when called into some kind of conflict "is happy as a lover; and attired with sudden brightness, like a man inspired"; he is "endued as with a sense and faculty for storm and turbulence." The Italian motion picture "Casanova 70" was about a man who could not perform sexually unless there was at least a modicum of danger connected with it; in the end, he climbed an outside ledge to his wife's bedroom rather than simply walk through the door to her. It has often been noted that to some men it is the excitement of the sexual chase and conquest, not final success, that is appealing.

A "Club Wow" solicits membership from "sophisticated men and women who want more out of life," who are "looking for adventure"; it promises "excitement" and "new adventure," "a more exciting tomorrow."[82] Its "Wheel of Fun . . . rolls past the dull daily routine and carries its followers to new horizons of adventure." The spokes in this wheel are: swinging, offbeat, unusual, sophis-

---

[81] A. C. Kinsey and his associates comment on the fact that the expression of men and women in the throes of sexual excitement is not one of smiling pleasure but of great stress, almost like that of a runner at the finish line. (*Sexual Behavior in the Human Female*, pp. 606, 622.) E. Franklin Frazier quotes a woman who found gambling a satisfying substitute for orgasm.

[82] Advertisement circulated through the mails.

ticated, freethinking, wild, bizarre, and exotic. In brief, a
kind of sexual eudaemonism. We are reminded that Dionysianism was originally associated with sexual orgies.
And the coupling of sex and violence in the mass media
has become one of their most pervasive characteristics. It
is not even vicarious eustress, as the spectators seem to be
active participators.

William and Marlene Park have made an interesting
analysis of one of the archetypical forms of this kind of
eustress, the James Bond moving pictures which are such
a spectacular popular success.[83] They note that the stories
deal with "a supranational conflict between good and evil
which takes us beyond the dull realities and limitations of
political life into the libidinous and exciting world of violence and sex . . . in which James Bond . . . acts as medi-
ator between the humdrum and the exciting and leads us,
imaginatively at least, to partake of dangerous joys."[84]
They conclude that the violence in these pictures serves as
a Freudian screen, filtering the sexual message in an acceptable way. ". . . his life must be fraught with violence
and . . . the most dangerous place in any of these movies
is his bed,"[85] for "there is a great deal of danger in making
love, obviously,"[86] because it is a different kind of sexual
encounter. It is not the traditional sexual chase. It is not the
stereotyped pursuing male and the fleeing female. It is,
rather, heterosexual love between two aggressive human
beings, a eudaemonistic woman[87] as well as a eudaemonistic man, a James-Bond heroine as well as the James-Bond
hero, James Bond himself:

[83] William and Marlene Park, "007—License to Love," *Sarah
Lawrence Journal* (Spring 1966), pp. 42–47.
   [84] *Ibid.*, p. 42.
   [85] *Ibid.*, p. 46.
   [86] *Ibid.*, p. 47. The authors suggest that these movies are allegories
about the triumph of sexual love (p. 43). They have to be kidding!
   [87] This eudaemonistic woman is quite different from the one popu-
larized by George Bernard Shaw early in the century in his play *Man
and Superman.* She was viewed as the embodiment of a great "life
force"; she was charged, figuratively, with reproduction. She must
pursue men in order to fulfill her own biological destiny. No personal eustress-seeking here, but blind implementation of a great
biological goal.

. . . the James Bond movies go far beyond any sort of puritanical or male fantasy and reveal something to their audiences even more alarming, something seldom shown in the movies, British, American, French, or even Italian. They show us a vision of heterosexual bliss in which a sexually aggressive male makes love to a sexually aggressive female, and in a sense is saved because of it. . . . Here there is no sexually gratifying but dominating woman as in American films; no brutal male and victimized female, as in British; no sexy but destructive women in French; there is not even the irony and incompatibility which have recently characterized love and sex in Italian films. Instead, there is mutual satisfaction. One sees women making sexual demands on Bond (this should be particularly upsetting to Americans), and Bond not only meeting these demands but making some of his own. Thus, after the chain of dangers and explosions—the explosion is the most typical form of violence in these movies—each concludes with Bond and the heroine lying down together and beginning to make love.[88]

The traditional sex difference that permits stress-seeking to men and denies it to women disappears; women are sexually as eudaemonistic as men.

THEORY'S DILEMMA: HOW TO COPE WITH THE EUDAEMONIST

Thinkers in a society governed by the Protestant Ethic find it difficult to accommodate their theories to the eudaemonist. He had no place in the Adam Smith system of political economy; he did not fit either the Jeffersonian type of democracy or the Federalist type of republicanism. Still, there he was. Practical people who had to deal with the man on the street saw him destroying wealth by dumping tea into the harbor or rioting in front of banks. The often state-supported, colonial churches of the eastern coast, which catered to the staid Establishment, recognized but repudiated him; but the nineteenth-century circuit-riding

[88] William and Marlene Park, *op. cit.*, p. 47.

preachers, serving the frontiersmen, knew him well and gave him Dionysian experience at camp meetings and harvested converts.

Social thinking and research, when it could neither ignore nor find a rationale for the eudaemonist, tended to relegate him to the student of collective behavior. When he has been studied by the psychologist he has been viewed as compulsive or in some sense pathological. Our concern with a rational model of behavior blinds us to open recognition of eudaemonism. When we study nonrational behavior we become concerned with pathology—the fight against evil—as the object of our research. "Fun" nonrationality is less of a social problem and therefore less likely to attract our attention.

To the extent that his behavior is unpredictable or inconsistent, the eustress-seeker is clearly not welcome in modern theories of conflict, which find him peculiarly resistant to scientific study. Modern behavioral science, influenced perhaps by the Protestant world view, finds exchange-type theories more congenial than those that imply the existence of fundamental nonrationality in man.

Much of recent thinking in the social and behavioral sciences has met the problem by obscuring the distinction between a rationalistic and a nonrationalistic emphasis referred to at the opening of this paper. Psychoanalysis *vis-à-vis* the individual and functionalism *vis-à-vis* societies tend to find even the seemingly most irrational behavior to be somehow or other contributory to the survival if not always to the well-being of individuals and social systems and—in at least this sense, if no other—as, in effect, "rational." Thus, for example, prejudice may be viewed as necessary for certain individuals; we destroy it at our peril: the prejudiced individual might collapse psychologically without the support of his prejudice. Or, functionalists find ignorance, crime, and practically any other kind of behavior to be performing some function for the ongoing social system and—again in this sense if no other—as "rational."

Even game theory, which began as *par excellence* a the-

ory of rational behavior, has come to provide for at least
some kinds of nonrational, even irrational, behavior.[89]
Not, however, for eudaemonic, or, for that matter, any
kind of violence.[90] It is difficult to fit eustress-seeking into
an intellectual system that posits decision-makers who count
costs.

Decision theory envisages at least two kinds of situations
with respect to information. If the probabilities of all one's
opponent's courses of action, or strategies, are known, the
situation for the decision-maker is one of risk; if not, of

[89] "Threats and responses to threats, reprisals and counterreprisals,
limited war, arms races, brinkmanship, surprise attack, trusting and
cheating can be viewed as either hot-headed or cool-headed activities.
. . . The assumption of rational behavior is a productive one in the
generation of systematic theory. If behavior were actually cool-
headed, valid and relevant theory would probably be easier to create
than it actually is. . . . Furthermore, theory that is based on the
assumption that the participants coolly and 'rationally' calculate their
advantages according to a consistent value system forces us to think
more thoroughly about the meaning of 'irrationality.' . . . Rationality
is a collection of attributes, and departures from complete rationality
may be in many different directions. Irrationality can imply a dis-
orderly and inconsistent value system, faulty calculation, an inability
to receive messages or to communicate efficiently; it can imply random or haphazard influences in the reaching of decisions or the
transmission of them, or in the receipt or conveyance of information;
and it sometimes merely reflects the collective nature of a decision
among individuals who do not have identical value systems and whose
organizational arrangements and communication systems do not cause
them to act like a single entity. . . . Some kinds of 'irrationality' . . .
can be accounted for within a theory of rational behavior. . . . As a
matter of fact, one of the advantages of an explicit theory of 'rational'
strategic decision in situations of mixed conflict and common interest
is that, by showing the strategic basis of certain paradoxical tactics,
it can display how sound and rational some of the tactics are that
are practiced by the untutored and the infirm. It may not be an exag-
geration to say that our sophistication sometimes suppresses sound
intuitions, and one of the effects of an explicit theory may be to restore some intuitive notions that were only superficially 'irrational' "
(Thomas C. Schelling, *The Strategy of Conflict,* Cambridge: Harvard
University Press, 1960, pp. 16–17).

[90] ". . . though 'strategy of conflict' sounds cold-blooded, the theory is not concerned with the efficient *application* of violence or
anything of the sort; it is not essentially a theory of aggression or of
resistance or of war. *Threats* of war, yes, or threats of anything else;
but it is the employment of threats, or of threats and promises, or
more generally of the conditioning of one's own behavior on the behavior of others, that the theory is about" (*Ibid.,* p. 15).

uncertainty.[91] The theory posits choices as involving another dimension also, in addition to probability: namely, the subjective valuation placed on outcomes—that is, the payoffs. An extremely highly valued outcome that has a very small probability will ordinarily not have as high an expected payoff as a less valued one that has great probability.

But some people like to take long shots. They choose a less certain or more risky outcome. In order to accommodate such eudaemonic individuals in decision theory, the concept of "the utility of gambling" itself is introduced. That is, the excitement of taking long chances, of acting against great odds, has value for some people in and of itself, quite aside from the possible rewards themselves. In this way theory can accommodate the player who ignores known probabilities and, in this sense, is not rational.[92]

SUMMARY

The existence of eustress-seeking as a given among human beings in societies above the subsistence level was taken for granted in this paper. As a form of human-energy consumption it was viewed as, in effect, an alternative to work. Class, age, cultural, and sex differences in the forms it has taken were explored. The effect of the Protestant Ethic has been to undercut the eudaemonist. At the same time, modern economies by their affluence release more and more energy for consumption rather than for productive uses. The result has been, allegedly, a great deal of "free-floating" eudaemonism all over the world, expressing itself in Dionysian violence. The controls operating in the

[91] R. Duncan Luce and Howard Raiffa, *Games and Decisions: Introduction and Critical Survey* (New York: John Wiley & Sons, Inc., 1957), pp. 280–86.

[92] An ancient truism in penology states that it is the certainty rather than the nature of the sanctions brought to bear against criminals which is important if they are to serve as deterrents to antisocial behavior. Capital punishment which has low probability is less deterring, it is argued, than a lighter sentence which is certain to be imposed. For some people, however, the risk-taking is itself worthwhile.

past—the provision of vicarious or simulated forms of eudaemonism and socialization of the young into acceptable role patterns—have not kept up with these changes. Since eudaemonism has great positive potential, the problem is not one of suppressing it but of providing currently suitable modes for its expression. Not too much help has been forthcoming from the social and behavioral sciences. Eudaemonism has not fit into their models and it has been relegated to the field of collective behavior for primarily descriptive study. Dr. Klausner's work subjects it to more rigorous study.

Charles S. Houston

Only a fraction of Charles Houston's story is told in his publications. He has been a practicing family doctor in a small community, leader of several Himalayan expeditions, a flight surgeon, and Director of the Peace Corps in India. *Five Miles High* is the story of the first American expedition which in 1938 reconnoitered the second highest summit in the world, K-2, reaching 26,000 feet. In 1953 he led another party toward that summit, but the party was trapped in a violent storm at 25,000 feet, and in evacuating a stricken member, one man was killed and the rest narrowly escaped. The story of this dramatic climb and tragedy is told in the book *K-2, The Savage Mountain*. The books describe vividly and with emotion the spirit of high climbing and contain appendices which may be helpful to others planning such expeditions. In 1950 Houston was one of a small party to visit the south side of Everest for the first look at the route over which later parties were to reach the summit.

The medical problems of man at high altitude are the natural concern of a physician-climber. As a Navy flight surgeon, Dr. Houston trained over 50,000 men in the problems of operating at great altitude, and directed the first major study of acclimatization to high altitude under controlled conditions: four men lived for thirty-five days in a decompression chamber in which the pressure was gradually decreased to simulate altitude increasing to 29,000 feet. Examinations of these subjects helped to define the process by which the human adapts to altitudes which would kill him in a few minutes without this adaptation. This work in high-altitude physiology is of value not only to those who climb, play, work, or fight in the mountains, but also to patients with heart and lung disease who are chronically short of oxygen.

Dr. Houston has also been active in the development of an artificial heart—a small pump that, inserted in the chest, can totally and permanently replace the human heart that can no longer maintain life. Working with Dr. Gerald Rainer, Dr. Houston built several such hearts and was able to sustain life in experimental animals for more than thirty hours.

Charles Houston's stress-seeker climbing in "The Last Blue Mountain" struggles under heavy baggage and against severe handicaps to "stretch his capacity" to do what few others can do—his capacity to bear the fear of falling and endure thirst, sunburn, frost-bite, blisters, fatigue, and the effects of altitude when "simple tasks become major struggles." Each step is evaluated in terms of the climber's control of the de-gree of risk. A less than deft movement endangering him or his companions is cause for a poor evaluation. Danger from a situation beyond his control is ab-horred; that is a test of fate, not of capacity. There is no abandon here, just controlled—rationally controlled —plodding and pulling. As Houston says, the aim is not to conquer, for mountain climbing is not a conflict between man and nature. The aim is to transcend a previous self by dancing a "ballet" on the crags and precipices and eventually, at very long last, to emerge exhilarated and addicted.

THE LAST BLUE MOUNTAIN

We are the pilgrims, master. We must go
  Ever a little farther, it may be
Beyond the last blue mountain, rimmed with snow.
                    James Elroy Flecker

Mountain climbing is one of the more obviously stress-seeking sports, and therefore an appropriate subject of study in stress. Nature rather than other men is the ad-versary in mountaineering. It is not a competitive game, it seldom brings material rewards. Recognition and fame are usually not accorded, unless by one's peers. Stress and the bright thrill of danger are ever present in climbing and are perhaps the principal call to climb.

Climbing offers many pleasures as well, although these take more gentle forms in other activities. Better physical fitness is gained from other types of exercise. The overwhelming beauty of mountains can be viewed just as well from easily attained summits and aircraft. Fame and fortune come more frequently to other sportsmen than to climbers.

Before trying to dissect motivation and reward, it might be well to describe climbing for the uninitiated. Those who tramp the hills are walkers; their enjoyment is great, but their risks are small, their stresses few. It is the climbers who cling like flies to sheer cliffs and who make arduous expeditions to remote ranges whose experiences and motivation we seek to understand.

Whether a brief *excursion* lasting a few days, perhaps over a short but difficult route, or an *expedition* that struggles for weeks or months toward a high summit in a wild region, it is mountain climbing; both offer similar stresses. Similar individuals participate in both, and for similar reasons.

Climbers, like other sportsmen, have developed an armory of special equipment suited to their needs. Among the obvious items are boots, warm clothing, tents, and sleeping bags. The climber's constant companion—his symbolic staff—is the ice ax. To his boots he may strap long spikes (crampons) for secure footing on steep ice and snow. He will drive special nails (pitons) into cracks or into holes drilled in the rock, and to these he will attach snap links (karabiners), through which runs the climbing rope each member of the party is tied to. On extreme climbs he will use ladders, stirrups clipped to pitons, or special sliding slings to give direct upward assistance where the rock offers no hold for hand or foot. He has hammocks in which to bivouac, slung from pitons. It is not unusual for a climber to be weighted down by forty pounds or more of such "hardware" when he tackles a particularly difficult climb, and to take many hours to gain a few hundred vertical feet. On longer expeditions such aids are a formidable part of the baggage.

The rope is the simplest of the protections used by climbers, and the subtlest. Two or three men may tie equidistant along a rope, moving one at a time over difficult pitches. Properly used, the rope protects all, but carelessly used it increases risk and danger. The rope has great symbolic value as well. Each roped man deliberately places his life in the hands of his companions, an added stress. After many or arduous climbs together, individuals feel deeply this kinship of the rope.

Such aids make routes that would be unthinkable without them possible and less dangerous. As in so many other sports, effort beyond the experience of one generation is commonplace to its successor. Refinement of equipment makes possible an escalation of effort within limits of acceptable risks. Stress is thereby deliberately increased. It is important to acknowledge that each older generation of climbers has resisted the development of advanced aids, perhaps foreseeing the ultimate day when equipment makes the presently impossible easily accessible to all.

It can be safely predicted that a determined climber with new devices could climb anything—even an overhanging wall of glass. We see, and some deplore, this happening every day, as more and more "impossible" routes are opened. The mountains are indeed passing through the three stages described by Mummery, the great nineteenth-century mountaineer: "An impossible peak, the hardest climb in the Alps, an easy day for a lady."

To add to stress and its headiness, climbers now make ascents at night or in winter, alone, or deliberately in bad weather. Do such variances gain more credit for the climber? Apparently so—at least among his peers. Where is the line between acceptable—i.e., controllable—risk, and that which is flagrantly foolhardy? What constitutes deliberate expansion of capacity, and when does this become unjustifiable gambling with life—not only one's own, but also the lives those who may have to rescue or retrieve the body? These are not easy questions to answer.

Most modern climbers believe that the proliferation of artificial aids is justifiable because they allow for greater challenge without increasing uncontrollable risks. The line is a thin one, as the following quotation suggests.

> Reports made the imagination boggle—the last great unclimbed north wall, a mile high, over-hanging, smooth, holdless, bolts all the way, sleeping in hammocks—impossible even! . . . The ascent of the wall was started on the 5th of July and during three days of hard labor in mist and rain, ropes were fixed up a thousand feet of steep introductory slabs and dangerously poised snow slopes. At the first bivouac, a hundred feet up the vertical wall, equipment was dumped. . . . As midnight approached, I reached the overhang. A perfect crack for channel pegs but as usual they were elsewhere. . . . Above we found a small snow ledge where we spent the last night with the summit ridge forming a black jagged skyline two hundred feet beyond.
> During the next weekend we gained about 400 feet more up the face (of this 2100-foot wall). . . . The next 250 feet . . . necessitated almost totally bolts. . . . The next 200 feet were very discouraging, all bolts again, and we were tempted to give up. . . . During the first sixteen days of climbing, except for one night spent on top of the Split Pillar, we descended each night so that much time was lost each day prusiking and unsnarling the tangles from the previous day. . . . Altogether we had used 138 bolts and we lost count of the pitons, although it was probably between 200 and 250.[1]

We must differentiate risk from danger. Experienced climbers understand, enjoy, and seek risk because it presents a difficulty to overcome and can be estimated and controlled. He equally abhors danger because it is beyond his control. Injury while crossing a slope swept by avalanche is unpredictable and dangerous, whereas the risk of an exposed climb up an overhanging face lies within his capability.

This constant stretching of capacity is one of the characteristics that distinguishes man from other animals and has led to his mastery of so many skills. When early explorers set out to sail across the apparently endless ocean, they

[1] Thomas F. Hornbein, *Everest—The West Ridge*, ed. David Brower, San Francisco: Sierra Club, 1965, p. 35.

were testing limits as much as the modern runner who tries a faster mile. We seem constantly to search for the ultimate test, perhaps to find as well as to test ourselves. Hornbein, writing of the great traverse of Mt. Everest in 1963, refers repeatedly to this ultimate: "Why was Willi here? With George he had made the top of Masherbrum. He had passed the Himalayan test—or had he? 'Not really,' he said. 'After all, Everest is the ultimate test—in altitude anyway.'" David Brower elsewhere wrote: "This inclination to inquire, this drive to go higher than need be, this innate ability to carry it off, this radiance in the heart when you carry it off, however brief in the infinite eternity, whether you do it, or Tom, or Willi, makes us grateful for the genius that man has and the beautiful planet he has to live on."[2]

The stresses or tests of new and more difficult routes are deliberately sought; other stresses adherent in mountaineering are accepted and controlled. Difficult climbs demand great exertion; long climbs bring the sensual satisfactions of conditioning—superb health, coordination, balance and nerve. The expert's dancer-like movements are beautiful to watch, continuous, unhurried, and never forced; his ballet is exhilarating and addictive. The novice, however, finds climbing exertion great and effort inefficient. He moves in jerks, clutching at holds far harder than necessary, and emerging spent at the end. But even he experiences the exhilaration.

There are other accepted stresses, some of which are also present in other sports. When every ounce must be carried, there is seldom enough to eat and drink. Thirst is a constant problem and dehydration the resultant stress. Sun temperature is high, while the cold is bitter, making frostbite as real a risk as sunstroke. Climbing severely taxes the heart and lungs, strains and cramps the muscles, and overstimulates the glands of internal secretion.

The psychological burden is also great. The fear of falling, considered one of man's basic phobias, is seldom far from the climber, but as he gains in skill it recedes, though it may explode after a near accident, in the form of a

[2] *Ibid.*, p. 21.

pounding heart, cold sweat, near-panic. To control such fear is a great satisfaction.

On long expeditions the stresses are multiplied by months of planning ending in the emotional frenzy of departure and the weeks spent on the approach march with its accompanying sunburn, blisters, injuries and sickness. From base camp upward the tasks are even greater. Although the goal—the summit—is sharp and clear, the route may not be. Weather changes violently. Loads must be carried on men's backs, camps stocked and occupied, logistics minutely planned. The game becomes work.

A major stress—the effect of altitude—appears still higher. Although few healthy individuals are adversely affected up to 10,000 feet, few remain unaffected above 14,000 feet. The percentage of oxygen in our blanket of air does not decrease with height, but its pressure does. Oxygen lack is incompatible with life above 20,000 feet except for the well-acclimatized person. There one upward step takes a dozen labored breaths, the heart races, and simple tasks become major struggles. There the climber is like a sick man walking in a dream. Do not believe the man who claims to enjoy climbing at the greatest heights; he has buried his recollections. Physiological limits are reached apparently at about the height of the summit of Everest. But is this really the limit? Could man go higher were there a higher summit? We can be sure that he would try.

The marvelous and intricate adjustments that enable man to acclimate to heights rapidly fatal to sea-level man cannot concern us here. They are physiological stresses overcome by the various parts of the body. Just as the lack of oxygen stimulates a series of adaptive changes that permit survival, stress develops dormant strengths that, emerging, make a bigger man. It is not appropriate here to dwell on the improvement of performance that comes when supplementary oxygen is breathed by mask, a climbing aid that, decreasing one stress, adds others.

High altitudes are usually cold and windy, and sunlight unfiltered by atmosphere is debilitating. Sleep is broken and brings little rest, so that the climber awakens, still tired, to fumble with frozen boots and melt snow for his morning tea, taking hours to ready himself for the exhausting labor of moving upward. Dehydration is severe. The cold air is completely dry and sucks moisture from skin and from each panting breath. There is never enough to drink when it takes precious fuel to melt each drop of water. Appetite decreases, food tastes flat, nourishment declines. It is usual for climbers to lose one pound per day spent above 20,000 feet.

Though less extreme, these stresses are also present on the lower mountains. Indeed, most of them are common wherever the limits of the known are explored, whether it be at the poles, on the seas, or in jungle or desert. Each venture toward the limits has its own pain and brings its own rewards. Nansen wrote: "Without privation there would be no struggle, and without struggle, no life."

Every mountain has an easier route to the top. Many may be climbed by car or train; others one can walk up. Yet climbers seek harder and harder routes to that summit, although they are not adverse to strolling down the easy way after hours or days spent laboring upward on a new or "impossible" ascent. On Long's Peak, for example, hundreds enjoy the easy way to the summit, but since 1964 twenty-three climbers have made six new routes on the "Diamond"—a desperately vertical face. It is the stress of the difficult, the call of controlled risk, that leads to this seeming absurdity. Such climbers are always seeking to find their own limits by ever-increasing stresses. The greater the rigors, the greater their pride in accomplishment, and perhaps the more honest their self-understanding.

Recently it has become fashionable to classify climbs numerically according to difficulty. A natural result has been the classification of climbers according to ability. It has followed with predictable certainty that individuals insistently try more difficult routes to test, and by testing to improve their ability and raise their classification.

Thus Herman Buhl, supremely capable, tried ever more difficult routes in the Alps alone, at night, then in winter, to prepare himself for the Himalayas, where he alone reached the top of man-killing Nanga Parbat. Later he died in a fearful storm while trying another virgin peak. Bonatti, after reaching the top of K-2, undertook fantastic rock climbs in the Alps. On one unclimbed buttress of vertical granite, he spent five days alone, and there were pitches where he roped *down* before resuming the ascent. Had he failed to reach the summit he could not have reascended these places and would have died hanging from the cliff. Few climbs can equal this solitary campaign in improvidence and courage, folly and endurance. No climber has shown more complete mastery of his medium under more appalling circumstances.

Lindbergh said, "A certain amount of danger is essential to the quality of life," and this is certainly true of climbing. As more and more difficult climbs are made, each new generation tests itself against still higher standards, at night, in winter, on skis. As I write, a party is attempting Mt. McKinley, which has been climbed by many routes over the years. Now it is challenged in winter with temperatures far below zero, and only an hour of dim, wintery daylight. Shall we see such testing carried to even further extremes? Will a party try Rum Doodle barefoot? Or make a first ascent with hands tied behind the back, or blindfold? How far can testing be carried before it becomes absurd?

There is a magic difficult to define about the highest standards of performance in any field. The desire to excel, to be supreme in one's chosen skill, is a very human ambition and has led man ever further in his growth and—I like to believe—in his knowledge of himself. Several generations ago the unattained ambition of thousands was to swim the English Channel; today it goes unnoticed. Shall we see man trying the Atlantic? More recently, the mile has been run in four minutes, a mark regarded unattainable a decade ago. Since one man broke that magic line, dozens have run still faster, and who shall say what the ultimate limits may be? Runners have not changed much, but their psychological knowledge of what is possible has changed. As known limits change, further limits are challenged.

Fifty years ago it was generally believed that man could not survive a night above 22,000 feet. That ceiling was rapidly raised, until we now know that a man may live on the 29,000-foot peak of Mt. Everest breathing air alone, after spending days and nights above 25,000 feet. Since the ascent, which defied a dozen parties for forty years, was accomplished by two men in 1953, it has been made by a score of others. Who can say that this is the ultimate in climbing? Though we know of no higher point on earth, what of the moon and stars?

The existence of a challenge has always stimulated response from man. And when the challenge exceeds known limits, the response brings increased capacity. Does the death of a climber make a certain mountain or route more attractive to others? The answer is probably yes, at least where the severity of the climb has been the prime factor in the accident. It is not necessarily true, however, where a fortuitous avalanche or sudden storm has been the killer. The north face of the Eiger is often tried despite its formidable death toll, because the accidents have been due primarily to the climber's failure. By contrast, the Marinelli Gully, whose avalanches have killed many, does not have the same attraction. The manageable risks that make a route difficult do attract climbers, while the uncontrollable dangers do not.

There have been tragic accidents where one or more climbers have faced life-and-death decisions. Should a man save himself after an accident, but only at the price of abandoning his companion who cannot be saved? Such a stress tears at the moral fiber. It is a known stress which each must accept if he is to try the great endeavors, and it is not evaded.

I must end as I began, by reiterating my conviction that climbing is one of the few human activities where the stress is clear, apparent, and freely sought. The goal is sharp and visible. There is no doubt when one has succeeded or failed. Mountaineering is more a quest for self-fulfillment than a victory over others or over nature. The true mountaineer knows that he has not conquered a mountain by standing on its summit for a few fleeting moments. Only when the right men are in the right place at the right time are the big mountains climbed; never are they conquered.

Climbers court and control risk, seek stress, but avoid

the uncontrollable dangers. By their repeated self-testing, capacity grows as it does in so many other and unrelated activities. By such expansion of capability, man finds that he has wider limits than we know.

One of the great modern climbers, John Harlin, wrote shortly before he was killed on a difficult climb: "I have used climbing as a medium for introspection into my own mind and have tried to understand my reactions to stimuli, particularly between emotion and muscle coordination. Before training, the coordination of mind and body is not stable when one is on a two-thousand-foot ice wall with a tenuous belay. After training, the personal understanding of oneself that occurs in the intricate alpine experience can be developed and used outside of this experience. In other words, it can be borrowed and projected. This ultimately leads to a physical and emotional control of one's self. I believe that this control is an important prerequisite to creativity."

The great George Mallory said of Everest: "Whom have we conquered? None but ourselves. Have we won a kingdom? No—and yes. We have achieved an ultimate satisfaction, fulfilled a destiny. To struggle and to understand, never this last without the other."

Samuel L. A. Marshall

Samuel L. A. Marshall has for some thirty years been criticizing the view that the armed forces are simply an arm of political institutions. Rather, they constitute relatively autonomous forces having their own role in the making of states and the shaping of civilizations. He has written widely on tactics. In *Blitzkrieg*, a battle analysis of the Second World War published in 1940, he attributed the rapid advance of the Nazi forces to the failure of the French and the British to adjust their military concepts to the new equipment being fielded at that time—particularly, to prepare for mechanized war.

Armies on Wheels, published a year later, attributed the success of the German thrust into Russia to the use of the heavy mobile tank. Military concepts, however, remain fluid. The advantage which mobile armor gave the Nazis was soon neutralized by the use of smaller antitank weapons. In this book "Slam" Marshall argued the case for independent air power operating in close association with ground power and ultimately responsive to the requirements of the ground commander.

Traditional military historians have given the lion's share of attention to strategy and tactical planning at the highest level. Marshall traced the working out of tactics and strategy in the behavior of the soldier in the field. *Island Victory*, a report on the battle for Kwajalein Atoll, was developed from postcombat interviewing data. He would assemble members of a combat unit as soon as practicable after a battle and interview them in groups. From these interviews he could reconstruct the events of that battle and so piece together the story of a particular unit under battle conditions. The interviews lasted an average of seven and a half hours per unit. With breaks for lunch this enabled him to complete the interviewing of a company. On one occasion, in which two battalions were intermingled, the debriefing lasted six days.

The postcombat interviewing technique was further developed during the Korean War, and *Pork Chop Hill* was written on the basis of such data. This book evaluates the response of infantry units to pressure—Marshall's official military task. The intent was to estimate whether troops were good or bad or the tactics right or wrong. Tactics had to stand the test at the level of their execution by the individual soldier and his unit.

Men Against Fire examines the relation of the command to troop performance in the field. The command sometimes errs in predicting the amount of firepower put down by an infantry company because they do not allow for the refusal of some soldiers to fire their weapons. The problem of refusal to fire led Marshall to write this psychological study of man in combat. The stage had been set in *The Soldier's Load,* a study of men under stress.

Sinai Victory, subtitled "Command Decision in History's Shortest War," recorded the advance of the Israeli Army across the Sinai Peninsula in 1956. Observation of individual men in action was combined with an analysis of the use of mobile armor and of men. Action in Sinai followed traditional military doctrine. Officers led their men, and maximum amounts of mobility were linked with an economy of fire.

Recently, *The Officer As A Leader* appeared as a revision of the *Armed Forces Officers' Manual* originally published in 1950. Intended for the officer who has completed formal training, Marshall advises that action is as contagious as fear or courage.

"Slam" Marshall's contribution to this symposium may well have been introduced with Lucretius' epigram, "What is food to one man may be fierce poison to others." All men live with fear but not all endure the same fears. The stress-seeker may run, toil, or fight, and yet these may be the most natural of tasks for him, though appearing stressful to the onlooker. One man may dread battle while another fears social encounters. Each may think the other brave. Men "recessive as barracks soldiers" may be courageous at the front. Depending largely on early habituation, some people are "natural" stress-seekers. For them, stress no longer hurts.

Stress-seeking is a "normal" portion of a considered life. Its alternative is "indolence," a return to the Dark Ages and to a matriarchate. Serenity coexists with peace of mind and rigor. Those who expose themselves to danger for kicks or vainglory are immature. The spectacular and dramatic forms of encounter with risk, such as the "lust of the athlete for success," differ from the simpler drives to "walk about" or "communicate with one's fellows" only in degree.

THE BETTER PART OF MAN'S NATURE

No better approach to the study and discussion undertaken here with my colleagues comes to mind than two sentences lifted from the writings of Rabbi Joshua Loth Liebman: "Grown men do not pray for vain trifles. When they lift up their hearts and voices in this valley of tears they ask for courage and strength and understanding."

The quotation is from his best-known collection of essays. He had begun by reciting how as a young man he had made his own inventory of earthly desirables, a list that included these words: "health, love, beauty, talent, power, riches and fame." Then an older and wiser scholar pointed out that he had overlooked the one boon precious above all others, putting it in these words: "Give me the gift of the Untroubled Mind."

Disclaiming any credit for original or hard-won wisdom, the sage said he was only paraphrasing such teachers of men as the psalmist David and the Emperor Marcus Aurelius, who said, "I have what the universal nature wills me to have; and I do what my nature now wills me to do."

Here are two lives cited by the philosopher as exemplary for their serenity of mind; yet they were still more noteworthy for the rigor, danger, and testing experience deliberately sought and overcome. He saw no contradiction in this, nor did Liebman; else the latter would not have noted that grown men pray for strength and courage. There is no need of either if there are no trials to be met, no sense of distance to be run, nothing to be sought except an outer tranquillity.

So it is that until I was invited to share in this study, it had never occurred to me that anyone regarded stress-seeking, in one form or another, as anything but a normal portion of a considered life. We are what we are only because throughout the ages certain men have willingly accepted nigh incalculable risks. I cannot imagine civilization enduring, much less advancing, without that spirit being present. Yet one cannot risk stresslessly.

I have participated in many so-called "stress" conferences with the military and its scientists, mainly because almost by accident I did pioneer work in this field and made at least one major original contribution to medical and military knowledge.[1] There, however, we were dealing with stress as it related to the physical wearing down of the soldier through the impact of fear, which is no less debilitating than road marching, trench digging, and other hard toil. The task was to determine what this signified in terms of load reform and adjustment, new principles in command, and the revising of operational theory and practice. The aim was purely practical and some extraordinary reform programs came of it, to the benefit of troops now fighting in Vietnam.

This stress study, while dealing tangentially with the nature of stress and its effects on man, is more directly concerned with penetrating the mystery of why male individuals primarily seek it. Inasmuch as I do not view that as a mystery, even after reading some of the papers that treat it as such, I cannot get my sights wholly in line with the target. The alternative to an acceptance of stress as the natural order of life is the seeking of indolence, pleasure, relaxation, surcease; the equivalents of which the average male in modern society is unable to command except at rarest intervals in his lifetime. That is the difference between him and the male aborigine in such an idyllic setting as Tahiti; in Captain Bligh's time he could gather the substance for existence from the trees of the forest or the off-

[1] Samuel L. A. Marshall, *The Soldier's Load and the Mobility of a Nation* (Washington, D.C.: Combat Forces Press, 1950).

shore coral reefs and live almost without stress until he competed in love with some brawnier, lustier savage. The same Tahitian, being free as a bird, can also be cited as an example of the perfect son of liberty. Still, all we know of him has no use as a measure of what attitude in man is required to extend the growth of an institutionally organized society, and thereby further the social and material progress of a great part of mankind. In earlier years I might have envied his existence, but age forbids that I dwell on possibilities no longer tantalizing.

That thought prompts one question: If stress-seeking is not a normal and natural urge toward the shaping of character and the doing of life's work, but must more properly be regarded as one means to the desirable ends of fame, fortune, and tranquillity, why do not all great warriors, statesmen, race drivers, and explorers joyously make the transition from full-scale participation to the shades of retirement? Rare indeed is the great adventurer, the strong competitor, who thereafter can rest easily on his laurels, though free of economic worry and amid surroundings designed chiefly to give him a sense of well-being. The explanation that he has been "conditioned" to high pressure or to stress-seeking simply does not wash; it is another way of saying that he has been made the victim of his whole life experience. There is no *a priori* reason not to believe that, but for stress-seeking, there would have been no halcyon years in his life.

Still, deliberate stress-seeking is not peculiar to what we call the civilized order. One finds it in the cultural patterns of some of the most primitive tribes. The Tarahumaras of Southern Chihuahua are much in the news these days because of famine. In 1925 I lived for three weeks among them—and speak of them as they were then. These people never walk; they run wherever they go. The males can jog one hundred and twenty miles or more without resting; the women can run from twenty to fifty miles. Either sex can run a deer to exhaustion. Persistence in toil is an absolute rule with them. When elders become so infirm that they cannot participate in work, they are, in all kindness, pitched over a cliff. Oddly enough, this is the one Indian tribe I

know where family devotion and parental love are as strong
and genuine as in the warmest households this side of the
border.

This may seem a digression. But, for the most part, the
conference papers I have read deal with stress-seeking as
if it were somehow virtually incompatible with man's best
nature, his well-being as a person, his significance as a contributor to his family's welfare, his environment and his
prospect of finding peace of mind. That is wherein I differ.
Stress is a natural condition and stress-seeking in man is
inevitable. Toil of any kind, or simply walking about, or
for that matter communicating with one's fellows begets
stress in some degree. It is an effort to walk two miles every
day to fetch a quart of milk, as I discovered at age ten,
but I learned to relieve this stress by becoming expert at
hitting any rock on the prairie with my spit at a ten-foot
range. Trying to get next to strangers is difficult, though it
may be essential to anyone's determination to keep on keeping on.

The key word in what I have said is *degree*. Some of
my collaborators seemingly see some vital, meaningful difference between stress-seeking in its simpler workaday and
truly unavoidable manifestations and its more dramatic,
spectacular, and if you will, mystifying forms. Personally,
I do not, nor can I understand how these collaborators
make a distinction between the simpler drives and impulses
and the athlete's lust for success in competition or the warrior's willingness to face a duty that is by nature disagreeable. Scholarship is not a tent under which we are permitted to disregard the relationship between the important
and the seemingly trivial.

Some of the papers pay no attention to the possibility,
or rather, the scientifically sustained proposition, that stress-
seeking is the natural and glandularly determined attitude
in the male, without which civilization might become
eclipsed by another Dark Age or revert to a matriarchate
as in the time of Sparta or the Five Nations.[2] So there is

[2] See Mathilde and Mathias Vaerting, *The Dominant Sex: A Study
in the Sociology of Sex Differentiation,* trans. Eden and Cedar Paul
(New York: George H. Doran Co., 1923).

the unavoidable implication that we are creatures of free choice and could will for ourselves a frictionless, stress-free sort of life. I do not believe that any honest male member of a college faculty would concede that he goes about his daily life and business making this his rule in meeting human problems, though it might be his heart's desire.

In "The Cowboy and the Lady," the late Gary Cooper said to the female, "I aims, ma'am, to be high regarded." It is a pat line that made that particular male character in no way exceptional. The phrases simply voice a common longing in mankind. Almost by the time we are through drinking mother's milk, we are permeated with the hope of turning out to be something different. Our parents give us that; the schools pound it home. We are schooled as competitors because there is little else all around us. The choice is one of taking to the sandlots or hiding in a corner at home. What happens after childhood may be determined by nothing more significant than the opening of opportunity, some odd chance, or a personal and unbeatable frustration. Accident, more than design, brings about our categorizations, launches us on some particular calling, and may ultimately bestow on us a reputation for being a certain "kind of man." We are all fearful about one thing or another; that is part of our destiny. When Franklin D. Roosevelt, paraphrasing Montaigne, said, "All we have to fear is fear itself," it wasn't even a half-truth. We all live with fear, and those of us who are most successful in coping with it may only have learned to fear it somewhat less.

However, there is a corollary, which could lead to a wholly false set of conclusions if not understood. Extraordinary stress, in its various forms, if undergone often enough may become so much a part of the routine of one's life that the stress is no longer present. The task may take such hold that the emotions are as normal as when one rocks on the front porch. There is no feeling of tension. For anyone looking on from the outside to call this stress-seeking, simply because he cannot understand the nature of another person or imagine himself being comfortable in the role, is hardly scientific.

In 1917 I had a recruit in my platoon, an Okie, one Stephen Wimberley. He could do nothing right. He would invariably start off on the right foot, fumble in shouldering arms, drop his rifle many times, and shake all over when I bawled him out. When the time came to weed out our culls, I kept his name on the list of men bound for France. The company commander, J. E. L. Millender, called me on it, saying, "I thought you said he couldn't soldier." I replied, "He can't, but he's so damned bad I want to find out what's wrong with him; besides, the men in the platoon all like him." Millender shook his head, but we took Wimberley along. At the front, this five-footer turned out to be a giant. He could take over the most dangerous detail and handle it so perfectly that we had to make him a sergeant. One night in the dugout I asked him about his past. Then it all came out. Now thirty years old, he had been a coal miner and dynamiter since age thirteen. Danger was his dish; he didn't fear it at all. But in that dark hole he had been away from the world of men. As we got to the front and he found out that he was superior to us in the one thing that counted most, there was an immediate wholesale change in his attitude. But on his many missions he was not stress-seeking; he was doing what came naturally.

Not unlike him was the late Staff Sergeant Edward N. Kaneshiro, a Hawaiian Nisei whom I met in Vietnam in late 1966. I was putting him in for the Medal of Honor for an incredibly bold action near the Soui Ca Valley. He shook with fright and could not answer coherently a single question I asked him. He said to my assistant, "I'd rather face fire." One month later, before the medal could be awarded, he was killed while once again charging a machine-gun nest ahead of his squad.

One finds this same attitude and reaction in our reservation Indians, many Southwestern Mexicans, and not a few recently arrived immigrants. They are reclusive, often badly disciplined and without initiative as barracks soldiers. At the front they perform confidently, courageously, and give it well-judged direction to other men. It is as if at last they had found their natural environment. It is self-apparent that these emergents do not feel the stress of other men. Is it then stress-seeking that they do duty of the hardest kind so admirably? Obviously, it depends on the point of view.

In my own case, I was an all-round athlete in school and the Army, and had some semipro experience; my sports were baseball, football, basketball and polo, although I weighed only one hundred and forty pounds. Having been a small boy with a small hand who could not spin a top, fly a kite, play marbles, roller skate, ice skate, or swim, I took to contact sports at the age of seven and quickly found that I was a good ball-handler. I enjoyed these things because I could do them well. It is true that we like to do those things in which we can excel, and the more we relish doing them, the less stressful we find them. The average professional college athlete, though he be college-trained, pursues his career because it is a good, lazy way to make a living, possibly the laziest he can find; he is not a stress-seeker or glory-hunter—though he may become a public hero.

I entered the Army at sixteen, and my first time in battle as a line sergeant occurred a year later. Prior to entry, I had the average adolescent's fear and apprehension of military service, had no interest in the Army, and could not think of myself as a soldier. Upon enlisting, I was surprised and delighted to find that everything in the military came easily for me, partly because the give-and-take in group sports was a good conditioner. At the front, I was again surprised to discover that artillery and machine-gun fire bothered me far less than other men; I didn't feel like ducking, though I soon realized it was the thing to do in the interest of self-preservation. I wondered about the difference between myself and my more nervous comrades: was it because we were of different fiber? One reason I kept going back to war, after another strange turn of the wheel landed me in the writing business, was my curiosity about the answer. Over the years I found it. Age and increased responsibility had nothing to do with it. What I was in the first place, I remained. In fifty years, I have gone to twenty-one wars, including two tours in Korea, and four in Vietnam. Always during the approach there is the same sweaty anticipation; I almost kick myself for doing it once again and worry about what I will find. I guess I have done this more times than any person alive. But because I know how to do my work and settle to it immediately, all of the moving-up stress lifts off once I arrive, even though my work is done in the combat zone. Can this be called stress-seeking, when experience has taught me that when at grips with the real thing I feel no stress? If I did, I could not get my work done. The rules of the game that I apply to myself are simple and inviolable: take whatever risk the doing of work requires; never take an extra risk just for the sake of risking. The last time out in Vietnam I had seventy-six hours of combat flying in Hueys during eight weeks. Every mission was essential to the work I had determined to do. It sounds strenuous, but I did not find it so. It was exciting and rewarding, and I felt more peace of mind than I ever know in New York City and slept better at night than I do at home. The pattern of my life is not at all unusual, because it enabled me to make the most of my small talents, an average desideratum. I can think of no easier or simpler way I might have made a good living or arrived at any reputation for doing original work. Writing was the easiest, least stress-filled thing I could do. (I had been an actor, soldier, bricksetter, underground surveyor, and, briefly, a cowpuncher in Sierra Blanca.) Only the first two occupations were agreeable. When I turned writer, I determined to specialize in military criticism, which I knew I had some real aptitude for. Either I had to keep going back to war to refresh my knowledge, or else find a small place among the so-called "military intellectuals," an idea I found repugnant. All else followed in due course. But I cannot say that my life has been stress-filled any more than I can think of myself as a stress-seeker. I just did what was easiest for me.

In the first war, I noticed with considerable astonishment that my regiment, a thoroughly conditioned outfit, would be beaten down by a twelve-mile approach march to the front on a balmy June evening. I had seen these men carry the same loads on a twenty-mile training march in far worse weather. I was even more mystified when three weeks later, after prolonged battle and heavy loss, the same men shouldered the same packs and marched thirty-seven miles effortlessly, going away from the front. Baffled, I still could not see what it signified. Much later, in 1943–44, during the invasions of the Gilberts and Marshalls, I began to put two and two together. A particular question haunted me: why did battle or near-contact drain the energies of men at an excessive and unaccountable rate? But it was only later, at Omaha Beach, that I realized for the first time what truth science and medicine had missed—fear was degenerative, not just mentally and emotionally, but like fatigue, was an invader of the physical temple of the person, a destroyer of bodily energy and willpower, a brake on the adrenal cortex. Since 1950, I have felt we should accept the fact and go on to its effects, so that in the military or elsewhere it could be used as a stepping-stone toward a correcting process. No man's time is long enough that he can afford to keep twanging the same worn string. I thought that it was because of this background of experience that I was invited to be with my associates at the conference. Most of what I have learned that applies in any way to the subject under discussion I have learned on my own, for which fact I mean no apology, for I go along with Kant's idea that most of what a person knows and can apply confidently he has learned pretty much for himself, out of what happens to him as a person.

I do not think that discussing Hemingway, Fitzgerald, or Crane, what they were and what their motivations signify, leads to any worthwhile end. It may be an entertaining exercise, but nothing more. Each man is a special case; and that the man as a writer happens to achieve a certain renown does not shade this proposition. Crane knew nothing of war until he served as a correspondent in 1898. So let us say he had an unaccountable instinct for getting at the roots of the male nature; how he got it no one has yet explained. As for Hemingway, whom I knew well, in combat action and less vigorous pursuits, nothing said of him touches bedrock. The writer accepts the myths and rejects the man as other men knew him. Surely there can be no gain to science through holding such a course, although we see the same thing being done by nonscientists writing of

MacArthur, the late President Kennedy, *et al.* There are
few, if any, balanced biographical writings or character
analyses of moderns of this stature. The essayists, where
they do not feed in the main on one another, set forth to
destroy or to ennoble, and winnow out the legends in accord with the aim. So there is little chance to view the subject through the smoke screen of how he thought of himself and wished to impress others, to say nothing of the
dust cloud raised by his various interpreters, each striving
to say something different if not sensational.

Hemingway was a man of tremendous physical courage,
and delighted in being tested. One does not go hunting big
game in Africa in old age unless stress-seeking comes naturally. Pictures taken in his middle teens show him holding
up a riddled woodchuck or porcupine, which, as trophies
go, are pretty small stuff at that age.

How durable that courage was, whether it would have
lasted over the long haul, there is no way of knowing. His
career as an ambulance driver in World War I was very
brief. Thereafter he knew war in person only as a correspondent and viewed it as such, though he would risk fire
boldly just for kicks, a foible in some correspondents but
rare among fighting men. Though he wrote much on the
subject, he did not seem interested in the nature of men
under fire; like most novelists who write on war, he assumed that he knew.

More astonishing than his courage and his penchant for
stress-seeking was his parading of these qualities, his vainglory. He wore his heart on his sleeve, or possibly it was
his complex. Amid bold company, he would go out of his
way to impress with his boldness. It was the least becoming
thing he did, and his friends loved him in spite of it; in that
he was still the boy, holding aloft a woodchuck, shot dead
center.

PART II

Fictional Analysis of Stress-seekers

Kenneth Burke

Introducing a revision of his first full-length book, *The White Oxen and Other Stories,* Kenneth Burke says that its stories gradually shift from the realistically convincing and true-to-life to those stressing the rhetorical properties of words. These rhetorical properties were to occupy Kenneth Burke for many years. With the disused science of rhetoric, he invaded the provinces of sociology, psychology, and history. In reaching back for a hoary literary technique to question the dominant scientific mood of his period, he balances the subtle sensitivity of the dramatic character against precise definition of the scientific concept. In *Counter-Statement* his words reflect the questioning of the dominant mood: "A writer establishes equilibrium by leaning (leaning as his age leans, or in the direction opposite to his age)."

From Kenneth Burke's pen, psychology was not the science of objective content analysis, but was rather a matter of form. Interest in the object of study was second to interest in the effect of psychological writing on an audience. Impressed by the persuasive qualities of rhetoric, he gave rhetorical knowledge priority over objective, referential knowledge. It is occupational diversity which accounts for the varied perspectives on the world. In *Permanence and Change* he allows that the foremost perspective should be poetic: because human beings are a symbol-using species, the poet takes precedence over the sociologist, the psychologist, and the historian.

Kenneth Burke's argument is the ethic of the gentleman disturbed by loss of style. Loss of style is blamed for freeing the competitive forces plaguing the world, for "increasing violence."

The Philosophy of Literary Form drew him closer to sociologists concerned with symbolic action. *The Grammar of Motives* asks what is involved when we say what people are doing and why they do it. The word "says" epitomizes the way the sociologists and psychologists put this question. Burke studies action through language used to describe action.

Human behavior may be understood dramatistically in terms of five elements: act, scene, agent, agency, and purpose. "Scene" corresponds to the sociologist's "conditions of action," and "agency" corresponds to "means of action." This terminological shift embodies Kenneth Burke's critique of social science. Science, he tells us in *The Rhetoric of Motives,* is concerned with "information." He is concerned with action, persuasion, identification—identification between both the agents who act and the other characters in the scene who constitute the agency whose action makes it possible for the agent to act. *Attitudes Toward History* deals with the history of human relations in terms of "acceptance and rejection" and "merger and division." Using this symbolistic framework, Kenneth Burke rewrites Western history as a five-act play, the names of the acts being Evangelical Christianity, Medieval Synthesis, Protestantism, Capitalism, and Collectivism.

For Kenneth Burke, the comic is the attitude of attitudes. Human antics are a comedy ever on the verge of tragedy. The following fragment of a poem, quoted from his *Rhetoric of Religion,* speaks prophetically to the problem of this symposium:

> If, to seek its level,
> Water can all the time
> Descend
> What God or Devil
> Makes men climb
> No end?

Kenneth Burke's stress-seeker is a divided self, troubled by necessity. He "must" create his own difficulties. Paradoxically, man struggles toward the enjoyment of Nirvana; yet to relax in Nirvana would be to allow his muscles to atrophy, and he would lose his ability to enjoy it. Thousands of years of adaptation have produced the need to seek stress. But more, in seeking stress he must risk that which he really possesses.

Several things may be learned from fictional writing about stress-seeking. The stress of fictional personalities may be an analogue of the author's stress as distilled and reshaped by the "stylistics of lamentation." The scientist employs the case history and the nomothetic report, each with its own literary form, to convey thinking and feeling about stress-seeking. The novelist commands a number of stylistic devices. He metaphorically conjures an image. For instance, the phrase "imposing fresh sharp sounds upon his own blunt echoes" conveys the contrast between the parts of a divided self, the part needing consummation and the part needing to endanger this joy. He uses images of self-violation, such as that of a sculptor "abusing granite." The writer may use a "principle of divisiveness," such as splitting the action or the motive into two literary roles, or use a "reflexive principle" by placing a story within a story to exploit their counterpoint.

Stress-seeking fits a literary form lying between tragedy and comedy. In Burke's words, "the sword of discovery goes before the couch of laughter." A minor reversal may be endured fictionally by turning a major calamity into a farce. The novelist may portray the "hilarious aspects of distress."

The writing process itself may be autosuggestive and induce stress-seeking. The attitudes an author expresses fictionally may be carried over into real life. A "homeopathic" spirit may try to destroy "tragic imaginings" by putting the self in jeopardy.

ON STRESS, ITS SEEKING

Comment by the author on his novel *Towards a Better Life: Being a Series of Epistles, or Declamations*, originally published in 1932 and recently republished by the University of California Press.

My first—and some might say my lamest—excuse for offering this article is that our inquiry has to do with stress-seeking and the article is concerned with a fiction featuring a character who is forever stressing his notions about stress —and thus distress—as a vocation, the deliberate answer to a "call."

My somewhat more justified but perhaps more embarrassing excuse for writing on this subject is that the fiction is a story of my own making and, since the story was originally published about thirty-five years ago, my discussion of it could have at least the advantage of being both *ab intra* and *ab extra*. For, in one sense, the book is nearly as alien to me as to anyone else. Yet I do know many things about it that no one else can. And since I have long been on the friendly fringes of the social sciences—much to the distrust of some colleagues—I dare hope that this area in common will have some effect.

The problem, basically, is this: first, I must set up an account of the work as viewed *ab intra*. Here several sheerly aesthetic considerations must be treated. However, since I take it that our inquiry should ultimately focus upon an approach *ab extra*—an approach that looks upon the work as symptomatic of something or other—even in the "aesthetic" section I keep incidentally pointing toward the discussion that is to follow.

All told, the article is concerned with three orders of motives, orders by no means mutually exclusive, though we can at times distinguish them clearly enough. These three orders of motives are: the aesthetic, or poetic; the personal, or psychological; and the environmental, or sociological.

Let's illustrate the three in their obvious distinctness:

(1) It's an aesthetic or poetic fact that a fiction might put stress upon a stress-seeking character because such a character helps keep a plot going. In this sense, the theme of stress is as handy to a storyteller as, for instance, vengeance, or excessive religiosity. And, in fact, when going over old notes that I had taken but not used in preparation for my novel, I found among them that gloriously resonant line from the *Aeneid,* Dido's curse (IV, 625): "Arise, some avenger, from our bones" (*exoriare aliquis nostris ex ossibus ultor*).

(2) It's a personal or psychological fact that—as will be noted at many points in our discussion—the author variously reproduced or transformed for purposes of the fiction material that was experienced by him differently in the course of living.

(3) It's an environmental or sociological fact that the book was written during the period immediately leading up to and away from the cultural and economic situation rife in the United States at the time of the "traumatic" market crash in 1929.

It is necessary to begin with a consideration of the work in its internality before gradually widening the range of our speculations to include the major psychological and sociological motives.

THE STYLISTICS OF STRESS

A man, who is envious and jealous, deliberately sets up the situation whereby a friend of his is surprised, on a fatal night, into sharing the same apartment with the woman whom he himself had coveted. He bitterly resents the union that he had thus strategically helped to consummate. And his resentment is aggravated by his claim that the lovers profited from a kind of unearned increment. First, he accuses them of carrying over into real life the roles they had played in a decadent drama about the incunabula of the Christian culture. (The play depicted Mary, for all her exceptional delicacy and love of her husband, as having been successfully courted by a fiery young Greek. The aging Joseph had known about this state of affairs, which he had sympathetically left unmentioned when the Wise Men came to honor the virgin birth.) Our Hero's other accusation against the lovers concerns the dignity they derived from their putative roles in plans for a colony. Though these plans never eventuate, for a while they look promising, particularly since Our Hero's rival suddenly comes into possession of the money that would make them feasible. In frustrated imitation, Our Hero starts extravagantly spending his own funds, on the hunch that something favorable will happen. Nothing does. Hence, at the end of Part One we see him bankrupt, and leaving town. He has picked a destination at random, in the country—antithetically to the metropolitan situation that has marked the conditions of his distress. The last two sentences of this section enigmatically foretell the subsequent developments of the story (p. 60):

> Reaching the little country station at dawn, in a valley still blank with mist, I stood on the cinders with my suitcase, in the chilly morning air, while the train continued on its way through the valley, and the vibrations of the engine diminished irregularly to silence. I noticed then the twitter of many unrelated bird-notes, with the rustle of water somewhere behind the mist—and a dog was barking, imposing fresh sharp sounds upon his own blunt echoes.

The middle section of this tripartite novel marks a notable turn in the direction of its motives. Here the narrator recounts the steps he takes, after he has left the city and married for money in the country, in arranging for a troupe of actors to give a performance at a nearby town. Among them appears the girl from whom he had fled. After he has been falsely boasting of an idyllic love affair, although they are actually still apart, she finally does spend the night with him, in her dingy room at a local hotel. His true account of this episode is of a wholly different quality. Breaking down, she tells him of various unsavory incidents in her life since his disappearance, including the fact that his friend had jilted her. The upshot of it all is that in his eyes she has lost her magic; and the section ends on his decision to see no more of her.

The final section (Part Three) unfolds the motives implicit in this change. "I had been pushing against a great weight," he says; "and with this weight gone, I fell forward. While her train hurried down the valley, I experienced such gloom as terrified me. For even a life of bitterness was desirable as compared with a life without purpose." She had made him live "as though . . . living were a vengeance." But now " 'You have no reason,' I whispered to myself, 'for doing any single thing' " (pp. 131–32).

Alone by the tracks, he begins turning his words "into a military rhythm," and "making a tune to fit at random." He calls his conduct "clownishness," and a "mechanical attempt to ward off the growth of melancholy."

"But melancholy came, like the fog even then rising from the river." Finally, "the arm of the nearby signal sank, showing that the track was free. 'I will do only what I have to do,' I said slowly into the emptiness, but I knew that this place would be henceforth unbearable" (p. 132).

The story now progressively reveals the nature of this "free" track, enigmatically indicated by the sinking signal. First, the narrator becomes engrossed "in chipping crude, unfinished shapes out of stone. . . . Then I would punish the grotesque things by smashing them with one blow of a mallet, though I do not know why I either made them or destroyed them" (p. 133). But surely their secret nature as vessels of a new motive is indicated when he says, "Since the beginning of my new pilgrimage, I have hacked at stone with venom. Let granite be abused, I have said, until its relevant particles drop from it, and it stands forth, a statue." In sum, this "store" which he "had accumulated unawares" and is now "tapping" is of an inturning, reflexive nature, a symbol of self-violation (p. 134).

At various places in the story there are references to another girl, who loved the narrator with a simple, defenseless devotion, and whom he treated badly. At this point he takes up with her again, takes her with him on his "pilgrimage," and mistreats her to the point where she finally leaves, abandoning him to his self-imposed self-torment. After her departure without farewell, he calls down this evil fate upon himself:

> If I were not myself, but something that looked down upon this that was myself, I should brand it, I should in quietude put an effective curse upon it, I should corrode it with the slow acids of the mind [p. 157].

The other aspects of the motivational recipe bear mentioning. At many points throughout the text a principle of divisiveness (a kind of "separating out") manifests itself. It takes many forms. Here I shall cite but a few:

> . . . need one who is uneasy on finding himself in two mirrors [p. 8]. . . . [while talking desolately in a phone booth, he is grinning so that] the man beyond the glass, waiting to speak here next [might not suspect his condition] [p. 22]. . . . it was at this time, on glancing into

the awry mirrors of a shop window, that I mistook
someone else for me. When the phone next door was
ringing, I thought it was ours [p. 45]. . . . he mentioned a bell which, installed at the door to announce the
entrance of new patrons, gratuitously marked their exit
[p. 53]. . . . I can remember stepping slowly into a
lake, until my eyes were even with its surface, the water
cutting across the eye-balls [p. 135]. . . . So, like a
ventriloquist's doll, I suffered injurious remarks to rise
unbidden to my lips [p. 146]. . . . the negligible shred
of comfort he had got for himself recently by talking in
two voices [p. 168]. . . .

This pattern of observations has its analogue in various
kinds of characters with whom the narrator feels a kinship,
sometimes hateful, because of traits or situations that he
finds duplicated in himself. Two in particular should be
mentioned. In the fifth chapter of Part One, there is the
despairing lover who, while the narrator offers no resistance, commits suicide. The incident is summed up thus
(p. 47):

> *"Incipit vita nova,"* he confided smilingly as he left the
> table for this Leucadian leap into the unseen litter of
> the courtyard. And I felt that the new life he spoke of
> was to be my own. "He died for me," I whispered with
> conviction, though he had not yet descended. And for
> days afterwards I found myself repeating, "He died for
> me."

In the third section there is a different but related mode
of identification (p. 166): "One evening when we were in
his apartment, and he had interpreted an operatic score for
me with unusual zest, after we had drunk somewhat, seeing
that we were alone, and not liable to be interrupted, like
youngsters we toyed with each other." Since this figure is
called "Alter Ego," in my present role as analyst I see it
as a roundabout way of distinguishing the pattern of self-
involvement by narratively splitting the motive into two
roles. For such is the direction in which the "free" track
is leading. And when "Alter Ego" vanishes, this is only
another variant on the theme of self-abandonment. An earlier variant is the ritual chapter in which the narrator ambiguously courts a "mad girl in white" (the sheer essence of

madness?). In keeping with the nature of the sinking signal, there are only dumb passes between them; here again he is with a woman in a dingy hotel room. And before that is a chapter in which Our Hero valiantly fights with friends, although he "could as easily have loved these people" (p. 145).

There is an interlude, a story by the narrator. We should note its ultimate internality even as sheer form, since it is a story within a story. In my subsequent criticism I have been much concerned with this aspect of the reflexive principle, whereby a work gets to the ultimate point of being inside itself. And as regards our sheerly sociopsychological inquiries here, I might point out that, although this chapter in its present form is the product of considerable revision, it stems from a story that I wrote as an adolescent student beset by an acute sense of isolation.

By then its development had reached a stage of "symbolic regression" that would attain its most accurate formal representation by reduction to a story within a story, a withinness-of-withinness that was ideal for my purposes, but that I could not have made to order. For I could not have so directly reimagined such conditions of my past that were now closed to me, so far as conscious retrieval was concerned. Yet here was the essence of the regression with which I was dealing. An accommodating fate had preserved one copy of the story and let me find it. And as regards content, I needed a kind of document that actually stemmed from a period of fierce male virginity, as experienced from within. Yet, in keeping with the nature of the work, it had to be a fiction. Among my unused notes I found a conceit that might be introduced figuratively: "The new application of this old story is as though, after learning a foreign language, I were to remember word for word a fatal conversation I had overheard in that language before I knew it."

One detail, however, is omitted. In the original version, the narrator thinks that he might throttle a boy he had seen clinging to the wooden figure upon which the victim of the "narrator's" story gets his fixation—in its nature as a rigid statue, guilty; but in its nature as a policeman, admonitory.

When I think of the choking in *Othello*, along with the reference to one whom Othello likened to himself and whom he "seized by the throat" precisely when killing himself, I realize that this detail of fantasy should have been left in. I took it out because at the time when I was working on the book I did not interpret the chapter as I do now, and I simply found the notion too repellent to retain.

Where next? The story within a story carries the narrator to the point where he is caught in a vicious circle. His loneliness begets loneliness, and there is no way out except for the flare-up of a compensatory fantasy, the vision of a mystic reversal whereby he is not alone, but is one with Universal Purpose.

Is his vision a lie, or not? At least, it comes to a focus in the image of an ark. Hence all this regression might somehow add up to rebirth? In the last chapter, the narrative ambiguously tries it both ways. The development may be inexorably back, back, back into silence—i.e., the womb in the absolute—or things may be directed towards resurgence, as some of the final jottings explicitly promise.

I think that we are here involved in vacillations ultimately having to do with the relationship between tragedy and comedy. The pattern is this: the character builds upon a cult of tragedy, deliberately designed to rule out the amenities of humor. "Under the slightest of reverses, I would welcome bad weather, would go out to scan a broad, lonely sky at sunset, saying, 'This I know; this is a return, a homecoming'" (p. 36).

There are two aspects of this motive. First: "There was gratification from the thought that I might derive even my defeat from within" (p. 55). Second: "Let us endure minor reversals by inviting major calamities; let us dwarf annoyances, or even melancholy, by calling upon life's entire structure to collapse" (p. 59).

All told, he celebrates his "despisals" as a "vocation," in which he must "persevere, even at the risk of great inconvenience" (p. 145). He chooses "to grow sullen where I might have dismissed a dilemma by laughter—laughter, which leaves us untried, which is a stifler in the interests of comfort, surrendering in advance, renouncing prior to ex-

cess, enabling a man to avoid the ultimate implications of
his wishes" (p. 198). A secondary effect arises thus:
"Though no one would choose failure, we may yet maintain that failure is a choice, since one may persist in attitudes which make his failure inevitable" (p. 200). And:
"one should live in such a way that he has with him these
three considerations daily: madness, the Faith, and death
by his own hand" (p. 168).

It becomes a question of purpose: "Place a man among
these streets, instruct him to choose some act which puts a
strain upon his temper. What work will he perform here,
if it is work in the absolute, and not the accidental matter
of flunkeying to an employer? If he does not mean by
work the earning of a little money through assisting in a
superior's blind purposes, but the straining of his resources,
what manner of living must he choose?" (p. 200) To which
his answer is: "How be called muscular if you would not
prefer the sewers and ratholes of the metropolis?" (p.
200); "Die as a mangled wasp dies—its body hunched, its
wings futile, but its sting groping viciously for its tormen-
tor" (p. 201).

The ultimate complication lies in his relation to money.
"Wealth and talent being complementary, neither will deem
itself enough without the other" (p. 57). "I have never
consented to console myself with the thought that we may
be rich in spirit while tangibly impoverished. Wealth—
wealth in love, money, the admiration of oneself and others
—is indispensable to those who would surround themselves
with the flatterings and stimulations of beauty" (p. 28).
Yet, in his "vision," at the culmination of his distress, he
boasts and/or pleads: "It is good that some men are
scorned by their fellows and made to feel homeless among
them, since these outcasts are, through their sheer worldly
disabilities, vowed to graver matters and could not, even
if they would, prevent themselves from pouring forth their
neglected love upon a formidable Father" (p. 206).

Throughout the book, he keeps moralistically fluctuating
between the paradoxical prosperity of poverty—a deliberate
cult of disaster—and the conviction that there is an ideal
need for a tradition of great wealth. And even at the last,

when he is reduced to a total destitution largely of his own making, he warns himself: "You cannot renounce, for none but the rich dare speak in praise of poverty" (p. 210). He ends in the condition that a stranger had described for him in the first chapter (p. 8):

> And upon my enquiring as to what he feared most of the future, he answered: "Destitution. Destitution of finances, destitution of mind, destitution of love. The inability to retort. The need of possessing one's opposite in years, sex, and texture of the skin; and the knowledge that by this need one has been made repugnant. The replacing of independence by solitude."

As regards the question of literary species, this fluctuant attitude involves a kind of grotesqueness that is midway between tragedy and comedy, or, in the narrator's words, "the hilarious aspects of distress" (p. 45). Many of the situations could be easily transformed into farce. Perhaps the most obvious instance is the episode about a compulsion to address the wooden statue of a policeman at the entrance to a store. He yields to the temptation, then fears that his act has been noticed (p. 190):

> I could have done the same under happier circumstances, but the meaning would not have been the same. It is quite natural to address inanimate things—it is no more foolish than confiding secrets to a dog. But as I looked about apprehensively, I saw that a woman had observed me. She was pretty, and insolent, and was watching me intently. There was no kindness in her eyes, nothing but cold curiosity. Her eyes, my dear, passed a terrible judgment upon me. And to escape her judgment, I repeated my greeting, this time leaning back, squinting, and waving my hand, as though I had been speaking to someone in the recesses of the store—but now I noticed that the clerk inside, with bewildered moonface, was staring at me glumly. I am now bending beneath eyes, the wooden eyes of the policeman, the cold, curious eyes of the woman, and the glum eyes of the clerk inside the store.

Perhaps these two preparatory notes indicate the pattern most clearly: "Be sure to have him boast of things for which he has attacked others"; and "He's all for setting up rules, but when they are applied to him he insists that the case is different." In this respect, the work adds up to a grotesque tragedy with the birth of comedy ambiguously in the offing (p. 217):

> . . . though you, in learning, brought trouble upon yourself, let no man discredit your discoveries by pointing to your troubles. Nor must you turn against your bitterness. The sword of discovery goes before the couch of laughter. One sneers by the modifying of a snarl; one smiles by the modifying of a sneer. You should have lived twice, and smiled the second time.

And the narrator's talk of lapsing into total silence is interwoven with his cry: *"Resurgam! Resurgam!* I shall rise again! Hail, all hail! Here is a promise: *resurgam."* Thus, personally, I look back upon the work as a kind of grotesque tragedy serving as a *rite de passage* into a cult of comedy, as explained in my preface to the new edition. But though I think that, in an ideal world, comedy would be the highest form of art, I find that tragedy leads most directly into the study of man's attempted solutions for his problems. I would but add the hope that, as with the ancient Greek theater, we sum up the analysis of "tragic dignification" by a satyr play, that is to say, a burlesque of the solemnities that have preceded it.

Before turning directly to the sociopsychology of our present concerns, perhaps I should mention one further point as regards the sheerly literary aspect of the book. At the time when I was taking preparatory notes, I was also doing much research in studies to do with the nature and etiology of drug addiction. As a result, I became interested in the notion that the case history could be readily adapted for purely poetic purposes. The form made for a kind of vignette with a strongly aphoristic aspect. Since the narrative is so designed that the plot gradually emerges from a sentarous context—though the aphorisms are "in character," hence not to be taken as strictly identical with the views of the author—I discovered that the case history, as a form, blends well with the aphoristic; a reader hardly notices when one leaves off and the other takes over. This relationship is of great assistance to the effect I mention in my preface to the first edition: "Lamentation, rejoicing, beseechment, admonition, sayings, and invective—these seemed to me central matters, while a plot in which they might occur seemed peripheral, little more than a pretext, justifiable not as a 'good story,' but only insofar as it could bring these six characteristics to the fore." (In the same preface I observe: "If my hero lacks humor, he does not lack grotesqueness—and the grotesque is but the humorous without its proper adjunct of laughter.")

So much for a view of the work in its internality. Let us now reverse things and approach it situationally, from without.

THE SOCIOPSYCHOLOGY OF STRESS

"Surely no one will fall victim to a form of insanity which he abhors," Our Hero speculates (p. 74) while willfully imposing upon himself a kind of stress that progressively tears at the edges of his mind, until his cult of quarrelsomeness and self-interference leads him into a self-perpetuating state of total isolation.

Since we ended the former discussion on purely poetic considerations, we might take them as our point of departure for this new phase. In Djuna Barnes's novel *Nightwood*, her major spokesman, the overripely perverted doctor, O'Connor, avows: "Calamity is what we are all seeking." On which I commented (in the Spring 1966 issue of *The Southern Review*), "Maybe yes, maybe no, so far as life is concerned—*but certainly yes, as regards the stylistics of lamentation.*" That is, I take it that, purely from the standpoint of literary appeal, lamentation is a pleasure. For "there is one notable difference between a Biblical jeremiad and a purely literary variant of the species. . . . However great the artistry of any document that gained admission to the Biblical canon (even so obviously literary an enterprise as the Book of Job), one should not approach a single sentence of the Bible purely in terms of literary entertainment." One should not, that is, if one is in the role of a devout believer. But "a *literary* jeremiad must somehow be fun." The same point is developed thus in my essay "Coriolanus—and the Delights of Faction" (*The Hudson Review,* Summer 1966):

> The dramatist can transform our moral problems into sources of poetic entertainment. . . . Many motivational conflicts that might distress us in real life can be transformed into kinds of poetic imitation that engross us. Thus in the realm of the aesthetic we may be delighted by accounts of distress and corruption that would make the moralist quite miserable.

I would assume that such delight begins in the preverbal solace of an infant sobbing itself to sleep. (Cf. my comments on the "three freedoms" of lamentation, praise, and invective, in my essay on Shakespeare's *Timon of Athens* in the paperback Laurel edition.) Calamity, or pathos, serves another function, which I have called "tragic dignification." I here refer to the rhetorical fact that one can dignify a cause by depicting serious people who are willing to undergo sacrifices in behalf of that cause. Suffering is a way of "bearing witness"—that is, in etymological literalness, being a "martyr." This stylistic strategy presumably ties in with the fear of boasting, a fear that runs counter to the norms of salesmanship, and that has often been rationalized along the lines of the notion that by lowliness one avoids the envy of the gods.

In the case of this particular book, since the whole cult of stress comes to a focus in what amounts to a roundabout courting of insanity—or more accurately perhaps, near-insanity, a state up to but not beyond the edge of the abyss —it might be relevant to quote some lines from the recently deceased poet, Theodore Roethke, regarding his desire "to break through the barriers of rational experience." Or again: "The only knowledge is reason in madness"; and "O to be delivered from the rational into the realm of pure song." This view of poetic insight obviously takes on a hierarchal dimension in his rhetorical question: "What's madness but nobility of soul/At odds with circumstance?" (The quotations are from an excellent article on Roethke by Denis Donoghue, in his recent volume *Connoisseurs of Chaos.*) In Roethke's case, the predicaments that he periodically got himself into were, in a sense, willed—for he deliberately cultivated a vigilant search for a kind of expression that would be in its very essence neoinfantile.

Here another strand ties in. I refer to the "aesthetic of alcohol," the desire to attain, in one's sober writing, the kind of effects that one feels one is getting when under alcohol's influence. In a sense alcohol thus acts as a kind of "call," which the sobriety of writing can never wholly answer. In particular, insofar as alcohol stimulates assertiveness, like heated argument it tends to simplify complexity, a recipe one can discern quite clearly in the author's use of the fictional device of writing letters not just *to* a former friend, but also *against* that same person—a simplified complexity further compounded by the fact that the man to whom they are addressed is a recipient only in principle, since the epistles remain unsent.

But there is a further issue, as I have observed in my article "Art—and the First Rough Draft of Living" (*Modern Age,* Spring 1964). Alcohol *qua* alcohol is not the same as alcohol during Prohibition—a notable aspect of the "cultural" climate prevailing during the years when this book was conceived and written. For those who were not bootleggers but who merely patronized bootleggers, alcohol under such conditions was in a penumbra of motives indeterminately lawless and sanctioned by custom. The chemical spirits were thus linked with a kind of spirit that had the aura of adventure even while being quite within the range of ordinary efforts and comforts. In any case, looking back now, I find it no accident that, in my preface to the first edition, I explain a problem in method in terms of an anecdote about "an illicit 'dive' in Greenwich Village." And I see no reason to retract my comment in the *Modern Age* article: "I incline now to believe that the whole of the F. Scott Fitzgerald enterprise would have collapsed without Prohibition and the illicit dispensing of alcoholic spirits that went along with it."

The clearest instance of this aesthetic is in Part Three, Chapter I, where Our Hero most energetically inveighs (pp. 140–46). Just as in some primitive tribes there are places where, without fear of punishment, one can go and curse the king, so alcoholic argumentativeness was taken for granted. Hence many things, however vehemently they were said, could be received like water off a duck's back, except for the unexpected occasion when somebody got clobbered for almost no reason at all.

All told, that complex composed a subpersonality within oneself, so that one was, as it were, "hearing a call" of that sort from within. In a sense, it added up to a vague, nagging kind of *vocation* for which no sheer *job* would be the answer. Furthermore, it could tie in with earlier motives that emerge and come to a focus in adolescence, a time when a "league of youth"—a band of heterosexual males—improvises modes of friendship that at the same time keep the members of the band sexually apart by quarrelsomeness. Such "simple" conditions necessarily drop away in later life, when one's financial and marital relationships, developed out of ties and obligations alien to the original situation, give rise to a set of "claims" no longer tolerant of such harsh sparring as was once the norm. (Perhaps the grandest instance of such a change is Falstaff's lostness when Hal becomes king and loses all sympathy with his clowning.)

An early story, "Prince Llan," in some ways illustrates the complexities of the case. The Prince, now mulierose, has become separated from his old friend, Gudruff, whose nature as a motive is most clearly revealed by this passage, written in, I hope, not too ungrammatical Latin—after the fashion of the *Greek Anthology*, which the author had studied extracurricularly while at college, and which gave English translations for all but the "indecent" entries:

> Suddenly, suddenly, *plena recognitio facultatum corporis latuit subito ei; se relaxabat, est molliter lapsus contra terram, deinde se dabat suorum temptationi inquinum.*
> The remainder of the morning he spent in reading.

The Prince, in trying to answer this call, dissolves as in a dream while he opens a door that leads to a door that allows him, "down a corridor beyond, the glimpse of a door" (*The White Oxen and Other Stories*, New York: Albert and Charles Boni, 1924). As I now interpret it, the incident represents a fantasy in which a later aspect of the author's self, in a mood of stocktaking, recalls an earlier adolescent identity, still surviving as a kind of subpersonality in the unconscious, and essentially identified with the poetic motive—in that our first literary methods are usually developed under reflexive conditions that are able to be ambiguously symbolized in terms of suicide, or "death by one's own hand."

As regards the full scope of the hierarchal possibilities here, we necessarily move into a socioeconomic sphere far beyond the muddled tie-up linking pro-poetic, prealcoholic adolescence with the beginnings of mature relationships— a change that often breaks up old friendships completely. I have been trying to indicate ways in which adolescence, alcohol, and a modified aesthetic cult of madness, however distressing, might all tie in with one another. Yet, thinking along these same lines, we are now ready to consider a much wider range of problems.

First of all, as regards our fundamental inquiry into stress-seeking, there is an unresolved conflict centering in what might be called a secularized version of the poor-Church principle—a view that comes to focus in the conviction that poverty is spiritual—in contrast with the cult of commodities without which our civilization could not last even until tomorrow. I take it that, although the narrator's surname, Neal, combines several motivational strands, a major one is "kneel." Contrast, in this regard, the conditions under which his name first figures—in connection with an act of cruelty, on p. 122—and the passage on p. 205: "He knelt while love poured from him, or poured into him from all outward things."

The author was raised in dingy suburban neighborhoods. To be sure, he didn't know how dingy they really were. For there was a scattering of weedy fields among the houses, and many years later he could write about them lyrically, nostalgically. (There was even a deserted, window-smashed haunted house with fascinating stories about it.) The author was among the poor relatives. And though he now realizes that there were no rich relatives, he took it for granted that his grandparents, who were so much better off, were rich, particularly since his grand-father had always boasted of great wealth when handing out a few pennies to the greedy, gratified grandson. And since the grandparents' house was obviously in a much better part of town than his parents', the difference meant *Wealth in the Absolute*—for those are the years when ab-solutes take form.

In brief, the poor-Church principle—prosperity of pov-erty—had to combine with the thought that wealth and aesthetic flowering needed each other. A devious fusion, or compromise, was attained by imaginary acquiescence to mental stress—mental distress—as a kind of ideal. (At least, such a development was to be welcomed as a sheerly aesthetic kind of risk.)

Also, although the actual story is a fiction from begin-ning to end, in principle it was "true"—at least in the sense that, as discussed in my first preface, it produced a "mon-ster" by magnifying some aspects of the author's character and minimizing others. In this alembicated sense, it was a perversely idealized self-portrait. The author was in a state of acute internal conflict owing to maladjustments in his personal affairs. He was caught in a kind of dilemma from which such imaginings seemed like a kind of escape, or at least relief, as on p. 211: "Speech being a mode of conduct, he converted his faulty living into eloquence. Then should any like his diction, they would indirectly have sanctioned his habits."

Thus these potentialities were intensely ambivalent. On the one hand, the fiction threatened to be autosuggestive, aggravating the very conditions for which it served as a relief. For the author's engrossment in its developments invited him to carry the attitude of the fiction over into real life, just as his protagonist had accused the fictive lovers of doing, when they endowed their lives with glam-our borrowed from their roles in the blasphemous play.

On the other hand, there was the homeopathic aspect of such tragic imaginings, along the lines of this formula-tion in Milton's preface to *Samson Agonistes:* According to Aristotle, Milton says, tragedy is designed "to temper and reduce" such passions as pity and fear "to just measure with a kind of delight, stirred up by reading or seeing those passions well imitated." And he continues: "Nor is Nature wanting in her own effects to make good his assertion; for so, in physic, things of melancholic hue and quality are used against melancholy, sour against sour, salt to remove salt humours."

At least, often the poetic usefulness of an author's personal quandaries does allow them to be faced. Some years back I suggested in the magazine *Poetry* that the myth of Perseus is particularly relevant in this regard. Although one cannot stare directly at the Gorgon's head of his entangled motives without being as it were turned into stone, their nature as material for art acts as a kind of protective reflector. By the subterfuges of form, one may be able to examine one's difficulties quite "realistically," even though the instrument also has the properties of a magnifying glass which can transform a tiny spider into a huge, glowering, hairy ogre about to seize and devour the observer, who somehow imagines himself dwarfed and defenseless.

On this score, when going over old notes taken at the time when the novel was *in utero,* the author was surprised to find a letter, written to a friend but never sent, in which, referring to a wealthy man in great mental difficulty, the author wrote with regard to his fears for his own welfare:

> I am battling like a fiend, battling for nothing less than
> my mind itself—and unless it is true, as I frequently tell
> myself, that [   ] went mad for me, that I can
> derive from his collapse vicariously my own rescue, un-
> less this is true (and the idea, I may convince you, may
> not be totally coocoo [sic], since I have in the knowl-
> edge of his errors the one stable point from which to
> orient my own), that unless this is true . . . [the sen-
> tence was left thus unfinished].

A notable feature about this statement is that the author is referring to a real person's mental collapse much as his Hero refers to the fictive suicide in Part One, Chapter V. And the book itself, as early as the second page, establishes the relevant convertibility of terms when saying that a person "may worry lest this day be the very one on which he snaps under the burden and, if not talented at suicide, becomes insane." The next sentence turns to the compensatory homeopathic principle: "Yet it is possible that by a constant living with torment, one may grow immune to it," etc. But here "constant living with" should be read as a quasi-temporal synonym for "radically imagining in principle." The fictive suicide, incidentally, killed himself in the cause of jealousy, a symptom that the author shared with his "smell-feast" protagonist, although in real life there was no such triangle as the plot is built around.

Perhaps I should pause here to say that when I state that this story is fiction from start to finish, I do hope that the reader will take me at my word. I am not merely using a stylistic subterfuge, for there would be no point to my lying, since all I'd have to do would be to leave these matters unsaid. What I am trying to get at, rather, is this: I am trying to make as clear as possible those respects in which a story that is totally false in its details can somehow be true in principle.

Consider, for instance, this kind of transformation from personal experience to fictive analogue: the narrator's notion that actors can derive unearned increment by reenacting offstage their roles onstage stems from early years of loitering about the fringes of the Provincetown Playhouse—on Macdougal Street in New York City. And whether or not the actors and actresses so thought of themselves, that's the kind of aura they had for me.

Similarly, although there was no actual plan for a colony, the congregating of artists and writers is always on the edge of "colony-thinking"—and the attack upon coteries is not far, by implication, from the renouncing of a practice that was attempted again and again in the history of our nation, and thus doubtless is inherent in the very trends that militate against it.

Or consider the narrator's mystic vision on pp. 111–15. I had in mind a place where I had actually lived for a time, on a hilltop. From there, one sultry afternoon, I had watched a storm, caused by contrary winds clashing and swirling in the valley. The ability to observe the sheer form of the downpour as a "happening" made an unforgettable impression upon me, particularly since the torrent was, as it were, the single outcome of conflicting currents in the air. Yet the situation was quite different from the lonely fury recounted in the book, while the nine white cranes are imported from memories of the morning after a storm at night in a wholly different valley under quite different circumstances. And who's to say that there were nine? One can only say that they somehow seemed like a message.

Nor did the author ever become the proprietor of a herd through marrying for money, to say nothing of stealing money from a woman whom he had coveted unsuccessfully. And above all, with regard to the cult of "straining" which Our Hero propounds so earnestly on pp. 200–3, please allow it to be a fiction when he says, "Prowling about the wharves, I have ministered to unclean men, for in this there was some ghastly decency, something beyond mere safety."

According to my tentative notion, all such fictions are "ideal completions" of personal experiences that are circumstantially quite different; but they contain some problematic motivational trace which, if isolated and made absolute, would be symbolized most accurately—or with most dramatic thoroughness, most "drastically"—by such a fulfillment as the fiction settles on. And I would tinker with the possibility that any such aesthetic imitating of motives prevailing outside the realm of art can have literal analogues involving persons who in effect make up such works of art but live them wholly in the realm of life itself, and without benefit of the formal reflector that Perseus had in his battles with the snaky-headed monster he could not dare to look upon.

But I should say more about the role of the economic motive in these imaginings. The author's early formative years coincided, I believe, with the time in our national history when the stress upon capital goods—rails, mills, mines, etc.—was just giving way to the rise of cheap, machine-made consumer goods—an emergent trend that was epitomized in the Woolworth chain of five-and-ten-cent stores. The corresponding slogan, which my father constantly repeated with a humorous twist whenever the women began talking of some new contrivance, was "Who would sit down and make it for that?" People marveled not only at the thing itself but also at its price, which they still considered in terms of the elaborate preparations needed if you had decided to assemble all the material and go through all the operations needed for the production of one such item.

During an era when a country is building up its industrial plant, there is necessarily a strong emphasis upon modes of thinking quite analogous to what I have called the religious stress upon the "prosperity of poverty." The sentiments in Benjamin Franklin's Almanac are probably the best example of such Puritanic abstemiousness, a set of secular norms religiously grounded, and still strong, though often best honored in the breach, as in the case of Franklin himself, who could become well-to-do by praising the austerities of poor men.

This sort of morality seemed natural to the author in his early years, even while feeling proud at the naïve thought that his grandparents were rich. Indeed, he even thought of them as a kind of alternate parenthood—a divisive trend sharpened by the fact that, often in the summer, his grandparents took him to some lake or the seashore, where, for a week or two, he was transfigured by life in the magic of a "rich" hotel.

His book was planned—and several early chapters written and published—during the fantastic bull market of the New Era. And although the author in a mild way got enough from his jobs and writings to feel that he too was in the swim, somehow it never seemed "natural" to him. He always felt uneasy, as though he had stolen his money and would eventually get caught. True, many persons like him did get caught in the smash of '29—but not the author; for even the few stocks he had bought at a time when people were gambling like crazy he bought outright and not on margin. So they could be held, and eventually in a mild way they recovered.

Yet the book was already far enough along to act suggestively upon the author himself. During the almost magical terror that followed the smash, he deliberately resigned from a well-paying job, having resolved to expend all his

energies on his writing, both the novel and the material
that went into his first book of criticism, *Counter-
Statement*. It so turns out that if he hadn't resigned, he'd
most likely have been dismissed a year later; for the entire
branch of the organization by which he had been employed
was discontinued. But the point is that when he quit he had
no thought of such eventualities. Thus, in effect, he put
himself in jeopardy as though by deliberate intention. And
the book was finished in a state of chronic financial terror,
intermingled with distress due to other emotional entangle-
ments. Yet this terror was mainly a matter of principle. For
although many kinds of imaginings to do with acute mone-
tary embarrassment keep recurring throughout the novel,
the author had some money in the bank and suffered no
actual deprivation. But even though his run-down farm in
the country was owned outright, without mortgage, and
he earned some money by reviews and articles, his little
hoard was dwindling slowly yet inexorably toward zero.
This was "destitution in principle," we might say pun-
ningly, for he was living on his principle.

But we have anticipated somewhat. It should also be
mentioned that, particularly during his connection with *The
Dial*, he had seen, in all its impressiveness, the magical
interweaving of wealth and talent, and many of the comments on this subject reflect observations about the marvelous assortment of persons that variously came and went
around *The Dial*'s offices. Here are typical comments: "I
knew one man who had applied his wealth to carrying
doubt into his very tissues. As birds, though out of danger,
fly with self-protective darts and veerings proper to their
kind, so he kept his statements guarded, even among
friends" (p. 57). Or the narrator's drunken statement of
policy (p. 197) to the effect that one should "make money
. . . before railing against wealth"; for "whatever he
would renounce, let him first acquire it in ample quanti-
ties, that he become immune to hecklers" (p. 197). Doubtless it was for this reason that, after Shakespeare's Timon
of Athens becomes a vicious misanthrope—when deserted
by his friends following the loss of his fortune—the drama-
tist arranges for him to find another treasure, which he

throws away like filth, thereby letting the audience see that Timon is now a universal hater on principle, and not just because of "sour grapes." Also at the offices was one man of great refinement whose wealthy upbringing had obviously put a great strain upon him, making him imperious even though he also had an almost pathetic desire to be frank and friendly. All told, it was a stable of racehorses if there ever was one—all swishing, and stamping, and tossing their heads nervously, all brought together by the resources of patronage, and all under the strain of their own temperaments, which were at once their assets and their liabilities.

Perhaps the most general grounding of all for the kind of outlook we are here considering could be called Nietzschean, as with writers bent upon "glorifying the problematical in art" and "stressing the state of tension in itself, picturing the dangers and discomforts in maintaining it, hence relying upon the *basic* military equipment in man as their last source of appeal—though differing widely in their selection of the symbols which would serve as the channels in which this original biologic psychosis would run."

I am quoting from my *Permanence and Change*, pp. 87–88, Hermes edition. I had in mind here an animalistic grounding (cf. p. 64). And in a section on "The Peace-War Conflict" (pp. 197–98), I tangle with the Nietzschean puzzle in which, though "the organism has developed an equipment for attaining the benign sluggishness of satiety, the very equipment for bringing about such a worldly Nirvana is in itself the essence of turbulence and struggle." Thus:

> We perceive here a contradiction at the very basis of behavior. For if the organism attained its state of quiescence permanently, the military equipment of nervous agility, of bodily and mental muscle, would fall into decay. On the other hand, to prevent such decay, one must exert himself in "warfare," abiding by the competitive genius of mind and body, thereby denying himself precisely that state of conscious death which he might derive from the booty acquired by his prowess.

It is a contrast that had long worried me. The titular story of my first book, *The White Oxen and Other Stories*, is built around a contrast between a lion and the oxen, in a zoo:

> Disdainful to the last, the lion retained his superiority while being fed. He greeted the attendant with a baring of yellow fangs which gave the impression of sneering; and he snatched the meat from the iron prongs with a growl, as though he were stealing it. He kept his eyes on his feeder until he had disappeared, and then began tearing the flesh from the bone by licking it with his rough, scaly tongue.

In contrast, it is said of the white oxen:

> They were chewing in deliberate contentment. At times they would move their heads to look in another direction; at such times they ceased their chewing, as though disapproving of too many simultaneous motions. But once their head was firmly established in this new direction, their chewing would be resumed. Calm, harmless, sleepy, they lolled about their cage. [And later] To them the supreme gift of God was to sleep and know that one is sleeping. He yearned to see things with their dull, slow-blinking eyes, to retire into their blissful sloth of semi-sensation.

Doubtless we have a considerable measure of vegetarian idealizing here. And, as I observe in a footnote (*Permanence and Change*, pp. 198–99), an overstress upon the contrast between the hunt and relaxation after gorging can mislead, in deflecting the attention from the humane realm of the sentiments. Also, in my analysis of Nietzsche's style, I tried to show that there are purely formal considerations involved in his use of what he calls "perspective"—a kind of sheerly terministic violence achieved by a method for wrenching words from a customary context and putting them in new, theoretical surroundings—a device for which I proposed the formula, "perspective by incongruity."

But the main point is this: insofar as the human organism is prepared by adaptations through thousands of years to undergo strain, such equipment must manifest itself as a need to be exercised, as in sports, horror stories, monastic disciplines, excesses of ambition in the building of financial or political empire, juvenile delinquency, and similar exertions *praeter necessitatem.* And there may even be a kind of reality about pain that is weakened by anesthetics, anodynes, soporifics, and the like.

One may question whether such conditions establish the psychological necessity for war. But they would imply grounds for a cult of conflict. War is but one species of conflict—and the kinds of war in which we have distinguished ourselves depend upon fantastically excess wealth, in contrast with the African tribe that lives in so sparse an area it exists wholly without intestine strife. Indeed, the food supply is so scanty, the tribe would by now be extinct if its members had not developed modes of peaceful cooperation to a maximum—for nothing less could save them. But, of course, the severity of their environment supplies all the conflict necessary to exercise the body's natural aptitude for the undergoing of stress. But just as delinquency can engage the efforts of spirited youths whose way of life otherwise—in an orderly, well-to-do suburb, for instance—would not sufficiently tax them, so wars help many in our times who, unbeknown to themselves, want not jobs but *vocations*—or, as I put it in a "subversive" poem I wrote in 1933 (see my *Book of Moments,* p. 59):

> We have even hoped for the trenches,
> That men might again be cronies.
> We have even told ourselves how by the wars
> We might again be brought together,
> By the helpfulness of slaughter.
> The wars are fuller than the peace
> In fellowship.

We should also consider the frequent compensatory tendencies—along the lines of "tragic dignification"—whereby our ailments can provide the makings for inverted kinds of boasting—engrossments of ours that we ask others to share, even though we may bore them to the edge of shrieking. And there's a wonderful variant of such matters in a documentary film I once saw (*Savage Splendor*), about which I once wrote thus (in "Hermes Scroll No. 7"):

A MORAL MADE MANIFEST

See *Savage Splendor,* a long documentary film too
soon over. And above all, don't miss the shot of the
300-pound king using for his throne the back of a
prostrate slave. The king further burdened himself with
200 pounds of ornaments, and some several hundred
wives, shown bunched in rows like a choir. And all told,
you could observe him being weighted down literally
with the responsibilities of office, only 500 pounds of
which he could transfer to the back of his slave. His
immobilizing fat was presumably a mark of exceptional
wealth and noble status, since only a personage of great
means could afford to be so sedentary in a jungle. It contrasted with the litheness of the dancers who had come
long distances to perform in his honor. You could see
before your very eyes a gross physical burlesque of the
Stoic scruples and meditative spirituality with which a
Marcus Aurelius might assume the burdens of empire.
And what directness of *realism* there was, in the
symbolism of the prostrate slave so heavily burdened by
the master! There was an indirectness, too. We refer to
the way in which the burdensomeness came back to
plague his lordship, a sufferance attested by the drawn
lines of the royal phiz, so very weary, and by the techni-
color of the bloodshot eyes. Another possibility: might
not the slave have felt *unbearably proud?* Surely he
lorded it over the other slaves, who were not thus sat
upon with such Distinction. And if he knew his Hegel,
he must have understood that he was, in his crouching
way, a world-historical figure, evolved by the Divine Idea
to fulfill this God-appointed task, as regards the heavy
responsibilities of Universal Order.

And since we are now on the verge of tragic farce, let's
include a reference to a practice of some current pitchmen,
who help reinforce your sense of guilt by selling you reme-
dies after first persuading you that you need them. Of
course you stink. So, adopt the most "natural" solution
possible; namely, obstruct the pores of your body murder-
ously, or gargle with poisons. Of course you stink. After
all, what are you for, if schemers can't get you to load
yourself with chemicals costly both in money and health?
In sum, think on all those stress-seeking, stress-sought deni-
zens of Madison Avenue, forever pleading with you; they
beg you to help ease their ulcers by being as stupid as you

can, in answer to their quack-quack. Madison Avenue stands for the very Priesthood of Stress. And it stands to reason: Of course you stink. Me too!

ADDENDUM: ON "SPARAGMÓS" AND THE EYE

As regards the enigmatic foretelling at the end of Part One in the novel, I take it that the sound of water behind the mist presages the final downpour—of both the ersatz mystic vision on pp. 111–15 and the book's last sentence: "Henceforth silence, that the torrent may be heard descending in all its fullness." Besides the flow of water, the whole range of connotations would probably include, at various places along the way, the flow of words, the flow of time, the frightened flow of urine, and what Coleridge called "the streamy nature of association," William James the "stream of consciousness." The passage most obviously linking words and downpour is near the beginning (p. 9): "I would speak as a gargoyle would speak which, in times of storm, spouted forth words." Its further tie-up is indicated by the fact that the narrator is on the subject of his scorn.

The dog barking, "imposing fresh sharp sounds upon his own blunt echoes," sums up the essence of the reflexive principle (including the chapter in which the narrator vilifies his cronies). The "twitter of many unrelated birdnotes" presages the disintegrative form of the last chapter. Borrowing from the Cambridge anthropologists' speculations on the incunabula of Greek tragedy, I'd want to contend that here, even in its very form, we find the "rending and tearing" that is necessary for a Next Phase, the ambiguously foretold turn from grotesque tragedy to a cult of comedy.

In the novel, for reasons which I hope I have made clear, this process of disintegration preparatory to reintegration takes place enigmatically and ambiguously at the end. But in my next book, *Permanence and Change*, which is explicitly concerned with questions dealing with the development from an earlier orientation to a new one, fittingly the "rending and tearing"—or *sparagmós*—takes place in the middle section, coming to a focus in the concept of "perspective by incongruity," which involves the Nietzschean clash of categories when a term that has come to seem natural in one context is suddenly jammed into a different and hitherto alien context. And to back this point, I should also mention, in my *Philosophy of Literary Form* (unabridged edition), my discussion of a painting by Peter Blume. For, as I interpret it, there is a similar kind of disintegration intermediate between two quite distinct motivational realms, although necessarily, by the nature of the medium, the observer confronts the three stages—of Before, During, and After—simultaneously.

Incidentally, as considered from the sheerly aesthetic or poetic point of view, the mimetics of breakdown in the last chapter are seen to be but the transformation of a writer's preparatory note-taking into a kind of culmination *in extremis*.

A fuller discussion of the book in its internality would have required the indexing of several other recurrent terms, such as the thesaurus of meanings surrounding the word "mouse," for instance, ranging from the "sickly and unsightly creature, a mouse-faced man" (p. 29), through "if she but stamped her foot you would, deep within you, scurry away like mice" (p. 149), to "would liken God to a little mouse" (p. 209). And the term "yield" ranges from yielding in guilt, through yielding in adjustment or accommodation, to yielding like Christ on the cross.

But one term at least I should pause to consider at some length, since it also bears strongly upon an experience outside the book. Inasmuch as any cult of conflict—or stress-seeking—is likely to take on moralistic connotations, eye-imagery can naturally figure, particularly if, like the author, one was constantly admonished as a child that God was always watching. How would this conceit manifest itself in sheerly secular terms?

We have already cited the passage from the story within a story. But on going through the book again, I note two others that are particularly relevant. On p. 72: "On dim, deserted streets I hurried through a city of eyes, under the surveillance of disparate objects which, as I passed, each transferred me to the supervision of the next. And there were real eyes among them, eyes of the cats that paused to note me with distrust (some of the cats stringy, others crouching in bunches behind their faces)." On p. 210, when Our Hero is *in extremis:* "There is an eye, firm as the eye of the newly dead. When I am alone, this eye inspects me." I cannot say for sure whether I already knew Emily Dickinson's lines on watching "a dying eye." But, to the best of my memory, I can say that after finishing the book, the author had an almost intolerable sense of an eye constantly bearing down upon him. He saw it so clearly in his mind's eye, at times he couldn't keep from looking for it outside him, even though he knew it was but a fantasy. And always, wherever he did look, it was still off to one side.

David Brion Davis

David Brion Davis is a historian of man's inner life who burrows beneath social movements to reveal the psychology of societies. He searches for American character through the fiction written by and for Americans. This fiction harbors themes of aggression and images of good and evil supermen. He has written of violence and social dominance in *Homicide in American Fiction, 1798–1860.* This book is a testament of a man of reason appalled by the lack of reason in the world about him.

Supermen act autonomously; they rise above society's institutions. David Davis' analysis disturbs him when it reveals that American society has accepted a philosophy holding that man is controlled by and depends upon nonintellectual forces. "Justice" rests upon an inherent passionate sense. This passion transcends reason and human desire.

The problem of moral perceptions is discussed in "Some Ideological Functions of Prejudice in Ante-Bellum America." Catholics, Mormons, and Masons have been treated as subversive groups. Davis tries to understand how the countersubversives come to feel that the subversive groups threaten their values or even their survival. He concludes that American culture is unable to accept the compatibility of national loyalty and special allegiances.

His most recent work, *The Problem of Slavery in Western Culture,* continues the historical exploration of moral consciousness. Painting a wider canvas, he examines moral and sociological problems of slavery across several millennia, asking why it is that, at a certain moment in history, a small number of men not only saw the full horror of a social evil to which mankind had been blind for centuries but also felt compelled to attack it through their personal testimony. This question added the study of abolitionism to that of slavery. The work contains a comparative analysis of the slave system in the Old World, the response to slavery in European thought, and the protest against

Negro bondage. Several sections of the book are devoted to the religious roots of the problem. The failure of Christianization of the African has been offered as a justification for slavery, while the abolitionist movement also had religious roots.

His conference paper follows the mood of *Homicide in American Fiction* in drawing its material from literature. Literature, he says, is not only the product of culture but may provide an imaginative illumination of its deepest tensions and conflicts. More specifically, literary conceptions of man's desires for stress and excitement often reveal significant historical shifts in interest, mood, and values.

David Brion Davis' *fin-de-siècle* literary stress-seeker walks a tightrope between death and death. On one side of the tightrope is the death established by the equation of individual salvation and material success, felt as confining and demeaning. On the other side is uncontrollable stress threatening to annihilate the self or drive the struggler to a suicide encountered in throes and flailing. Balanced precariously, he strains against an opponent approaching from the opposite direction. Then struggle is a fierce occasion to find meaning, a sense of immediacy, and a tingling of living. Character is proved through struggle unrelated to material reward. Sometimes the battle is blind and purposeless, sheer vitalism in a sea of indifference. But, in the struggle, the fear of death may be conquered; the ruthless strong man has an opportunity to release titanic energy and impose his will on the impersonal audience gaping from below. The elemental struggle, the basic reality of life, brutalizes and regenerates. Yet, by struggling, he may feed the fire that will consume him.

STRESS-SEEKING AND THE SELF-MADE MAN IN AMERICAN LITERATURE: 1894–1914

It is difficult to imagine a body of literature built on the model of man as a wholly rational creature who calmly defers pleasure, accepts temporary pain, and always chooses the most appropriate means to his end of maximum happiness. It would also be difficult to write an interesting novel about men who seek nothing but peace, contentment, and security. Even in utopian literature the most vivid scenes deal with cataclysms which precede the millennium. And who is to say whether the apocalyptic vision of Armageddon is a means of enhancing the value of a New Heaven and making man worthy of salvation, or whether the vision of final peace is a means of justifying a subversive delight in orgies of lust, clashing armies, seven-headed beasts, earthquakes, eclipses, fire, smoke, and brimstone? Whatever the reason, from the earliest times men have been fascinated by imaginative projections of danger, strife, terror, and violence.

Since Western literature has so often been preoccupied with man's demonic and aggressive impulses, one must be cautious in relating literary themes of stress-seeking to a supposed historical context. In the nineteenth century, for example, American tales of roving adventurers and border warfare probably owed more to Byron and Scott than to the conditions of frontier life. American writers have seldom portrayed a compulsive young truth-seeker without alluding to Hamlet, or an amoral and defiant rebel without suggesting Milton's Lucifer. Nevertheless, literature is not only the product of a culture, but may provide an imaginative illumination of its deepest tensions and conflicts. And there can be no doubt that literary conceptions of man's desire for stress and excitement often reveal significant historical shifts in interest, mood, and values. Thus the roving, lonely protagonists of Hemingway, Faulkner, and Thomas Wolfe bear a resemblance to the homeless Ishmaels and solitary Adams of the American literary tradition. Yet it is only after the First World War that we find such archetypal figures rendered impotent and hopeless by the trauma of past events, or in desperate search of stresses that can be manipulated and controlled in order to keep the self from being annihilated by waves of meaninglessness. According to Jack Burden, in Robert Penn Warren's *All the King's Men,* "the dream of our age" is that all life is "but the dark heave of blood and the twitch of the nerve." Although Jack is obviously a descendant of Hamlet, and discovers that truth always "kills the father," he also comes to see that the man of ideas, Adam Stanton, and the man of fact, Willie Stark, were doomed to destroy each other "because each was incomplete with the terrible divisions of their age." It is the lesson of Warren's masterpiece, which was written after the impacts of the Great Depression and the Second World War, that man is neither a free, rational agent who can make the world conform to his highest ideals, nor an irresponsible robot who responds to the strongest impulse or twitch of nerve. The conclusion that man must accept the burden of the past and the awful responsibilities of time—that he must, in short, "live in the agony of will"—is surely a reflection of the world of the mid-twentieth century.

With the perspective of time we are beginning to see that the period from 1890 to the First World War was not only marked by extraordinary scientific and artistic creativity, but also witnessed what John Weiss has recently termed "the origins of modern consciousness." In a stimulating essay on "The Reorientation of American Culture," which appears in Weiss' volume,[1] John Higham has shown that in the 1890's American popular culture was suddenly permeated with a sense of liberation from stifling norms and restrictions. From popular songs and fads to serious literature and even foreign policy there was a celebration of youth, vigor, ruggedness, and virility. The new ideal was defined at the end of the decade in a famous speech by Theodore Roosevelt on "The Strenuous Life." It found expression in a national enthusiasm for combative sports; in the bicycle craze and the physical culture movement; in the wilderness cult and the yearning for an outdoor life of fishing, hunting, and camping; in a fascination with military exploits; in a new contempt for sissies, stuffed shirts, and effete manners; in a glorification of the New Woman, who, if less sexually aggressive than Fleming's heroines, was nevertheless shockingly bold, vigorous, and athletic. Higham points out that the spirit of exuberance, restless-

[1] In *The Origins of Modern Consciousness,* ed. by John Weiss (Detroit: Wayne State University Press, 1965), pp. 25–48.

ness, and rebellion extended to such intellectual innovators as William James, Frederick Jackson Turner, and Frank Lloyd Wright. In every sphere of culture there was a zest for new experience, an emphasis on man's unlimited energies and creative powers, and a joy in breaking through the confining walls of custom and routine to "boundless space."

Before turning to an analysis of stress-seeking in representative novels of the 1894–1914 period, we should consider the significance of this pervasive shift in attitudes and values. Why should strenuous activity take such precedence over sensual indulgence, domesticity, or intellectual discipline? One might answer that Americans had always been activists, that the task of clearing the wilderness and building a nation, coupled with the Protestant Ethic, had always made them value vigorous striving and a determination to overcome all obstacles. But this explanation does not account for the sudden obsession with virility, toughness, and combativeness, and the rejection of the ideal of tender-hearted sensibility, which had actually been most popular among the middle and upper classes when there was still a wild frontier to be won. Another possible answer might lie in the consequences of rapid industrialization. By the 1890's there was a growing consciousness of the intensifying struggle for economic power, both among nations and between capital and labor. In his speech on the strenuous life, Roosevelt concluded that "it is only through strife, through hard and dangerous endeavor, that we shall ultimately win the goal of true national greatness."[2] There can be no doubt that Roosevelt envisioned a vigorous and manly middle class as an antidote to socialism and anarchism and as an indispensable support for advancing and protecting America's interests abroad. Just as the English had been prepared for greatness by their imperial responsibilities, so Americans had been toughened by their frontier experience to meet the challenge of world power.[3] Yet such pragmatic

---

[2] Theodore Roosevelt, *The Strenuous Life* (New York: Century Books, 1900).

[3] David H. Burton, "Theodore Roosevelt's Social Darwinism and Views on Imperialism," *Journal of the History of Ideas*, Vol. XXVI (January–March 1965), pp. 103–18.

thoughts could not have been in the minds of the promoters of college football or of the Americans who were thrilled to read how Gentleman Jim Corbett knocked out John L. Sullivan in the twenty-first round. It is doubtful whether the cyclists and mountain climbers thought of toughening themselves for future combat against anarchists or foreign enemies. Even Roosevelt saw national greatness as only an indirect product of the strenuous life. If certain "virile qualities" were necessary to win in "the stern strife of real life," they were also goods in themselves. The important thing was manly character—"unselfishness, courage, devotion to duty, honesty"—and these were virtues threatened by the sloth and self-indulgence that comes with wealth.

In his misgivings over the effects of economic success Roosevelt revealed one of the most profound and complex sources of the cult of the strenuous life. That Americans have valued individual success is so much a truism that we have failed to appreciate the enormous tensions and conflicts entailed by the ideal of the self-made man.[4] What so many writers on the subject have been unable to see—and what Justin Kaplan so brilliantly documents in his recent biography of Mark Twain—is that an American could internalize the ideal of economic success and frantically pursue every opportunity to make money, and still know that wealth corrupts and despise a society in which money is the ultimate measure of human worth. This conflict could lead to self-punishing and self-defeating action; painful stresses seemingly endured for rational goals might be chosen for their own sake.

The origins of this paradox were deeply embedded in the religious past, especially in the Protestant rejection of salvation by good works, which meant that the moral risks and stresses of self-discovery must always transcend worldly goals and achievements. Originally the Protestant was free to pursue material rewards precisely because they were irrelevant to his spiritual pilgrimage. The crucial problem was the state of his soul in withstanding the tests of life.

[4] Some of these conflicts are imaginatively explored by John G. Cawelti in his *Apostles of the Self-Made Man* (Chicago: The University of Chicago Press, 1965).

Even in nineteenth-century America, where the drama of salvation had been largely secularized in terms of individual success, the apostles of the self-made man warned against the sin of making wealth an end in itself. Young Americans were told to emulate the successful man not because he was rich but because he had proved his character by struggling with adversity.

Irvin Wyllie and John Cawelti have noted that the tracts, sermons, and manuals that preached self-help and the duty of economic success made little reference to practical skills or techniques for accumulating wealth. The emphasis was rather on such religious and moral virtues as faith, strength of will, self-discipline, and perseverance. Cawelti has also pointed out that in popular novels celebrating the self-made man, including those by Horatio Alger, Jr., the hero's rise from rags to riches is not due to his virtues of industry and self-reliance, but to the unexpected aid of a benevolent patron or some other providential force. The hero proves his worth and deserves success, but he is not directly responsible for it. Cawelti might have added that this device was obviously a vestige of the Protestant doctrine of election. Upward mobility could be justified only if it were untainted by egoism or by a desire for wealth and sensual gratification. The stresses that proved one's moral stamina could never be directly linked with material goals.

To be sure, the prophets of success always recognized a certain correspondence between moral character and worldly success. It was necessary to find some material corroboration for one's inner, spiritual progress. According to Ralph Waldo Emerson, for example, the American environment was a testing and liberating force which at once stimulated and rewarded self-reliance. Nevertheless, Emerson was deeply aware of the inadequacy of wealth and material success as goals in themselves. If one of the meanings of American opportunity was to give a material basis to free and unlimited grace, there were grave dangers in materializing spiritual goals. Material success could easily absorb all other motives and stultify man's vision of life. And as too many business apologists were to show by the late nineteenth century, one could easily arrive at a simple equation of wealth and moral character.

Yet, in Western culture wealth had long been associated with sybaritic decay. In America the quest for material success was always balanced by traditional middle-class suspicions of aristocratic luxury and by ancient Christian denunciations of avarice, mammonism, and voluptuaries. The apostles of the self-made man make it clear that the second and third generations could expect no benefits from their fathers' struggles with adversity. John Cawelti has found that the novels of success are filled with rich snobs and lazy, arrogant youths who were born with the proverbial silver spoon in their mouths. One of the most frequently recurring figures in American literature is the effeminate, good-for-nothing son who breaks the heart of his otherwise omnipotent father. It was a major paradox of American life that the two forces of regeneration and progress—the frontier and economic success—were self-consumptive. By the end of the nineteenth century the crucial problem was how to retain the ideal of America as a material paradise offering unlimited opportunities for individual salvation, and yet keep success from polluting the very process of redemption. How could one cultivate the virtues associated with upward mobility without becoming enslaved to material goals or softened and corrupted by wealth? One answer might be the strenuous life.

The problems of wealth and success had long been felt with particular acuteness by American writers. The values most esteemed in the Western literary tradition—culture, wisdom, courage, honor, selflessness, martial vigor and prowess—were traits of nobility. It is significant that writers like Cooper and Parkman attacked both the *nouveau riche,* who were boorish and materialistic, and the effete New World gentry, who shrank from conflict and responsibility. The natural aristocrats of Cooper and Parkman, men like Leatherstocking and La Salle, were proved by extreme physical stress to be men of strength, courage, and fortitude, who could never be demeaned by petty goals.

But from the time of Cooper and Scott literature was

itself an appealing route to material success. For writers like Mark Twain, Jack London, and Theodore Dreiser it was a means of spectacular upward mobility. American writers have been so personally committed to the ideal of success that they have been unable to treat the subject without great ambivalence.[5] By the end of the nineteenth century the mainstream of American literature had absorbed a hostile view of the conventional self-made man and a deep suspicion of the corrupting power of wealth. And one of the major themes of American novels from the 1890's to the First World War was a search for alternatives to material success in adventure, self-knowledge, social reform, loyalty, or the zest of youth for culture and experience. One should add that American writers from Stephen Crane and Frank Norris to Jack London and Ernest Hemingway have often been ardent stress-seekers themselves, and have tried to prove they are tough knowers-of-life by dashing off to foreign wars or other hazardous escapades.

If American writers never emancipated themselves from the popular dream of success, popular culture was itself eager to adopt strenuosity as an antidote to the debilitating aftereffects of wealth. Irvin Wyllie has concluded that, even on the popular level, Americans' faith in the traditional image of the self-made man was severely shaken between 1890 and 1914;[6] in the same period John Cawelti has traced a shift in the literature of self-help from an ascetic moralism to a new emphasis on willpower, initiative, personal magnetism, and a relish for competitive struggle. Money was less an end in itself or a sign of divine favor than a symbol of personal power. Economic failure was the result of weakness of character and failure of nerve. With the increasing impersonality and rationalized organization of an industrial and corporate society, it was essential to live at full throttle if one were to create a distinctive identity and preserve the immediacy of life. By the 1920's Bruce Barton could win fame by telling Americans that Christ

[5] See Kenneth S. Lynn, *The Dream of Success* (Boston: Little, Brown & Company, 1955).
[6] *The Self-Made Man in America* (New Brunswick, N.J.: Rutgers University Press, 1954).

was not a namby-pamby moralist but a man of magnetism and potency who imposed his will on history.

The need for preserving the immediacy and vitality of experience suggests another source of the American vogue of strenuosity, although this aspect of the subject is so immense that it can barely be mentioned here. For some time historians have recognized that at the turn of the century Western literary and philosophic thought was curiously divided between a delicious *Weltschmerz,* a *fin-de-siècle* savoring of decay, hopelessness, and degradation, and a fierce will to believe, a buoyant intoxication with the *élan vital,* a Dionysian joy in the throbbing intensity and passionate struggle of life. It seems fairly clear that both postures, which could be assumed at different times by a single man, were responses to what Robert Penn Warren later called the modern dream that all life is "but the dark heave of blood and the twitch of the nerve," to an uncompromising positivism and materialism that reduced human aspirations and consciousness to the mechanistic movement of individual particles of matter in a universe totally lacking in purpose and indifferent to the fate of man.

Of course, philosophic materialism has often been used as a weapon to liberate man from superstitious fears and ignorant submission to vested authority. In the early twentieth century many American writers embraced an eclectic and half-baked materialism as a refreshing alternative to the anemic idealism of the Genteel Tradition. Yet it was difficult to avoid moments of doubt and gloom as one contemplated the cold abstractions of mathematical science, the apparently certain dissipation of kinetic energy, the appalling waste and blind fortuity of the Darwinian system. In the eyes of Anatole France and Henry Adams life was an absurdity made tolerable only by lies and illusions. Even William James, who from youth was intensely alive to the wonder and beauty of life, experienced the crushing loss of purpose, the anomic failure of commitment, and the yearning for suicide that were so common among intellectuals of the late nineteenth century. Yet it was James, along with figures like Bergson and Nietzsche, who helped to provide a new faith for the generation that matured in the early twentieth century. Bergson was applauded by Theodore Roosevelt for restoring hope to philosophy. It was James who celebrated the spontaneity and exhilaration of life, who preached of the limitless energies of men, and who searched for moral equivalents of war that would create risks to challenge the human spirit. As young American rebels selected and blended elements from the thought of James, Bergson, Nietzsche, Herbert Spencer, and Ernst Haeckel, they arrived at a kind of misty vitalism that gave philosophic reinforcement to the strenuous life. For in this amalgamated world view life was to be stripped of abstract ideals and pretentious rhetoric, of mean calculations, dull routine, and bourgeois fears. Only then could man live joyously and dangerously, and open his soul to the full, rich immediacy of experience. Not surprisingly, Americans tended to envision this liberation in purely individualistic terms. If a Mussolini could later cite William James as one of his favorite philosophers, it is a gross distortion to see seeds of fascism in American vitalism, with its built-in bias against institutions.

As Americans of the 1890's pondered the meaning of success in a world transformed by industrialization, economic consolidation, and Darwinian notions of struggle and natural selection, they often looked back to the great Civil War of their fathers' generation as a key to their national identity. From its beginning the war had been recognized as a crucial test; as America's great Passion, it was constantly reenacted in ritualistic ceremonies as well as in ponderous histories and memoirs, as if a vicarious participation in national suffering could mitigate the self-indulgence of the Gilded Age. Yet the meaning of the war was almost immediately obscured by sentimentality, high-flown rhetoric, and political or constitutional abstractions. It was for this reason that Stephen Crane, at the age of twenty-one, achieved such instantaneous success by recreating a psychological response to Civil-War combat in language perfectly tuned to the mood of his generation.

For Crane the Civil War was the agency of self-discovery; his tale was almost a parable of America's quest for identity and justification in a critical moment of stress, or in what young Henry Fleming calls "one of those great affairs of the earth." The overriding question in Fleming's mind, as in the mind of any soldier approaching combat for the first time, is how he will respond. Still enticed by literary images of heroism and Homeric struggles, which were so appealing to a middle-class, commercial society, Fleming knows that this is real life and not fantasy, and that no one can be certain how he will act. By mathematical calculation he tries to prove to himself that he will not run. But the "monster of fear" grows as the moment of judgment approaches.

Fleming's problem is total self-absorption. As an isolated, individualistic American he is on his own and must prove himself against the entire universe, without the comfort of genuine communion with his fellows. Each soldier is walled up within his own internal foxhole, where his fears feed upon themselves and generate autistic images of reality. In the first confusion of combat Fleming is swept by feelings of impotence, rage, and self-congratulation. Then suddenly the entire battle and war seem aimed at destroying his own being; annihilation threatens from all points. Fleming runs in wild and unashamed panic.

He is now not only alone but is overwhelmed by crushing guilt. Like a sinner who wishes that the entire human race might be damned, he momentarily hopes that the Union Army will suffer defeat so that his dishonor can be shared. Even nature offers no reassurance, for in the serene forest groves he stumbles upon a ghastly corpse. Wandering through the swirling chaos on the edge of battle, Henry Fleming seems a totally alienated soul in a purposeless void. But after experiencing pangs of self-hate and a wish for death, he suddenly forgets that he is "engaged in combatting the universe" as he comes upon panicked troops fleeing as he had done, from the front. Fleming tries to stop one of them to ask questions, and is crushed in the head with a rifle butt. The receipt of this wound, this "red badge of courage," is the turning point in Fleming's life. As Bernard Weisberger has noted, the wound had been wished for and

might as well have been self-inflicted.[7] Fleming slowly realizes that it does not matter where the blow comes from or
which side one is on. There is no purpose to war or life.
Man has no control over his fate, which means that he is
released from responsibility, guilt, and fear. Weisberger
shrewdly observes that this is a perfect negation of Protestant faith. Yet the naturalist Stephen Crane was the son
of a Methodist minister, and if Fleming's crisis was a "con-
version in reverse," it nevertheless leads to a purging of
egoism and to a discovery of life through a heedless risking
of life.

Henry Fleming fights like a devil once he has been emancipated from guilt and fear. Temporarily he loses all sense
of self-consciousness. He rushes forward, blind to the odds,
with other men who are wild with the "enthusiasm of unselfishness." Like the others, Fleming is eager to show his
willingness to take further risks. With no thought of heroics
or of the meaning of the war, he fights with the reckless
daring of a savage. Then suddenly the engagement is over.
The men retire from "the place of blood and wrath" to
momentary tranquillity. The battle had been blind and purposeless, but Henry Fleming has conquered his fear of
death and has found his identity in a feeling of quiet self-
confidence and sturdy manhood.

In a sense Henry Fleming was a self-made man who won
success in the meaningless strife of war. As an alternative
to war, the Great West had long been regarded as a place
where a man might prove his character without becoming
tainted by avarice or the decadence of wealth. In the words
of Owen Wister, who did much to shape the conventions of
popular Western melodrama, the West was the realm of
the "horseman, the cowpuncher, the last romantic figure
upon our soil." Wister's *The Virginian* (1902) is wholly
lacking in the psychological subtlety and impressionistic
realism of *The Red Badge of Courage* (1894). But it is an
interesting expression of the ethic of the strenuous life, and

[7] In *Twelve Original Essays on Great American Novels,* ed. by
Charles Shapiro (Detroit: Wayne State University Press, 1958), pp.
96–123.

was appropriately dedicated to Wister's friend, Theodore Roosevelt.

The novel offers a forthright rejection of sentimental democracy. In the Virginian's words, "equality is a great big bluff." The true American creed is that all men should have equal liberty to find their own level, and "let the best man win, whoever he is!" Molly Stark Wood, the young heroine of the tale, comes from the natural aristocracy of New England. Her character has been formed by family pride and pluck, and by "struggling with hardship." This was all in line with the self-help manuals and the values of Horatio Alger, Jr. But by the 1870's America had begun to change. Despite their pride and natural merit, Molly's family had fallen on hard times and the girl was tempted to marry a man she did not love in order to help her family. In the South, the Virginian's lazy brothers sat around talking "hawgs and turkeys," and seemed unwilling to take chances. For men and women of ambition, the West was the only escape from decadence and vice. The Eastern narrator, who travels to Wyoming and follows the Virginian around in unembarrassed adoration, observes that the West sees more of death but less of vice than the East. He is entranced by the "wild and manly" faces of the cowboys, and by their "daring, laughter, [and] endurance."

The Virginian himself is a slim young giant who exudes strength and personifies the chivalric code of the West. Deferential and shy toward women, he is also a humorous prankster and a deadly realist in his attitude toward life and death. It should not bother anyone to have killed a man, he says, "when he'd ought to have been killed." He is a bit bothered, however, when he participates in the lynching of his friend Steve, because Steve is easygoing and "game" to the end. If it is only justice to hang a cattle rustler, the Virginian cannot help admiring a man who "took dying as naturally as he took living. Like a man should." But when the Virginian is plagued by nightmares of Steve, he is ashamed of being "that weak."

The drama of Wister's novel turns on an epic conflict of will between the Virginian and the bully Trampas. From the moment that Trampas first backs down, after the Virginian makes his now classic utterance—"When you call me that, *smile!*"—it is inevitable that the two must meet in mortal combat. The Virginian courts trouble by humiliating Trampas with a practical joke and by refusing, as ranch foreman, to dismiss his enemy in order to avoid further conflict. Since the Virginian never knows the fear of a Henry Fleming, the only complicating factor is his love for Molly Wood. For it is on the day before their wedding that Trampas publicly slanders the Virginian and issues an ultimatum that he leave town before sundown. The sympathetic bishop advises the hero to observe the higher law of love, and to leave town with Molly. Molly flatly says that "fear of outside opinion" cannot justify killing in cold blood, and that therefore "if you do this, there can be no tomorrow for you and me." But the Virginian cannot resign his manhood. After he shoots Trampas, even Molly's New England conscience "capitulates to love," which is a good thing for her since the Virginian eventually becomes a prosperous man who is "able to give his wife all and more than she asked or desired." Presumably the Virginian, having once proved his selfless courage and manhood, could be perfectly satisfied with the wealth that came with railroads and the discovery of coal on his ranch.

But what of the later generations who could receive no moral benefit from the Civil War or the vanishing frontier? In 1895, while still in college, Frank Norris wrote a semiautobiographical novel, *Vandover and the Brute,* about the sensitive, artistic son of a self-made man. Like his creator, Vandover is a shy and awkward lad, looked upon as a sissy by other boys and psychologically dominated by his immensely strong and upright father. Vandover's father had devoted his entire life to business, and though now a wealthy "old gentleman," he has reentered the sordid business world as the only escape from the "mortal ennui and weariness of the spirit" that had plagued him in a brief retirement. He has no capacity for enjoying anything but the challenge of competitive life, and in his new venture as a builder and real-estate developer is soon an enormous success. Nonetheless, the father is not lacking in sympathy for Vandover's artistic aspirations, and except for substituting

Harvard for Paris as a more suitable moral environment, he encourages and supports his son's unconventional career. He continues to do so even after Vandover has left Harvard and has confessed to grave sexual sins which culminate in the suicide of a young girl.

Like Norris himself, Vandover associates virtue with success and social respectability, and yet is strangely drawn to vice. Norris places great emphasis on the fact that Vandover's mother had died when he was eight, which meant there was no feminine influence to counterbalance the perverse and vicious ideas, the "brute" that began stirring within him in his teens. Norris' later novels rely on powerful Amazons who, like Moran in *Moran of the Lady Letty*, are virginal superwomen who beat up villains and help the frail hero become a man. The one force within Vandover that keeps the libidinal brute from plunging him into total degradation is his hallowed respect for women. Nevertheless, "as the desire of vice, the blind, reckless desire of the male, grew upon him, he set himself to destroy this barrier." He deliberately tries to corrupt his impulse to idealize women, which has been his only saving grace.

In one sense Vandover is the very opposite of a stress-seeker. In the manner of Zolaesque determinism, Norris pictures him as simply a weak and pliable youth who, being unaccustomed "to doing hard, disagreeable things," submits to the strongest impulse and adjusts to the most sordid environment. Yet, as a student, he does not know why he gets drunk, since he enjoys drinking no more than his father enjoys leisure. Sleeping with a cheap girl does not bring pleasure but an agonizing repentance. Vandover continually hurts his father with confessions of sin, and is hurt in return by his father's kindly understanding. When his father dies and Vandover inherits the hard-earned fortune, there is no check to his idleness, self-indulgence, and decline. Ostracized by friends, he no longer fears the opinion of others and feels free to do anything he chooses. Needing violent and untried excitement, he develops a mania for gambling and finds that he must continually raise the stakes in order to maintain interest and excitement. His fortune dwindles and the brute within him grows, destroying first his artistic

creativity and then his reason, until Vandover has halluci-
nations that *he* is the beast itself. A victim of lycanthropy,
Vandover suffers a ghastly punishment which, Norris informs us, he brought upon himself: "His whole life had
been one long suicide."

If Vandover's choices bring him to the point of imagining
he is a wolf, his friend Charlie Geary is a wolf of another
kind. Originally one of the youths who caroused with Vandover and helped to corrupt him, Geary is a pushing, am-
bitious, domineering figure who lives by the motto, "Every
man for himself . . . the weakest to the wall, the strongest
to the front." If this is only a Darwinian version of the
Virginian's "let the best man win," Geary shows what success has come to mean in Vandover's generation: "anything to be a 'success,' to 'arrive,' to 'get there,' to attain
the desired object in spite of the whole world . . . trampling
down or smashing through everything that stood in the
way." It is Geary who moves in voraciously to grab what
he can of Vandover's property, and who finally hires the
demented man to clean and scrub some filthy tenements on
land he had formerly owned. It is as if Geary were the
punitive agent of Vandover's father.

Vandover and the Brute contrasts the success of a ruthless strong man to the failure of a weak artist who is driven
to dissipation and madness by the temptations of affluence
and by internal compulsions that seem provoked by a father
and a society wholly committed to material success. Theodore Dreiser's *The Financier* (1912) and *The Titan* (1914)
chart the repeated successes of a man who possesses the
same strength and ruthless code as Charlie Geary. One
might assume that novels modeled on the career of a great
tycoon, in this case Charles T. Yerkes, would present a
man who calculates rational strategy to achieve his goals,
and would thus be irrelevant to the theme of stress-seeking.
But Dreiser's Frank Cowperwood is as much an artist as
Vandover, and is a rational goal-seeker in only a superficial
sense. If he pursues money, power, and sex, it is only because they provide means for releasing his titanic energies
and for imposing his will on an otherwise impersonal and
meaningless world.

Theodore Dreiser, who knew the taste of failure and came close to suicide in 1903, was always dazzled by the glamour of wealth. His articles on great Americans, written for the magazine *Success*, showed that the self-made man was not necessarily a cramped, bourgeois moneygrubber. Instead of looking for an alternative to the self-made man, Dreiser worked a transvaluation of values and pictured Cowperwood as a Nietzschean superman, as the strongest product of evolutionary struggle, as a modern counterpart to Lucifer, Don Juan, and the greatest of Renaissance princes.

Cowperwood's father represents the limits of success within the framework of traditional values. A moderately prosperous banker, he is content with his station in life. His vision is restricted by excessive caution and conventional morality. But his son Frank lives by the rule, "I satisfy myself," and knows no law except that imposed upon him by his inability to think. Completely free of the self-doubts of a Henry Fleming, the only thing he dreads is inactivity. Frank Cowperwood is at once an intellectual, an amoralist, and an egoist; he is a man of enormous will and personal magnetism whose hypnotic eyes overpower other men and captivate women. He can simultaneously manage a number of illicit sexual affairs while manipulating politicians and bankers, dealing with strikes and labor unions, bonding and equipping tunnels for his street railways, and mapping the grand strategy for his conquest of Chicago. When a stubborn property owner blocks the construction of a tunnel, Frank simply has the building demolished on a Saturday afternoon, knowing that a court will not act until the following week, when he can protect a *fait accompli* with legal delays. If a mayor is elected to combat corruption, Frank simply engineers his seduction by an attractive prostitute, and then threatens his supposedly respectable enemy with the exposure of love letters and a suit for breach of promise.

Frank's cool sense of strategy makes it appear that his behavior might be explained by a theory of games. For example, when he is confronted by a Mr. Sohlberg, who is suspicious of Frank's relations with Mrs. Sohlberg, Cowperwood first tries the gambit of threatening to reveal what he has discovered about Sohlberg's own love affairs. When this fails, Cowperwood escalates the conflict by asking what Sohlberg would do if his suspicions proved to be true. Sohlberg replies that he would kill Cowperwood. Prepared for this, Frank pulls out two small revolvers, flatly states that he has been sleeping with Mrs. Sohlberg, and says, " 'Now if you want to kill me here is a gun. . . . Take your choice. If I am to die you might as well die with me.' " This proposal, coupled with a look of cold steel, undermines Sohlberg's nerve, as Frank knew it would. Cowperwood now denies the affair and tells Sohlberg that he will be shot on sight if he says anything more, but that he will be amply rewarded if he gets out of town.

But game theory, while perhaps relevant to Cowperwood's strategic use of power, cannot explain why he gets into such positions in the first place. Even as a young man in Philadelphia, Cowperwood is not simply the shrewd, calculating financier that the bankers take him to be. He is so reckless in his risk-taking that a financial panic exposes him to enemies who are able to send him to prison. Two years after this punishment he is back in the same room at the stock exchange where he was once ruined, again taking chances in a time of crisis, and now triumphing. Upon arriving in Chicago, he boldly seeks out the president of the largest bank, and after impressing the man with his wealth and personal magnetism, coolly informs him of the conviction for embezzlement, the prison term, and a recent divorce. Although Cowperwood knows nothing about the manufacture and distribution of natural gas, he is attracted to the field because it presents the opportunity for a big fight and for bitter lawsuits, both of which Frank says he loves. Even in the social sphere Frank and his new young wife Aileen take the risk of plunging immediately toward the upper strata, although they know that by pitching a lavish party much will be at stake both for them and their suspicious guests. Neither prudence nor patience is among Frank's virtues. This is because he is attracted only by the "complications" of life: "Nature was beautiful, tender at times, but difficulties, plans, plots, schemes to unravel and make smooth—these things were what made existence worthwhile." Life was essentially a battle without ultimate purpose; the only meaningful question was "whether the world would trample him underfoot or no."

Cowperwood is a great admirer and collector of paintings, and achieves a certain aesthetic satisfaction from his financial manipulations. This "artistic" bent is also expressed in his passion for beautiful women. Nothing could have been more foolhardy than his decision to pursue Aileen Butler, the daughter of a Philadelphia contractor who had the political and financial power to crush him. Not only was Frank heavily dependent on Butler, but he was a married man in a society that put sexual transgression on an altogether different plane from simple graft and corruption. Cowperwood is "almost nervous" after his first overture to Aileen, and realizes he is contemplating "a very treacherous thing." Yet seduction has much the same appeal as some daring financial challenge. He is thus thrilled to watch himself deliberately, calculatingly pump the bellows that heighten his flames of desire, "to feed a fire that might ultimately consume him—and how deliberately and resourcefully!" Later on, in Chicago, he repeats the performance by seducing the wives and daughters of some of his principal supporters. And if Cowperwood is a "buccaneer" on a "sea of sex," it is not because he really seeks either beauty or sex. He is not dissatisfied with Aileen in either way. Rather, he must continually test himself against the will of the very best women. He must respond to every challenge and every risk as he pursues an ultimate ideal of perfection and mastery that can never be found. Frank Cowperwood is, in short, an embodiment of the *élan vital* that can never find an object or goal commensurate with its unlimited energy. In the end, Cowperwood's powers are diffused and become self-destructive as they fail to find limits that can give them meaning.

Theodore Dreiser accepted both the American ethic of success and a pessimistic materialism. Yet he clearly identified himself with Frank Cowperwood, who, by seeking stresses that would test his own will and capacity for transcending the deterministic flux, defiantly challenged both the materialistic world view and the narrow equation of

morality and success. The same intriguing pattern can be
seen in the work of Jack London. Born in illegitimacy and
destitution, hardened as a physical laborer, oyster pirate,
hobo, and sailor, London made a fortune by writing forty-
three books in sixteen years, crowned his success by building a patriarchal estate and instructing his Korean servant
to call him "Mr. God," and then committed suicide at the
age of forty. London's uncertainty over the meaning of
success was matched by his confusion in philosophy. His
reputation as a Socialist speaker and writer was based on
his indignation at the authority structure of a capitalistic
society, especially at the so-called custodians of culture; but
Marxist rhetoric could not conceal London's deep contempt
for the masses. A self-professed disciple of both Spencer
and Nietzsche, he was at once a materialist, a Social Dar-
winist, and a believer in the creative energy of a kind of
elemental life-force. Essentially he agreed with the elitist
philosophy of Frank Cowperwood, and held that the race
is to the swift and the battle to the strong. But instead of
looking to the strife of business or the vanishing frontier,
he treated the themes of success and failure within a framework of decadent civilization and regenerative savagery.
Writing at a time when even the Far West had settled into
the dull and repressive routines of civilized life, London
found the last life-restoring stresses in Alaska and the Pacific. His best-known character, Buck, the self-made dog,
moves from the boredom and soft decay of the Santa Clara
Valley to a fierce contest for survival in the Klondike, and
finally finds a richer and freer life by responding to the
call of the wild and becoming a leader of the wolves of
the forest.

As we have seen, when Vandover became a wolf it was
a sign of the ultimate moral degradation, the triumph of
the "brute" over reason and sensibility. Yet Dreiser frequently described Cowperwood as a predatory animal.
Jack London wanted people to call him "Wolf," and even
named his mansion "Wolf House," presumably to justify
its luxury with a primitivistic label. His most memorable
protagonist, Captain Wolf Larsen of *The Sea Wolf* (1904),
is a kind of Cowperwood in the rough. Like Cowperwood,

his magnetic eyes fascinate and dominate women until they surrender. The very archetype of virility, he is a man of massive build and titanic strength, the savage, ferocious strength, we are told, that one associates with wild animals or with our own "tree-dwelling prototypes." He embodies the "potency of motion" that is the essence of life, the "elemental stuff of which life's forms are molded." Although only a sealer and a kind of pirate, Larsen has read widely in literature and philosophy. From Spencer he has learned that life is a struggle in which only the fit survive. But he has rejected Spencer's sentimental notions of self-sacrifice for the benefit of children or the human race. Life, he says, is yeasty and crawling, and totally without purpose. It is absurd to lose one crawl or squirm of life through self-denial or sacrifice. Larsen's version of "I satisfy myself" is more brutal than Cowperwood's. Since he thinks that might is right and weakness is wrong, he enjoys inflicting physical pain on others, and is totally indifferent to suffering and death.

If Wolf Larsen is a more primitive, sadistic Charlie Geary, his foil, Humphrey Van Weyden, is a more effete Vandover. But in London's tale, the brutalization of the sensitive artist is a process of regeneration. When "Hump" Van Weyden is taken aboard Larsen's hell ship, he is a bookish dilettante, a self-confessed "sissy." In Wolf Larsen's eyes he is "a miserable weakling" who allows himself to be bullied by the entire crew until he finally proves his nerve by sharpening his knife in preparation for a fight. It appears that London could not decide whether Larsen was an admirable figure whose amoral philosophy was essentially correct, or whether the ideal was some kind of synthesis between Larsen's brutal realism and the traditional values of humanity. Various members of the crew rebel against Larsen's tyranny, and in so doing represent the struggle of idealism against the view that life is "but the dark heave of blood and the twitch of the nerve." A sailor named Johnson, for example, says that he would die for what is right, if necessary, in order to be true to himself. Van Weyden sees this as a triumph of spirit and principle over flesh, as a refutation of Larsen's materialism. But Larsen tells Hump that Johnson is only "a bit of animated dust" that defies him, and succeeds in breaking the sailor's will by a savage beating. Hump is both toughened and enlightened by his contact with Wolf, and becomes a kind of admiring fag.

The crew's resistance and plotting are hardly an affirmation of the human spirit. For a time Van Weyden sees something "sublime" in the defiance of young George Leach, whose denunciations of Larsen recall the moral courage of the Hebrew prophets. But Leach, like other members of the crew, regresses more and more to the level of the snarling animal. Why, Hump asks, is Larsen content to beat Leach to a pulp, when the sailor has tried so often to kill him? "There seemed a certain spice about it, such as men must feel who take delight in making pets of ferocious animals. 'It gives a thrill to life,' he explained to me, 'when life is carried in one's hand. Man is a natural gambler, and life is the biggest stake he can lay. The greater the odds, the greater the thrill.'" Larsen adds that he is really doing Leach a favor: " 'The greatness of sensation is mutual. He is living more royally than any man for'ard, though he does not know it. For he has what they have not—purpose, something to do and be done, an all-absorbing end to strive to attain, the desire to kill me, the hope that he may kill me. . . . I doubt that he has ever lived so swiftly and keenly before.' "

Wolf Larsen thus defends a philosophy of pure stress-seeking as a means of responding to an amoral and materialistic world. He says that he would like Van Weyden more if he joined the crew in their murderous plots. It is only fear that keeps Van Weyden from trying to murder the Captain, and he is thus a hypocrite who sins against his "whole pitiful little code." Hump inwardly knows that this is true, but he is faced with a great moral dilemma. His contact with Larsen has hardened his mind and body to the world of brutal reality; in a storm he finds that he is no longer afraid of death, that he will risk his life to carry out the Captain's orders. Yet, in accordance with Larsen's code he should try to kill Larsen, but finds he lacks the nerve.

Apparently London was unable to resolve this dilemma

without ultimately endorsing Larsen's philosophy, and consequently he sought escape in an absurd fantasy which nevertheless illuminates his conceptions of culture and the strenuous life. At the most unlikely moment, the hell ship takes on board one Maud Brewster, who turns out to be a famous and beautiful writer. Maud represents wealth, manners, and genteel culture. She stands, we are told, at the opposite end of the evolutionary ladder from Wolf Larsen. Yet Larsen more than holds his own with her in philosophic discourse, and lectures her on the sins and hypocrisy of the leisure class. Hump Van Weyden lectures her on the utter futility of "moral courage" against Wolf Larsen, but then leaps to her protection when Larsen tries to rape her. The rest of the story is too silly to summarize, but two themes deserve mention. After fleeing the ship, Maud and Hump land on a deserted seal island where the two literati are purified and regenerated by a reversion to caveman existence. Hump finally becomes a man as he learns to club seals and protect his "mate"; Maud becomes a woman as she sews skins and blows up the fire for the evening meal. It should be added that, despite their deep love for each other, Maud and Hump lead ascetic lives and even build separate huts to sleep in! The second theme concerns the morality of killing, when Wolf Larsen's ship, with only the blinded Captain aboard, washes ashore. Wolf tries to keep Hump from repairing the damaged vessel, but calls him a slave to conventional morality for not daring to kill a blind, unarmed man. While Hump has learned to club defenseless seals, he resolves not to shoot Larsen unless Larsen attacks. It is finally the newly toughened Maud who knocks Larsen over the head when Hump has been trapped by deceit. And though Wolf later tries to kill them both, just "to be the biggest bit of the ferment to the end," Maud comes to admire him and to sympathize with him before he dies. The conflict between brutal impulse and culture, between id and superego, is resolved in sentimentality.

Wolf Larsen never had a chance to test his powers in the realms of business and culture, and for that reason the novel is more concerned with the implications of materialism than with the implications of success. But in Jack London's autobiographical *Martin Eden* (1908), a Wolf Larsen-type hero pursues success and confronts a Maud Brewster-type heroine on her own ground. Martin Eden is not a cruel sadist, but like Larsen he is a man of indomitable will, whose muscled body is a "mass of quivering sensibilities." A former sailor, cowboy, and oyster pirate, he is a rough man of the world who is cut off by the widest chasm from Ruth Morse's world of wealth, polite manners, and formal education. Nevertheless, Martin knows that he is superior to the sailors, dock workers, and cheap cannery girls who have never understood him; his body sings with strength and vitality; he yearns for self-fulfillment and beauty. Although Ruth seems to be an ethereal spirit, untouchable and impossibly remote, Martin is confident that he can leap the gap to a higher sphere of culture. For her part, Ruth is moved by an unconscious instinct "to tame a wild thing," and is also drawn to Martin's virility by "a primordial force." Thus she coaches him in grammar and reads him Browning.

As Martin furiously pursues his self-education, he stumbles upon the unity of all knowledge in the works of Spencer. He is now desperate to write about "the stress and strain of life, its fevers and sweats and wild insurgences . . . to glorify the leaders of forlorn hopes, the mad lovers, the giants that fought under stress and strain, amid terror and tragedy, making life crackle with the strength of their endeavor." In 1908 Jack London was writing about just such things, and making over sixty thousand dollars a year from it. Martin tells Ruth that he wants to become famous, as part of the adventure: "It is not the being famous, but the process of becoming so, that counts." But unfortunately, the magazines are not interested in the stress and strain of life, but rather in glorifying "sordid dollar-chasers" and "commonplace little love affairs of commonplace little men and women." Martin Eden receives nothing but impersonal rejection slips, and has no one to turn to for advice. Even Ruth fails to understand the great creative force that moves within him. Her literary values are those of genteel society; her ideal of success is her businessman father.

But though Martin faces starvation, he knows that the world belongs to the strong and that he can eventually lick the editors just as he once licked a bully named Cheese-Face when he was a boy. In a powerful scene that is similar to the fight to the death between Buck and Spitz in *Call of the Wild,* Martin recalls the circle of bloodthirsty boys, "howling like barbarians," as he and Cheese-Face confronted each other in deadly combat. For eleven years Cheese-Face had beaten and bullied him. Now the two fought like Stone-Age savages, and Martin was glad that even after his arm had been broken, the gang let the battle go on until he finally pounded Cheese-Face to a senseless blob. Such an elemental struggle, in Jack London's eyes, was the basic reality of life. And for all his life Martin Eden would have to pit himself against a cosmic Cheese-Face, his "eternal enemy."

After studying and writing for nineteen hours a day, as Jack London himself had done, Martin begins to find that the culture represented by the Morses is shallow and pretentious. The lawyers, bankers, and army officers who gather at the Morse's have read very little and make pompous pronouncements about writers and ideas they do not understand. Martin's quest for knowledge and culture leads him into ever sharper conflicts. When he preaches Nietzsche to the dull Republicans at the Morse's dinners, they think he is a Socialist and are perplexed when he argues that they are closer to Socialism than he. When Martin denounces the ignorance of a judge who insults Herbert Spencer, Ruth tells him he is unbearable. Nevertheless, she comes to love him and he keeps up his furious but apparently hopeless pace of writing in order to prove himself to her.

Then suddenly Martin becomes a tremendous success. Editors clamor for his work, money keeps flowing in, his name is on everyone's lips. Seeking temporary escape from fame, he tries to return to his old crowd of drinking, dancing, fighting friends. But though he is exhilarated by a gang fight and is sentimentally touched by the love of a lowly girl, Martin finds that books and culture have exiled him from his former companions. On the other hand, he is

crushingly disillusioned by the sudden adulation of the
bourgeoisie. The same editors eagerly compete for the
same stories they had once scorned. "Fawn or fang," it
was all a matter of chance. He was the fashion of the
hour, and even the Morses, who had broken off his tentative engagement to Ruth and had forbidden him to enter
their house, try to woo him back because of his fame and
wealth. Everyone wants to feed him, when before they
would have let him starve. After struggling so hard to
prove himself, Martin Eden is sickened by the symbols
and consequences of success. His success, he feels, is in-
valid, since he is not really appreciated for either his work
or his own being. He has become so much a public fad,
a mere symbol, that he feels an acute sense of nonbeing.

The climax is when Ruth arrives on what she represents
as a daring mission to declare her love, regardless of her
family's feelings. Martin knows that she had liked him for
himself; yet this simple human attraction had given way to
her bourgeois standards of success. She had opposed his
writing and had urged him to get a conventional job and
work for conventional symbols of success. She had wanted
to make him afraid of life, as she and her class were, and
remold him in the image of timid, repressed, bourgeois
respectability. When Martin confronts her with these truths
and asks if love is so gross a thing that it must feed on
publications and public notice, Ruth confesses her sins and
begs forgiveness. She loves him now, for what he is; and
in order to prove that she can liberate herself from the
values of her class, that she can be a traitor, as she says,
to all that had previously made her a traitor to love, she
offers him her virginity in free love. Martin is impressed
by this gesture and says that she has redeemed herself. Yet
the nonbeing of success has drained him of all desire and
aspiration. He knows now that he had never loved the real
Ruth Morse but only an idealized Ruth of his own creation.
His disillusion is hardened when he finds that Ruth had
lied about coming to see him alone, and that she had really
been brought by her brother, obviously with her family's
consent.

Whereas Martin Eden had once grasped every moment

of life in its maximum intensity, he now sees every day as a bright light that hurts his soul. Instead of begrudging the moments lost in sleep, he yearns for rest. On a voyage across the Pacific he quietly slips out a porthole and into the night sea. He is amused by the way his instinctive will to live checks his resolution to die. Finally, he takes a deep breath and dives as deeply as he can. He knows that death can bring no suffering, that the pain in his chest is the last blow that life can deal him. When he inhales the sea and his hands and feet churn the water, in a desperate, reflexive effort to lift his body to the air, he knows that he has fooled them.

Erik Erikson has said that a creative man "must court sickness, failure, or insanity, in order to test the alternative whether the established world will crush him, or whether he will disestablish a sector of this world's outworn fundaments and make a place for a new one."[8] We have seen that in American literature the cult of the strenuous life was linked with a desire to break out of the confining and demeaning patterns set by the equation of individual salvation with material success, and to bring to man's quest for identity some of the dangers and unpredictability of the unknown. This search for new challenges that would restore a sense of the immediacy and richness of experience was also a response to a materialistic philosophy that reduced spiritual values to the level of animal desires and impulses, and thus destroyed the traditional Protestant ideal of a balance between moral character and material success. Unfortunately, in America it was difficult to test one's will and character, in the sense of Erikson's statement, without resort to the conventional canons of success. There were so few institutional channels and boundaries that when a stress-seeking man, that is, an identity-seeking man, tried to move beyond success, he became an embodiment of sheer vitality in a limitless void, a Martin Eden beating his arms and legs in the depths of a dark sea.

[8] Erik Erikson, *Young Man Luther* (New York: W. W. Norton & Company, Inc., 1962), p. 46.

PART III

Empirical Analysis of Stress-seekers

Samuel Z. Klausner

Early in his career Samuel Z. Klausner was studying the relation between personality and society, more specifically between "Social Class and Self-Concept." A harbinger of his concern with problems of stress is his study of "Immigrant Absorption and Social Tension in Israel." This paper discusses problems of formerly relatively wealthy Jews of Baghdad who immigrated to Israel.

The psychology and sociology of sexual behavior, another theme of his work for several years, combined with his concern for the acculturation of immigrants to produce an article on "Inferential Visibility and Sex Norms in the Middle East." Although initially their sexual patterns contrasted with those of native-born Israelis, within two to three years after entering Israel the sexual behavior of Iraqi immigrants converged with that of the native Israelis. Since the sexual norms are not manifestly communicated, the immigrant infers them from the cultural symbolism of, for instance, clothing and even from missing symbols such as the infrequency of sexual graffiti.

"Sacred and Profane Meanings of Blood and Alcohol" reported a cross-cultural study based upon data from the Human Relations Area Files. The use of alcohol was correlated with attitudes toward blood. Light rather than heavy drinking in secular situations was found to be associated with an attitude that blood is holy.

The influence of the sociology of religion was apparent in *Psychiatry and Religion,* a sociological study of counseling. It traces changes in counseling orientation among ministers under the impact of psychological thought and of psychiatrists.

"Rationalism and Empiricism in Studies of Behavior in Stressful Situations" combined a concern with research methodology and the sociology of knowledge. Concepts from studies of stress were classified according to whether they were related directly to observables, or were placed in a rather long chain of conceptual imagery. The empiricistic approach was more common among researchers lacking an attitude of "certitude." They tended to be young or working in a field not their own.

The Quest for Self-Control is a series of papers on the problem of self-control in stressful situations. The papers in this book treat stress as a response to environmental press upon an unwilling individual. The present symposium recognizes that some people endeavor to raise their tension levels rather than striving for a steady state. In this sense Klausner's paper is a critique of the equilibrium model in the social sciences. The term "stress-seeking" was selected to highlight arousal or excitement connected with fear and the subjection of the organism to disabilities. The stress-seeker may be seduced by the symbolic challenge of a job or by the more physical challenge of a mountain. Aside from obvious differences, both these types of stress-seekers share common psychological qualities. Both approach their task rationally; both tend to be egocentric and to repeat the difficult task or successively seek new ones. The characteristics of rationality and egocentricity suggest that the behavior is dominated by ego processes in which the self as effective actor is the primary focus. The tendency to repeat may be a symbolic reenactment of a fear-conquering drama.

The basic paradox of the stress-seeker lies in his apparent engagement rather than avoidance of the painful. This paradox may be resolved by the fact that pleasure and pain both draw upon the same reservoir of underlying excitement. Depending upon the intensity of the excitement or upon the conditions surrounding it, the arousal may be appraised as either pleasurable or painful. As one moves through a stress-seeking act, the appraisal may change, so that excitement which at first seemed painful may be experienced as pleasurable.

The stress-seeker is socially supported, lauded, and legitimated ethically and philosophically. The stress-seeker is also socially controlled. Interpersonal social manners remove inciting symbolism. Territorial division keeps rivals apart. Incipient conflict between stress-seekers may be diverted into competition. Systems of law give higher authorities a monopoly on the more extreme forms of violence and so limit violent expression in society at large.

THE INTERMINGLING OF PAIN AND PLEASURE: THE STRESS-SEEKING PERSONALITY IN ITS SOCIAL CONTEXT

THE CHARACTER OF STRESS-SEEKING

ESCAPING THE STEADY STATE: THE PROBLEM SETTING

Stress has been a fashionable topic among behavioral scientists for two decades. Under aliases such as tension and anxiety this topic has dominated a respectable scientific literature for half a century.[1] Its broad compass has been matched by its disagreeable connotation. Stress has referred to the suffering of individuals while imprisoned, exposed in the Antarctic, or caught between incompatible value directives. Stress has also referred to the relations between competing nations, the effects of maldistributed wealth, and the explosive potential of ambiguous lines of organizational authority. Stress situations are seen as unwanted deviations from a steady state, the fault of some pernicious environment or tragic circumstance denying to individuals and groups their natural state of tranquillity. The afflicted individual or group is pictured as hopefully holding these pernicious or tragic forces at bay.

The theoretical structure of this tradition in the study of stress is informed by an equilibrium model. This model's paradigm is borrowed from physical mechanics. Systems are conceived of as running down, like a taut rubber band snapping back, when released, to an equilibrium state—a state of minimum tension. The system may tend toward absolute rest or toward a dynamic balance of forces. Walter

[1] See Samuel Z. Klausner (ed.), *The Quest for Self-Control* (New York: The Free Press, 1965).

Cannon's advocacy of the case for homeostasis in physiology[2] has had a profound influence on theoreticians of personality, society, and culture. When the body's stable state is upset, mechanisms are set in motion to reassert a balance. Body temperature rises in the struggle with fibrosis; moisture is excreted on the skin surface and its evaporation cools the body. When blood is being lost, a clotting process is set in motion to seal the lesion.

The equilibrium model locates evidence of personality adaptation to its external environment or of adjustments among its internal conditions. This model has been useful for conceptualizing deterministic systems such as the natural sciences may present, or for theoretical, psychological, or social systems which, for heuristic purposes, may be assumed to behave deterministically. However, equilibrium theory has been reified as a model of conscious motivational systems. People are said to strive for a consistent self-image, though it be a bad one.[3] Some people may seek this internal equilibrium some of the time but not all people do it all of the time. At times people may act to reduce the tension or stress they are experiencing, but there are also times when they act to increase their tensions.

Unquestionably, the reduction of tensions, particularly those due to interpersonal and intergroup conflict, is a contemporary social goal. In our times, the search for battle, particularly battle between nations, is viewed publicly as an evil. One need not, however, retrace many years to arrive at a time when men could seek a military engagement with social approval. The change in the motives of many men has not kept pace with this change in social values. This is not surprising. The contemporary derogation of conflict derives more from intelligent contemplation of a future holocaust than it does from changes in our social relations —the hearth in which most of our motives and values are forged. The subjection of interpersonal and intergroup relations to the values of peace is not aided by the assumption

[2] *The Wisdom of the Body,* revised edition (New York: W. W. Norton & Company, Inc., 1963).
[3] See Prescott Lecky, *Self-Consistency: A Theory of Personality* (Hamden, Conn.: The Shoe String Press, Inc., 1951).

that all people have, *a priori*, personal commitments to these values. It is incumbent upon us to examine man as a stress-seeker in order to establish the social conditions for his tranquillity. Where individuals seem intent upon upsetting the steady state, the reified equilibrium model is no longer paradigmatic.

For several years I have been studying the behavior of sport parachutists.[4] This study was originally designed to explore ways in which individuals cope with internal disequilibria occasioned by environmental press. It became apparent that some sport parachutists were not the victims but the pursuers of stress—seekers after situations that would stress them. This seeking is epitomized in the character of their airplane ascent and parachute jump.

Stress-seeking is a species of the genus arousal-seeking. This latter term neither implies unpleasantness nor suggests potential danger for the organism. Stress-seeking may be defined as behavior designed to increase the intensity of emotion or level of activation of the organism. The term will be retained to draw attention to people who seek arousal in ways that expose them to fear and to disabilities. Evidence will be presented to show that both fearful and pleasant emotions draw upon the same energic reservoir. The degree of arousal, activation, or emotional intensity may be assessed from behavioral measures of gross movement and task engagement, or by physiological measures such as those based on the Galvanic Skin Response or electroencephalogram.

Arousal may be attained by pitting oneself against an unusually difficult or threatening situation. One consequence, and sometimes the aim of such behavior, is to disequilibrate some physiological or psychological processes. This is arousal-seeking by stress-seeking. Stress may be sought by engaging a symbolic challenge such as a demanding job, a physical challenge such as climbing a mountain, or by inciting the opposition of other persons—engaging in

---

[4] Samuel Z. Klausner, "Fear and Enthusiasm in Sport Parachuting," in James A. Knight and Ralph Slovenko (eds.), *Motivations in Play, Games and Sports* (Springfield, Ill.: Charles C. Thomas, Publishers, 1967).

conflict. Upon committing such acts, the individual will trigger in himself the series of stressful responses and the adaptational responses to stress so well described by Hans Selye.[5] These stress and adaptational responses may be automatic, but they are precipitated by the active, purposive, self-initiated behavior of the stress-seeker.

Motivation involves an inner state and some external objects around which the inner energy is organized. This paper will emphasize the dynamic aspects of stress-seeking, leaving the question of objects in the background—though only analytically in the background—for the moment.

THREE ILLUSTRATIVE STRESS-SEEKERS

The realm of sports, which originally drew my attention, is but one of those where the stress-seeker performs. The role of entrepreneur has been consistently attractive to stress-seekers. Despite a high failure rate among their predecessors, modern societies continue to find new aspirants for this role. "Creating a business . . . is no easy task. It requires motivation bordering on obsession—a drive that possesses a man and keeps him struggling toward his objective in the face of obstacles, frustrations, and discomfitures."[6] Collins, Moore, and Unwalla, in their study of the enterprising man, assert that no one would undertake the development of a new business unless he had compelling reasons. The glittering attraction of the entrepreneurial way of life is not among the reasons.[7] If other roads to status are blocked by low education or an impoverished childhood, a candidate for this role is more likely to precipitate into it. These conditions are influential but not determining; many individuals affected by them do not become entrepreneurs.

A puzzling image of the entrepreneur emerges from the Collins study. The entrepreneur drives himself but does not

[5] *The Stress of Life* (New York: McGraw-Hill Book Co., Inc., 1956).
[6] Orvis F. Collins, F. David G. Moore, and Darab B. Unwalla, *The Enterprising Man* (East Lansing, Mich.: The Michigan State University Press, 1964), p. 37.
[7] *Ibid.*, p. 246.

"love" his work. Unable to submit to authority and having an intense need for autonomy, he finds it difficult to work with others, he breaks partnerships, and he may exploit his sponsors when his success or that of his enterprise calls for it. He abhors a structured situation such as that enjoyed by managerial executives, and obsessively pursues the new idea or the new deal. In moments of crisis, he does not seek security but tends to increase his insecurity. To the question of what makes the enterprising man tick, David McClelland *et al.*[8] reply with the concept of the need for achievement. To approach a complete understanding of the enterprising man requires dramatic language, the language of agonistic struggle. The psychic drive of stress-seeking is blended with moral and ethical force. The entrepreneur pits a sense of right and virtue against the power of evil and sloth.

Seeking stressful situations may be incidental to the attainment of economic, political, or other goals. The value of these other goals may be enhanced by blocks to their attainment. The entrepreneurial situation is one in which the importance of economic or organizational goals exceeds that of the stress-seeking.

Stress-seeking may become an end in itself. Economic and political goals may serve to legitimate stress-seeking. In the area of sport, however, the meeting of challenge need not be justified in terms of other values. In fact, when sport is justified in terms of character building or body building by the sportsman, we recognize these as rationalizations after the fact—the fact expressed in the English term "fun."

Ernest Hemingway was one type of sportsman stress-seeker. He repeatedly tested his own mettle and used his pen to sketch the brave and the cowardly. Charles A. Fenton,[9] a literary biographer of Hemingway's early years,

[8] D. C. McClelland, J. W. Atkinson, R. A. Clark, and E. L. Lowell, *The Achievement Motive* (New York: Appleton-Century-Crofts, 1953).

[9] *The Apprenticeship of Ernest Hemingway* (New York: The New American Library of World Literature, Inc. [Mentor Book], 1961; originally published by Farrar, Straus & Cudahy, Inc., 1954).

describes his instinct to win as almost a reflex. In Paris during the First World War, he sought areas where shells were impacting to get his news stories, or, at least, Fenton assigned this motive to his behavior. He joined the Red Cross Ambulance Corps in 1918 and then was bored when not stationed at the front lines. He persuaded his officers to allow him to bring supplies directly to Italians in the trenches. On one such mission a shell-burst gave him two hundred and twenty-seven separate wounds. A. E. Hotchner, a biographer of Hemingway's later years,[10] reported him in Havana during the 1950's as full of enjoyment, seeking action, expounding the three basic qualities of a good matador—courage, skill, and grace in the presence of death—and displaying his wounds.

When stress-seeking is enlisted in the service of overshadowing aims, it is difficult to extricate its contribution to action from that of the motives attached to these other aims. This is particularly true when the stress-seeker is engaged in political action—as Theodore Roosevelt was. In the words of William H. Harbaugh, "Roosevelt's is the story of a man driven: of a man whose strength came from the conquest of fear, not from the lack of it; of a man compelled again and again to prove himself and possessed, happily, of the moral and physical stamina to do so."[11] Struggle was itself a virtue. The battle hard won had an uplifting influence. William James judged Roosevelt's bellicose emotion as a sign that he was still mentally in the *Sturm und Drang* of early adolescence. Historians who espouse the "great man" concept of events doubt that we would have declared war on Spain but for Roosevelt's impetuous drive to strike blows. Roosevelt is quoted as saying he would have left his wife's deathbed to have answered this call to "cut my little notch on the stick that stands as a measuring rod in every family."[12] Refusing an inactive retirement during the Taft administration, he was drawn more

---

[10] *Papa Hemingway* (New York: Random House, Inc., 1966).

[11] William H. Harbaugh, *The Life and Times of Theodore Roosevelt,* revised edition (New York: Collier Books, 1963), p. 15.

[12] *Ibid.,* p. 104.

and more into the leadership of the Progressive Party, although, as a gentleman aristocrat, he felt little affinity for its liberal fellowship. Wilson's refusal to intervene against Germany earlier in the war drew his scorn. His last years were consumed by anger against Wilson, who, when war arrived, refused him permission to raise a division of infantry and cavalry for service in Europe.[13]

RATIONALITY, EGOCENTRICITY AND REPETITIVENESS AMONG STRESS-SEEKERS

These vignettes of stress-seeking in business, sports, and politics expose some general characteristics of stress-seekers. First, their behavior is carefully planned; second, they tend to be more responsive to internal than to external imperatives; and third, they return again and again to the stressful situation.

Not to plan rationally for a stressful situation is to court self-destruction. The masochistic or suicidal individual illustrates a pathological type of stress-seeker. None of the above types were seeking self-destruction. The sportsman stress-seeker strains to develop his skill, to improve his technique, and is forever concerned with safety procedures—learning to look around before swinging a golf club, or practicing the reach for the rip cord on an emergency parachute. Hotchner writes that Hemingway planned fun as seriously as he did work. The entrepreneur schemes the creation of new organizations and the marketing of a new product. Rational accounting is the heart of his endeavor, and each business risk is examined, weighed, and hedged, if possible. Theodore Roosevelt planned battle tactics with care. As a member of the Civil Service Commission, he pressed for a merit system and for salaries instead of fees, and fought patronage in public administration.

The stress-seeker's rationality is the type that Weber called *wertrationale*—the means for attaining a goal are subjected to a rational rule while the choice of a goal of action

[13] George E. Mowry, *Theodore Roosevelt and the Progressive Movement* (New York: Hill and Wang, Inc., 1960; originally published by The University of Wisconsin Press, 1946).

remains unquestioned. Sport parachutists do not debate whether they should jump, but exert effort in training, in checking procedures and the safety of their equipment, and in practicing precision falling and landing. Where stress-seeking is an adjunct of dominant political and economic goals, these goals are more likely to be rationally evaluated.

The stress-seeker's greater responsiveness to internal than to external imperatives is reflected in a peculiar accent to his rationality. While committed to procedural rules, his own interpretations of those rules may take precedence over interpretations imposed by an authority. For example, Roosevelt, as President, refused a request to use federal troops against striking miners. Instead, he dispatched the troops to operate the mines in receivership; according to prevailing interpretations, this procedure was unconstitutional. Roosevelt declared, however, that the Constitution was made for the people and not the people for the Constitution.[14]

This internal imperative is reflected in an insistence upon personal autonomy. An entrepreneur is distinguished in this respect from an executive in a large business organization. According to Collins *et al.*, the entrepreneur early in his career may even rebel against the authority of an older sponsor, and is notoriously prone to refuse to share authority with his partners when that partnership seems no longer vital. This theme of autonomy is blatant in the careers of Hemingway and Roosevelt. Neither was capable of being either a follower or a peer.

At some point this attention to the internal imperative becomes self-infatuation or narcissism. Stress-seekers may demand center stage. The entrepreneur can put his name in neon. Theodore Roosevelt was seduced into political error by his weakness for adulation. While considering the Progressive Party's offer to nominate him for the Presidency, he had occasion to meet with the overseers of Harvard University. Emerging from the meeting, a crowd of eight thousand cheered him as the next President. This experience is reported to have changed his mental attitude, leading him

[14] Harbaugh, *op. cit.*, p. 176.

to a politically unwise choice.[15] Hemingway and his bull-fighters sport their wounds and accept the plaudits of the crowds at the bullring. Sport parachutists develop complex techniques for photographing themselves in midair.

The stress-seeker's tendency to return again and again to the stressful situation develops, in the extreme, an obsessive quality. He does not simply repeat the act but engages in more and more difficult versions of the act. Sport parachutists jump from higher and higher altitudes, each time increasing free-fall time and attempting more complex maneuvers.

THE DEPENDENT STRESS-SEEKER: AN ANTIPHONAL TYPE

Another type of arousal-seeker should be mentioned in passing. He seeks arousal as part of a crowd, and/or through symbolic identification with a larger society or transcendent self. He may join the cheering mob or throw himself into religious ceremonial. The courage of the individualistic stress-seeker rests on self-affirmation in the face of danger. The courage of the group stress-seeker, his antiphon, is in readiness to abandon his self, to risk losing integrality. Often, group arousal is preparation for facing some greater or individual stress, for taking a business risk or fighting a war.

The characteristics of the group stress-seeker complement those of the individualistic stress-seeker. Not a rationalist, he allows logic to dissolve in crowd enthusiasm.[16] Not striving for autonomy, he depends on the crowd about him or upon a charismatic leader. External authority is not onerous. Not personally narcissistic, he rejects self-aggrandizement. On the contrary, through self-effacement he enjoys the power of the crowd, living through a more encompassing "social narcissism." In the pathological extreme, like the individualistic stress-seeker, he may become self-destructive or even sadomasochistic. He may also re-

[15] Mowry, *op. cit.*, p. 199.
[16] This aspect of his character is described by Sigmund Freud in *Group Psychology and Analysis of the Ego,* trans. James Strachey (New York: Bantam Books).

peat the experience, but his repetitions have another quality. The individualistic stress-seeker appears compulsively driven to repeat the experience; he appears more hysteric, characterized by energy release and catharsis.

The dependent, self-effacing type of stress-seeker enters into a symbiotic relationship with the individualistic stress-seeker, providing the latter with one source of social support. Their relationship is that of leader and led. They meet one another's needs. At one level, their relationship may recapitulate that so often observed between hysteric and compulsive personalities. At another level, the self-effacing stress-seeker may look upon the individualistic stress-seeker as a charismatic leader. The individualistic stress-seeker may charge him with heresy if his leadership is not accepted. In either event, the individualistic stress-seeker looks with disdain upon the dependent, self-effacing type. This self-effacing type will be discussed further in this paper only to the extent that he interacts with the individualistic type.[17]

THE RELATION OF PAIN TO PLEASURE: THE KEY TO THE PARADOX OF STRESS-SEEKING

THE COMMON EMOTIONAL RESERVOIR OF PAIN AND PLEASURE: A PSYCHOLOGICAL INTERPRETATION

Contemporary psychological research contributes to an understanding of the individualistic stress-seeker. In this and the following three sections the paradox of stress-seeking as such will be discussed. Following this, psychological roots of the three general characteristics of stress-seekers, as noted above, will be suggested.

Stress-seekers find pleasure in situations that most people would agree are fear-provoking. This would not seem as

---

[17] Group arousal as a preamble to individual courage is the subject of the author's "A Social Psychology of Courage," *Review of Religious Research,* Vol. 3 (1961), pp. 63–72; and "A Social Scientist's Thoughts on Religious Worship," an unpublished paper presented to the Social Science Symposium of the Union of American Hebrew Congregations in October 1960.

strange if we did not categorize fearful avoidance and enthusiastic approach as radically distinct. Epstein and Fenz, in some of the best studies of sport parachuting, conceptualize the jumper's experience in terms of an approach-avoidance conflict, the simultaneous presence of these seeming opposites.[18] Both fearful and pleasurable, aversive and attractive experiences seem intertwined. Further, evidence is accumulating to show that an individual interprets the same underlying energy or arousal negatively under one set of circumstances and positively under another. Berlyne[19] finds that arousal accompanies states of distress and punishing stimuli as well as pleasant emotional excitement and rewarding stimuli. N. E. Miller[20] argued that appetitive reactions are nothing but disguised aversive reactions. James and Marianne Olds[21] found that electrical stimulation applied to the forebrain of a rat would induce a positive feedback, so that a rat quickly learns to stimulate itself. They conclude that the brain areas associated with self-stimulation are not merely substrates of appetitive behavior but substrates of all operant responses.

In the light of this new experimental work, the pain-pleasure distinction, which has played so significant a role in motivational theory, begins to blur.

THE INTENSITY OF AROUSAL

A common general substrate of excitement may be experienced as positive or as negative and may be associated with either approach or avoidance behavior or with behavior containing elements of both. Whether the excitement is experienced as pleasurable or as painful may depend, among other things, upon the intensity of the ex-

[18] "Theory and Experiment on the Measurement of the Approach-Avoidance Conflict," *Journal of Abnormal Psychology*, Vol. 64 (1962), pp. 97–112.
[19] D. E. Berlyne, *Conflict, Arousal and Curiosity* (New York: McGraw-Hill Book Co., Inc., 1965), p. 174.
[20] "Experiments on Motivation," *Science*, No. 157 (1957), p. 1271.
[21] "Drives, Rewards and the Brain," in T. M. Newcomb (ed.), *New Directions in Psychology II* (New York: Holt, Rinehart & Winston, Inc., 1965), pp. 329–410.

citement and upon the attribution of meaning to the excitement. This section and the one following discuss each of these influences on interpretation of excitement.

The relationship between intensity of arousal and experiencing it as positive or negative seems to be curvilinear. Either too high or too low a level of excitement will be experienced as aversive. The nineteenth-century psychologist Wundt proposed a curvilinear relation between the intensity of a stimulus and the way it is experienced. As the intensity of a stimulus rises, pleasure rises along with it until a point is reached after which a further increase in the intensity of stimulation becomes unpleasant. Berlyne argues that too little excitement, as in the case of sensory deprivation, is apprehended as aversive because external stimulation functions to hold down, or make one less conscious of, internal sources of stimulation. In the absence of external stimulation, the internal factors produce a level of arousal that the cortex is incapable of keeping within bounds. In Freud's terms, the organism may be flooded beyond its capacity, creating an anxiety-like situation. Excessive stimulation from external sources may also induce such an overload.

Berlyne made the observation of a curvilinear relation between intensity of arousal and evaluation of that arousal central to his theory of curiosity and exploratory behavior. A minimal level of arousal is required to keep an organism from being bored; this he calls "arousal tonus." To maintain the level of arousal tonus a particular rate of influx of arousal potential is required. The tonus rises or falls with this rate of influx. When there is a departure from tonus level, drive increases and, as a result, the organism regains its tonus level. Drive renews tonus level by inciting exploratory behavior. Berlyne distinguishes three types of exploratory behavior, each associated with a given level of arousal. If high arousal potential is sought to reduce boredom, diversive exploration may increase influx. If anticipatory arousal becomes too high, then the organism may engage in specific inspective or inquisitive exploration. Inspective exploration extends exposure to the stimulus and thus serves, paradoxically, to reduce arousal. This paradox occurs because familiarity reduces the arousal potential of a stimulus.

A drop from a high level of arousal may be brought about by specific exploration. An increase in arousal followed by a drop, Berlyne calls the "arousal jag." Jumps in the level of arousal become pleasurable as a consequence of the drop that terminates them. Petty gambling satisfies the conditions of the arousal jag. There is a small stake and uncertainty that is relieved quickly. This is typical of the situation of the stress-seeker. An aversive experience is induced by attaining a high level of arousal, and then pleasure obtained by dropping the intensity to some optimum level. Certainly, there must be a negative arousal jag which begins by a deprivation, an ascetic act, in which an aversive experience is induced by dropping to too low a level of arousal, and then pleasure obtained by allowing the level of arousal to rise to the optimum. Arousal jags are initiated by stress-seeking behaviors that exploit the curvilinear relation between intensity of arousal and its evaluation. One does not "enjoy" remaining at his equilibrium tonus level but "enjoys" returning to it after he has upset the equilibrium.

THE COGNITIVE APPRAISAL OF AROUSAL

Arousal may be experienced once as pleasure and again as pain without a corresponding change in its intensity. Magda Arnold's comprehensive study of emotion supports the notion that the aversive or appetitive quality of emotion depends on the appraisal of the experience.[22] She distinguished feelings, immediate intuitive responses to perception, from emotions, which depend upon an appraisal of an object as good or bad. The same underlying energy or feelings can be differently appraised. K. M. B. Bridges arrived at a similar position using developmental psychological data over three decades ago.[23] He identified a gen-

[22] *Emotion and Personality*, Vol. I: *Psychological Aspects* (New York: Columbia University Press, 1960).
[23] *The Social and Emotional Development of the Preschool Child* (London: Routledge & Kegan Paul, Ltd., 1931).

eral excited reaction in young infants which later develops into recognizable distress or into joy and delight. The same energic basis underlies contrasting emotional states.

Experimental evidence supporting this contention continues to accumulate. Richard S. Lazarus reports an experiment in which individuals were shown a film on subincision.[24] Varied sound tracks interpreted the action either in ways to catalyze the traumatic impact of the visual images, or to lead the viewers to intellectualize or deny their feelings about what they were seeing. The viewers' degrees of psychological stress were assessed by measures of skin conductance. They were less stressed when encouraged to intellectualize than when the trauma-suggesting sound track was used. The sight of a subincision was sufficient to arouse the viewers. The interpretation of the sight—that is, of the arousal—determined whether the emotion would be stressful. A sight is threatening when understood to betoken harm.[25]

Schacter describes an experiment in which physiological arousal was induced by epinephrine.[26] The aroused subjects were then exposed to varied social conditions. Some were provided an angry companion and others a joyful companion, and in both cases were asked to report how happy or angry they felt. The state of arousal seemed, in itself, to be neutral. The characteristics of the precipitating situation labeled the stirred-up state. The perception of emotion is also dependent on the apperceptive mass of the individual, his own predisposition for interpreting the situation. Cognition steers the perception of emotion. "It is the cognition which determines whether the state of physiological arousal will be labeled 'anger,' 'joy,' or whatever."[27]

[24] "A Laboratory Approach to the Dynamics of Psychological Stress," in George H. Grosser, Henry Wechsler and Milton Greenblatt (eds.), *The Threat of Impending Disaster* (Cambridge, Mass.: M.I.T. Press, 1964), pp. 34–57.
[25] *Ibid.*, p. 56.
[26] Stanley Schacter, "The Interaction of Cognitive and Physiological Determinants of Emotional State," in Leonard Berkowitz (ed.), *Advances in Experimental Social Psychology*, Vol. 1 (2 vols.; New York: Academic Press, Inc., 1964), pp. 49–80.
[27] *Ibid.*, p. 51.

The individual's predisposition to appraise personal, or libido, energy in one or another way has been a focus of psychoanalytic research. Balint, substituting an "object relations" theory for the traditional libido theory, also describes the common routes of fear and pleasure.[28] He considers, among others, pleasures associated with dizziness, vertigo, loss of stability, and games of chance found in "fun fairs." Here the individual exposes himself to aggression for "fun." Balint rejects the libido theory explanation that these pleasures derive from oral identification with the aggressor—that is, that one enjoys an attack on the self by identifying with the feeling of the aggressive inflictor of that attack. The individual at a fun fair also acts as an aggressor by breaking and mastering objects. The environment rejoices in its own destruction. Those who expose themselves to excitements such as riding a roller coaster have three characteristic attitudes: (1) they are aware and afraid of external danger; (2) they expose themselves voluntarily and intentionally to this external danger and the fear it arouses; and (3) they have the more or less confident hope that the fear can be tolerated and mastered, the danger will pass, and they will return to safety. "This mixture of fear, pleasure, and confident hope in the face of an external danger is what constitutes the fundamental element of all thrills."[29] The farther we are from safety, the greater the thrill. Balint calls one who enjoys such thrills a "philobat." Other characteristics of the philobat are that he enjoys friendly expanses but sees them as dotted with dangerous objects to be negotiated. He is thought of as a robust and conquering type. His heroism tends to be narcissistic and he has a need to repeat the thrilling act. Balint relates philobatic thrills symbolically to the primal scene. Symbolically, he interprets the primal scene as a going out for a daring deed and a safe return to mother earth.

Individuals who cannot stand swings or switchbacks, and who prefer to clutch something when in danger, Balint calls "ocnophils." Ocnophils fear expanses, and clinging to

[28] Michael Balint, *Thrills and Regressions* (New York: International Universities Press, Inc., 1959).
[29] *Ibid.*, p. 23.

"part objects," like a drowning man to a straw, they unrealistically clutch certain limited aspects of the objects in their environment. Their real aim is to be held by the object. The philobat is similar to the individualistic, autonomous stress-seeker. The ocnophil is similar to the self-effacing, dependent stress-seeker. For both, the thrill involves fear and pleasure.

THE TRANSFORMATION OF PAIN TO PLEASURE

As the previous cases show, the interpretation of emotion may depend on personality predispositions—such as being an ocnophil or philobat—or on a perceptual, cognitive, informational input: the sound track with the film, or the attitudes of companions. The latter experiments exposed different groups to each condition. If changing conditions are presented sequentially to the same group, a reappraisal or a shift may occur in the interpretation of the aroused feeling. A real threat may pass; a perceived threat may be reevaluated as nonthreatening.

In successive stages, the same arousal may be experienced as primarily fearful and then as primarily pleasurable. Both fear and pleasure may be present simultaneously. Their relative dominance may shift as an individual goes through an action that changes the real or perceived nature of his situation. As described by Balint, the action may symbolize going out and returning. The sequence of appraisals need not be simply a consequence of a changing real or perceived environment of the actor. The very fact of acting, of the individual setting himself in motion, may produce the attitudinal change—the reinterpretation of arousal. Acting changes the relation of the actor to his situation, and insofar as it is in pursuit of a goal, the act has an inherent fulfilling quality. A most general formulation of this was given by Pierre Janet in 1928. Janet said an action stopped too soon results in melancholy; an action carried through to the end results in joy.[30]

[30] Pierre Janet, "Fear of Action as an Essential Element in the Sentiment of Melancholia," in *Feelings and Emotions: The Wittenberg Symposium* (International Symposium on Feelings and Emotions;

My study of sport parachutists provides an example of the changing appraisal of emotion as the succession of acts constituting the parachute jump are executed.[31] Self-reports were used to assess the quality and the intensity of emotion experienced by sport parachutists at various points during the jump. As they prepare for the jump, board the plane, and ascend to jump altitude, the level of arousal increases. During this preparatory phase the arousal is experienced primarily as fear. The level of arousal remains relatively stationary while the jumper prepares for exit. However, the feeling of fear decreases while the feeling of enthusiasm correspondingly increases during this time. After exiting there is a sharp decrease in fear and a corresponding sharp increase in enthusiasm. Just before the parachute opens, fear increases and enthusiasm decreases. After opening, with the level of arousal still remaining about the same, enthusiasm increases again. Fear displaces enthusiasm just before landing; upon landing, enthusiasm becomes dominant again.

At any given point during the jump phase, fear and enthusiasm are negatively correlated. The peak level of fear, which is experienced at the inception of the jump run, is positively correlated with the level of enthusiasm at subsequent points. The more frightened the skydivers are at the start of the jump run, the more enthusiastic they become later. Since the level of arousal is fairly constant throughout, it is the jumper's appraisal of the situation and of the task remaining before him that changes from point to point. Under one set of conditions the organism's excitement is experienced as fear, and under other conditions this same energy, arousal, or excitement is experienced as enthusiasm —this is a "transformation" of fear into enthusiasm.

The transformation of fear into enthusiasm begins at the point when the pilot starts the jump run, not after the

Worcester, Mass.: Clark University Press, 1928), quoted in James Hillman, *Emotion* (London: Routledge & Kegan Paul, Ltd., 1960).
    [31] "The Transformation of Fear" (mimeographed; Washington, D.C.: Bureau of Social Science Research, Inc., 1966); a brief version of this paper appears in the published report of Symposium 13: Motives and Consciousness in Man, Eighteenth International Congress of Psychology, Moscow, USSR, August 1966.

jumper has exited and so literally entered a new situation. It is at the start of the jump run that the final commitment to act takes place. The jumper, who has been seated in the plane, begins to rise and move toward the door. As he steps out on the strut in preparation for his actual jump, his fear has already begun to abate and his enthusiasm to increase. It seems odd that the sport parachutist's fear is decreasing while he approaches the objectively most dangerous points of the jump. In acting, however, the jumper's appraisal of his role in the situation changes. To act, to be in the process of encountering or engaging the stress becomes, in itself, pleasurable. Observing that he is able to master his own fear and the environmental obstacles contributes to his situational reappraisal. The pleasure in acting may be quite separate from that of the simultaneous or retroactive consideration of succeeding or winning.

The reappraisal may take place after the act has been completed. This is illustrated in a more intellectual context. Jon D. Jecker[32] compares dissonance-reducing behavior before and after a decision. In each event the alternatives involved in the decision may be reevaluated so that dissonance is reduced. If the cognitive processes before differ from those after a decision, the "act of decision" itself has psychological import. The "act of decision" in this work is comparable to the commitment at the beginning of the jump run in the parachuting situation. Jecker finds that a reevaluation favoring the chosen and disfavoring the rejected alternative, or both, is a postdecision phenomenon. The act of deciding precedes, and perhaps it promotes, the cognitive reevaluation. In the example of the subincision film, the individual is a relatively passive recipient of information. As he appraises the information, cognitively evaluates its meaning for him, the meaning he attributes to his aroused emotion changes. In the parachuting and cognitive dissonance experiment, the individual's active role in engaging the situation contributes to changing the quality of his emotion. Through his action, his self, in relation to its situation, is reappraised.

---

[32] In Leon Festinger, *et al.*, *Conflict, Decision and Dissonance* (Stanford, Calif.: Stanford University Press, 1964).

The Fenz-Epstein studies suggest that the drop in fear or increase in enthusiasm is a result of drive reduction. Pleasure is the concomitant of reducing the level of arousal. Berlyne accounts for the pleasure of the arousal jag in the same way. However, this interpretation would not account for the pleasure accompanying a negative arousal jag. Affective deprivation is followed by a return to optimum tonus; that is, pleasure would be associated with the phase of rising arousal or tension. This return to optimum tonus might be a return to an equilibrated level but could be thought of as drive reduction only in the sense that the influx of external stimuli really reduces the arousal caused by previously unbound internal feelings. The interpretation of the parachuting situation is that the enthusiasm results from a shift in the meaning of the excitement that the parachutist is experiencing. If the parachutist experiences pleasure due to drive reduction, this would occur only after the landing phase, when there is a tapering off of the level of arousal or drive.

FURTHER ATTRIBUTES OF STRESS-SEEKERS

RATIONALITY

The above theory fragments contribute to a general understanding of the stress-seeker. What of his specific characteristics: his rationalism, egocentricity, and drive to repeat the performance? Robert White explored the rationality of the stress-seeker by observing that individuals became concerned with reality independently of instinctual needs.[33]

EGOCENTRICITY

Traditional psychoanalytic theory explains interest in the world in terms of libidinal cathexes for objects. Interest,

[33] Robert White, "Ego and Reality in Psychoanalytic Theory: A Proposal Regarding Independent Ego Energies," Monograph 11, *Psychological Issues*, Vol. 3, No. 3 (New York: International Universities Press, 1963).

in these terms, is tied to satisfactions obtainable by, for example, orally incorporating an object. Drive-reduction theory in academic psychology makes a similar claim in stating that interest in objects depends upon their meeting the organism's needs. It would follow, from either point of view, that after a need had been met, the individual would lose interest in the object. If, for example, we take the need for food as signaled by hunger, this is indeed the case. Freud accounted for the persistence of a male-female relationship in the interval between sexual relations on the basis of anticipated needs. This type of explanation ignores the broader, socially based motives involved in a male-female relationship.

White calls attention to play and exploration in animals and children, behavior that is not easily explained by libido or drive-reduction theory. An infant manipulating an object is not motivated by a known organic need. White suggests that this play is part of a general relation of *effectiveness* which the child seeks to establish between himself and the environment. The child possesses capacities for action. These capacities rely upon energies of the ego that are independent of libidinal energies. These independent ego energies prompt the child to keep trying out his capacities for action. Pleasure arises through the sense of competence he obtains by establishing his effectiveness.

Placing the burden for the motivation of stress-seeking behavior on ego energies—seeing it as a function of the ego, the reality-related aspect of the personality—clarifies the source of rationality of the behavior. The ego is the seat of judgment and rational planning in the relation of the organism to its environment. Emphasis shifts to action, to doing things with objects; this is *effectance*.

Continuing this line of reasoning, we perceive a basis for the egocentricity of the stress-seeker. Effectance does not prompt attachment to the object itself but to what can be done with it. Objects may be set aside coolly when their manipulative possibilities have been exhausted. Interest is principally in the self as an effective actor. This casts light on the self-centered qualities of the stress-seeker.

Balint, replacing libido theory with "object relations" theory, arrives at a similar conclusion. He says that philobats—individualistic stress-seekers—develop exaggerated ego cathexes, are preoccupied with personal skills, and neglect development of lasting object relationships. The ocnophils, on the other hand—dependent, self-effacing stress-seekers—develop exaggerated object cathexes and neglect the independent ego.

THE DRIVE TO REPEAT

The repetitive side to stress-seeking could follow inherently from the nature of stress-seeking. To obtain arousal pleasure one would have to engage increasingly difficult situations. Some situations may lose their arousal-producing potential once effectiveness has been established. This is suggested by both White's ego-energy theory and by Berlyne's concept of the arousal jag. This is probably only part of the story. Certain situations in which there is an element of fate involved, that is, where the outcome may be affected by circumstances of nature beyond the control of the individual, may have the same arousal potential with each repetition of the same situation. Thus, experienced skydivers may be just as afraid as the novices. This could be explained most simply in terms of reinforcement theory. The mastering of fear and of the environment is pleasurable and therefore remains attractive.

To a certain extent, however, the stress-seeker aims to conquer doubts about his own abilities. Freud considers stress-seeking as a mode of handling a traumatic neurosis.[34] The individual obsessively recalls the trauma by symbolically reenacting the original situation to reassure himself that it no longer holds its dangerous potency. Otto Fenichel analyzed this as the counterphobic attitude.[35] In counterphobic behavior an individual is repeatedly drawn to per-

[34] Sigmund Freud, *Beyond the Pleasure Principle,* trans. James Strachey (New York: Bantam Books, 1959; originally published 1920).

[35] Otto Fenichel, "The Counterphobic Attitude," *International Journal of Psychoanalysis,* Vol. 20 (1939), pp. 263–74.

form an act he fears. Each repetition reasserts his mastery and keeps his fear at bay. Freud observed[36] that a child fearful of losing his parent, or being lost by his parent, symbolizes the problem and manages his fear by repeatedly throwing away a plaything and retrieving it with pleasure. The philobat, according to Balint, over and over again leaves the object, enjoys the friendly expanse, and returns to the object. The basis of the effectiveness of these repetitions lies in the individual's assuming an active rather than a passive relation to the traumatic situation, one that puts it under his control. The child troubled by fear of losing his mother may obtain mastery of the situation or even assertiveness in sending the mother away. The Freudian traumas are related to infantile situations. This approach does not account for the sometimes observed rising crescendo of stress-seeking. The crescendo aspect is perhaps best understood in White's terms. Once a challenge is met and a sense of competence obtained, one continues to push on to test yet another or greater capacity to obtain further pleasure of effectiveness.

The arousal jag, as conceived by Berlyne, is implicitly rhythmic or repetitive. It is not, however, obsessive. Berlyne illustrates by referring to artistic productions that involve expected patterns, such as meter in poetry and scale and tonal patterns in music. The artist, by meeting or not meeting this expectation of pattern, may endlessly exploit arousal and relief.

THE SOCIAL CONTEXT OF STRESS-SEEKING

SOCIAL ENCOURAGEMENT OF STRESS-SEEKING

The stress-seeker is cheered on and legitimated by prevailing philosophies, myths, and ethical norms. He is applauded by both spectators and followers. For the spectator, who intends no action, he is a source of vicarious

[36] *Op. cit.*

pleasure. For the follower, who does intend a course of action, the stress-seeker provides leadership and encouragement. The relation between the spectator and follower, on the one hand, and the individualistic stress-seeker, on the other hand, has undergone historical development. The competitive impulse, according to Johan Huizinga, shifted from the spectator to the protagonist during the Greek and Roman periods.[37] The protagonist represents and fights on behalf of the spectators. Reciprocally, the supporting crowd is an extension of the protagonist's self. By elevating the crowd through his action, it, in turn, elevates him.

The effect of the charismatic leader on his followers has been well documented. The reciprocal action of the followers on the leader has received less attention. Actors report that the mood of the audience affects the quality of their performance. Every speaker is sensitive to "good" and "bad" audiences. Mowry provides an illustration of the effect of an audience on Theodore Roosevelt. Before accepting the nomination of the Progressive Party, Roosevelt debated the issue with himself. In part, Roosevelt's doubts were related to personality and ideological differences between himself and the members of the party. In part, they reflected his uncertainty about the party's ability to win. When the Progressives met in Chicago, Roosevelt, in an address entitled "A Confession of Faith," appealed to the radical elements in the party.

> As he stood on the platform in his old familiar attitude, his body swinging with delight, his left hand in his pocket and his right hand vigorously waving a reply, fifteen thousand people roared their welcome. For fifty-two minutes wildly waving red bandanas, they cheered him as they had never cheered anyone else. Here were no claques, no artificial demonstrations sustained by artificial devices. None were needed. Men and women simply stood on their feet for an hour to welcome a man because they liked him and believed in him. When Roosevelt finally sought to stop the demonstration, the crowd once more broke into song:

[37] *Homo Ludens: A Study of the Play Element in Culture* (Boston: Beacon Press, Inc., 1955).

Thou wilt not cower in the dust,
Roosevelt, O Roosevelt:
Thy gleaming sword shall never rust,
Roosevelt, O Roosevelt![38]

Though not convinced that he would win and not fully comprehending this enthusiasm, he nevertheless threw himself into a strenuous, and ultimately ill-fated, campaign.

Support for the stress-seeker is not usually demonstrated so personally and forcibly. General cultural support, however, is available to the struggling and achieving man in our society. He is a cultural hero of American myths. David Brion Davis,[39] in his analysis of American literature, depicts the mythical struggler as a superman. The superman was not the figure of the dominant religion—a suffering servant with strength to bear the sins of the world. The superman was self-sufficient and autonomous and in a state of war with the rest of society—an ideal villain, a sublime rebel, an abrupt fissure in the great chain of being, one who commanded awe and wonder.[40] The superman was guided more by an inner necessity than by social law. He was an exceptional person.

The attitude toward the mythical superman is as ambivalent as that toward the stress-seeker in general. Supermen could be evil, insane scientists or members of an organized conspiracy. Though a villain, he commands respect. This ambivalence projects an aspect of modern American national character. "Americans of the mid-twentieth century seem to think of themselves as a highly aggressive people who never commit acts of aggression, in spite of their imaginative interest in bloodshed."[41]

The stress-seeker enjoys social legitimation when engaged in conflict and competition, even when its intensity increases to the level of violence. Davis traces the philosophi-

---

[38] Mowry, *op. cit.,* p. 264, based on reports in *The New York Times, New York Sun,* and *Chicago Tribune,* August 7, 1912.

[39] *Homicide in American Fiction, 1798–1860: A Study in Social Values* (Ithaca: Cornell University Press, 1957).

[40] *Ibid.,* p. 49.

[41] *Ibid.,* p. vii.

cal roots of the legitimation of violence in nineteenth-century America. He says that the nineteenth century was characterized by a decreasing reliance on intellectual factors in the explanation of human behavior and, as a consequence, a decreasing sense of personal responsibility for behavior. Phrenology was in vogue. Behavior was considered a function of the physical brain condition over which the individual had no control. When, late in the century, character was believed determined by environmental experience, man was freed from personal accountability. The violent man was forgiven and tolerated when his action could be attributed to a ruling passion or to "hot blood," a type of "spirit" that imposed its will upon him. These philosophical-attitudinal developments were promoted by the conditions of frontier life, where a loosening of social ties, lack of institutional barriers to crime and violence, and personal acts of vengeance were permitted in accord with the principle of talion. In the literature of this period, vengeance was often presented as an inevitable expression of righteous law. The avenger was for one moment free from external morality, from public opinion, and political justice. These factors conspired to legitimate violence on the part of the stress-seeker.

The principle was easily shifted from the individualistic to the dependent, mob-involved stress-seeker. "Just as a personal insult temporarily suspended the social contract, requiring an honorable man to defend his reputation, so a mob of men could strive for unity and purpose by abrogating constitutional justice and by using violence to exorcise agents of the devil."[42] Not everybody in a society would join such a mob, but some individualistic stress-seekers wait for an opportunity to lead it, and some self-effacing stress-seekers wait to follow.

Darwinism provided philosophical legitimation for some stress-seeking activities. Darwinism was anti-intellectual. Human development was traced to nonrational forces. The

[42] *Ibid.*, p. 276.

determinism inherent in the theory undermined the conception of responsible action. Scientific descriptives were taken from Darwinian theory and put to work as moral directives. Richard Hofstadter[43] describes how terms such as "struggle for existence" and "natural selection," originally applicable to the biological order, were applied to legitimate the social order. In justifying force-determined relations, Social Darwinism became a conservative philosophy of those in power. Hofstadter quotes Max Nordau: "Since the theory of evolution has been promulgated, they [militarists] can cover their natural barbarism with the name of Darwin and proclaim the sanguinary instincts of their inmost hearts as the last word of science."[44]

Ethical approval has also rested on the popular notion that evolution is inherently progressive; the selected species are "superior." Centuries before Darwin, some theologians identified virtue with victory. A struggle could be a test of virtue. As the theological basis for this norm declined, Darwinism gave it new life by "demonstrating" that it was rooted in the natural order. As long as certain rules are followed, virtue, honor, and moral superiority are the struggler's companions.

The stress-seeker's prestige is associated with that of the knight. The knight or the gentleman must not shrink from a fight. Stress-seekers may take the role of the champion, the one who struggles in the name of others. The champion, who represents the society as a whole, may come from a lower social status. His rewards may be prestige and social mobility. The elite he represents may extend its aristocratic aura to him.

The autonomous stress-seeker may enjoy the adulation of the self-effacing stress-seeker. This recipient of adulation may return disdain. This is the disdain of the aristocrat for the masses, of a Republican Roosevelt for the Democrats,

---

[43] *Social Darwinism in American Thought* (Boston: Beacon Press, Inc., 1955; originally published by the University of Pennsylvania Press, 1944).

[44] In "The Philosophy and Morals of War," *North American Review*, Vol. CLXIX (1889), p. 794.

of the hero for the coward, of the conservative for welfare recipients who beg out of the stressful arena. This is a social aspect of the pleasure-pain ambivalence of the stress-seeker. He needs and indeed enjoys the support of the audience he disdains. In fact, this very audience may serve as a screen upon which he projects the cowardly elements in his own character.

The group may go beyond cheering, the normative approval of action, to goad its members into stress-seeking behavior. The stress-seeker himself may command his environment to incite him, as in the case of an individual who challenges another to strike the first blow. If the other responds to the challenge, retaliation is legitimate. More importantly, this creates the stress-seeker's needed opponent. A nonresisting object of aggression provides little satisfaction to the stress-seeker. Just as the stress-seeker is not a masochist, he is also not a sadist. He is out to humble the environment and give it the pleasure of being mastered by him. The stress-seeker commands the environment to inspire fear in him. This fear is the form in which his energy is mobilized. Then, acting against the source of fear and overcoming it, he enjoys the sweet taste of enthusiasm.

The nature of the social support meshes with the psychological characteristics of the stress-seeker. The philosophical anti-intellectualism and determinism not only protect him from criticism but they tame the social environment in preparation for his application of rationality. The myth of the superman, virtuous and moved by inner necessity, provides the free atmosphere in which he can struggle. This myth also permits him to affirm his own ego in the face of society. The public's attitudinal ambivalence toward the stress-seeker complements the emotion of the afraid-enthusiastic, destructive-constructive stress-seeker. In fact, the relation between the individualistic stress-seeker and society is an extension of his relation to the self-effacing stress-seeker. The relation is dramatic, with the public sometimes playing the antagonist while he is protagonist. Sometimes a more tamed public takes the role of the Greek chorus, reflecting antiphonally, but in all events providing the conditions for his action.

THE STRESS-SEEKER'S SOCIAL CONTRIBUTION

Why should society support the stress-seeker? One answer may be given in terms of the social function of the stress-seeker. However, not everything that is socially functional enjoys social support, nor does social support necessarily imply functionality. Stress-seeking subserves some manifest functions. For example, the public shares the esteem accorded the champion. The struggle itself—a good fight or a good drama—provides vicarious pleasure. More fundamentally, the stress-seeker manifests the active energies that society identifies with its constructive development. In this he contributes to the general optimism that society will indeed have the strength to achieve its goals.

When stress is sought through interindividual or social conflict, its functions are not as immediately apparent. Social attitudes toward conflict are ambivalent, as they are toward all stress-seeking. A bounded conflict may have latent eufunctions. Some of these have been delineated by Georg Simmel.[45] Simmel viewed conflict as a form of sociation aimed at achieving social unity even though one of the parties may be annihilated as a result. Conflict clarifies group boundaries and so contributes to their integrality as well as to their integration. The ranking of group members is an outcome of conflict. Simmel and many other sociologists believe such stratification is essential to the working of society. Lewis Coser recalls Gumplowicz', Ratzenhofer's, and Oppenheimer's contention that, by establishing boundaries and internally integrating a society, conflict is associated with the genesis of the state itself.[46] Coser here quotes Churchill in a way that relates boundary-defining and internally integrative functions:

[45] In *Conflict*, trans. Kurt H. Wolff (Glencoe, Ill.: The Free Press, 1955).
[46] Lewis A. Coser, *The Functions of Social Conflict* (New York: The Free Press of Glencoe, 1964; originally published 1956).

The former peacetime structure of society had been . . . superseded, and life had been raised to a strange intensity by the war spell. Under that mysterious influence, men and women had been appreciably exalted above death and pain and toil. Unities and comradeships had become possible between men and classes and nations, and had grown stronger while the hostile pressure and the cause endured.[47]

These social functions have their analogy on the animal level. Konrad Lorenz[48] describes how ritualized fights among fish serve a species-preserving function. These are token duels and in that sense "ritualized." The loser is not destroyed unless the combatants happen to be of equal strength. Aggressive combat and interindividual cohesion seem to be associated phenomena. Peaceable herd creatures do not develop permanent friendships. A personal bond is found only in intraspecifically aggressive animals. The more aggressive the particular species, the firmer the bond. Evidence drawn from reptiles suggests that intraspecific aggression is an older form of sociation than love. Lorenz concludes that there may be aggression without personal friendship but there is no love without aggression.

The above argument suggests that stress-seeking contributes to the formation of social groups. The direction of relation may be reversed. Social groups may be formed to provide an occasion for stress-seeking. The sports team is an example of a group established to satisfy stress-seeking needs, among others. Lorenz says "humanity is not enthusiastically combative because it is split into opposing political parties, but it is divided into opposing camps because this is the adequate stimulus situation to arouse militant enthusiasm in a satisfying manner."[49] These struggle groups may become functionally autonomous and, as such, mongers of destructive conflict. Society has an interest in controlling such developments.

---

[47] Winston Churchill, *The World Crisis*, Vol. IV: *The Aftermath* (6 vols.; New York: Charles Scribner's Sons, 1963–64), quoted in Coser, *op. cit.*, p. 90.

[48] *On Aggression*, trans. Marjorie Kerr Wilson (New York: Harcourt, Brace & World, Inc., 1966).

[49] *Ibid.*, p. 53.

SOCIAL CONTROL OF STRESS-SEEKING

Social support of stress-seekers contains the seed of their social control. It will be instructive to examine "social" control mechanisms among animals. Lorenz offers some good examples of the control of aggression among animals. As an ethologist, he is especially concerned with behaviors that are inborn rather than learned. These behaviors remain potential until elicited by specific stimuli. "If stimuli normally releasing such behavior fail to appear for an appreciable period, the organism is thrown into a state of general unrest and begins to search actively for the missing stimulus."[50] In this sense, some stress-seeking behavior among animals is unlearned.

The eliciting stimuli are paralleled by a set of conditions that inhibit stress-seeking. A cock exposes his red comb to elicit or incite aggression from another against him. Contrariwise, the cock hides the red comb to inhibit the aggression of another. Young animals inhibit the aggression of older ones toward them by nuzzling, pawing, and licking—generally submissive behaviors. Mere acquaintanceship with a fellow member of the species may exert an inhibitory effect on aggressive behavior.

Lorenz generalizes from these observations to man.[51] Man's trouble stems from his being a basically harmless, omnivorous creature lacking in natural weapons with which to kill big prey. Therefore he is also devoid of the built-in safety devices that prevent "professional" carnivores from abusing their killing power by destroying members of their own species. Artificial weapons upset the equilibrium between killing potential and social inhibitions. The deep emotional layers of our personality simply do not register the fact that the crooking of the forefinger to release a shot tears the entrails of another man, Lorenz reminds us.

If man lacks these built-in safety devices, he has developed cultural mechanisms for controlling stress-seeking be-

[50] Lorenz, *op. cit.*, p. 53.
[51] *Ibid.*, p. 241.

havior. He has developed forms of ritual control—social manners. These may be considered symbolic variants of the inhibiting signals of the animal world. Manners define the area of permissible human interaction. They decrease misunderstandings by establishing well-known forms. Smiling, handshaking, and friendly verbal exchanges are token obeisances which reassure the other person against aggressive intent. These rules complement those by which man signals aggressive intent and that define acceptable forms of struggle.

Control is also exerted by territorial division. Animal ecology is patterned in a way that reduces the probabilities of attack. The notion of private property and the juridical specification of personal rights seem to have a similar function. In the most general sense, partition plans between hostile nations reduce conflict. Juveniles divide territories for gang roaming.

Perhaps the most common form of control is by channeling or redirecting the energy, or shifting it to another object of aggression. Simmel points out that conflict may be avoided by replacing it with competitions. In competition the effort is directed at a possession rather than at the other party. Under cover of competition, individuals may allow themselves means they would be ashamed to use in direct conflict.

Thus, just as there is ethically based support for stress-seekers, they are also ethically controlled. In a broad sense, an ascetic philosophical orientation will reduce the striving itself or reduce the desire to possess. The stress-seeker in an ascetic culture would appear self-indulgent. An altruistic ethic will inhibit stress-seeking by discouraging gain for the self at the expense of others. The stress-seeker in an altruistic society would appear avaricious. A fatalistic ethic would undermine the notion of the worthwhileness of the striving and so make the stress-seeker appear foolish. Interestingly, in fatalistic societies such as that of India, the worthwhileness of striving for possessions is doubted, yet control of desires (a form of stress-seeking) through Yoga is accepted practice.

Written codes play a very significant part in containing stress-seeking in modern societies. These are formalized extensions of the rules of sport, the rules that define the game. In the economic sphere, government agencies regulate competitions, and in the political sphere the types of efforts considered legitimate in a political campaign are controlled by legislation. Law controls interpersonal aggression by giving a monopoly on the use of violence to representatives of the government. Control by concentrating the means of violence may be extended to international relations.[52]

The basic social problem is to encourage sufficient stress-seeking to get the work of society done, while exerting control of the stress-seeker so that his drive does not eventuate in social destruction.

[52] Richard A. Falk, *Law, Morality and War in the Contemporary World* (New York: Frederick A. Praeger, Inc., 1963).

Elton B. McNeil

During his professional career, Elton McNeil has turned from the study of the deeper layers of personality—the latent dispositions—to the study of manifest behaviors and their implication for social life. An early study, reported as "Handwriting and Psychosexual Dimensions of Personality," employed Blacky pictures to test the validity of graphologists' personality assessments. The Blacky test interpretation involves the projective interpretation of stories written in response to animal pictures. Graphological interpretation of personality has evolved separately from that of projective techniques. Graphological signs for interpreting personality include the size of the handwriting and the way the individual letters are connected. The relation between the inferences from these two techniques was found to be small but positive in some cases.

More recently, Elton McNeil has been concerned with educating the gifted. In "The Paradox of Education for the Gifted" he declaims against the "academic crazy quilt" of theories current in our society for educating talented youngsters. Today, he charges, education neglects creativity and, in fact, systematically excludes the possibility of its development.

He has edited an issue of the *Journal of Social Issues* in which he compares aggression at the animal and at the human level. The latter is elaborated in a discussion of aspects of aggression in human society. *The Nature of Human Conflict* contains further contributions to the study of human aggression. Its papers represent work at the interface of personality and society. It raises issues regarding a relation between personality factors in aggression and international societal relations and ends with a call to social scientists to cooperate in solving some problems of international human relations.

His recent book, *The Concept of Human Development*, is an introductory psychology text. Its special feature is a discussion of the interrelationship of social and physical factors in personality development. His early interests in deeper levels of personality and his later interests in manifest aggressive behavior are joined in an article entitled "Aggression in Fantasy and Behavior." Studying disturbed boys, he found no significant link between aggressive behavior and aggressive fantasy as measured by the Thematic Apperception Test. However, he did discover a significant positive association between a fantasy in which the hero suffers and a behavioral tendency to be friendly and reject aggression.

Elton B. McNeil accepts aggression as inherent in human existence. It embodies the action and vitality of living. His contribution to the present symposium is written in this spirit. He spotlights the world's leaders, who hold the fate of our planet in their hands. These individuals achieve power, in part, because they are stress-seekers whose personal charisma matches the spirit of the times. We should not be misled by the American tendency to deny the desire for leadership. In other countries there is no embarrassment in equating power and leadership. Some leaders seek stress through aggression and violence; some of these are creatures of impulse. The psychologist has a social duty to study such individuals, since they are empowered to decide the fate of others.

Elton McNeil finds that some world leaders share with juvenile delinquents the methods, techniques, and psychological view of what is necessary in life. Both rise by structuring power through the use of aggression and violence. Both may suffer from inability to shun conflict. Both may require immediate gratification, and both may succumb to excitement and group intoxication. Elton McNeil finds no evidence that even the great leaders of the past had stable psychological qualities. Thus he challenges the image that the leader plans rationally, being a person with a strong ego. For these people, stress is a visceral experience, a matter of the "juices of life" and blood coursing through their veins.

Stress-seekers must be sorted according to whether their social contributions are positive or negative. One approach to such sorting is through discrimination between those stress-seekers with effective and those with defective egos.

THE EGO AND STRESS-SEEKING IN MAN

That some men seek stress for its own sake and find it pleasurable is perfectly obvious. This is as it should be, for this element of small- and large-scale adventuring with fate is incontrovertible evidence of the vigor of a society that encourages an individual and personal definition of the way life ought to be led and of the risks that are reasonable to take. Stress-seeking—whether aggressive or sexual—has proved to be continually and enormously pleasurable to a humankind unconvinced that youth must be spent before true contentment can be experienced.

Man has always sought stress because no saccharine substitute has ever proved adequate and because "moral equivalents" of conflict have been exactly that—moral, not visceral equivalents. Shakespeare purloined from the ancients the notion that the condition of peace is antithetical to the fundamental nature of the human organism. Blood coursing through one's veins was thought to prevent the achievement of rational and peaceful solutions to human disagreement. This century has witnessed again and again the militancy with which peaceful objectives have been pursued, and the aggressive quest for nonaggressiveness has proved to be an interesting paradox of our age.

Man's cross-eyed view of stress is one that insists that in its eradication is salvation. Yet, Western man has never constructed a utopia that any red-blooded male would care to visit even for a brief period of time. As Mark Twain noted, even heaven is sexually inert. In addition, I might add, heaven makes no provision for stress of any sort. As Mark Twain put it, "Heaven for climate and hell for society!" The devil wisely selected aggressive impulses as his most potent weapons in the titanic struggle for men's lives because, like sex, the thrill was renewable.

This is not to say that aggression or sex should be equated with moral evil or considered to be no more than tools of the devil. As Freud perceptively noted, man is, for better or for worse, a biological organism that becomes civilized primarily by the diversion of these drives into socially acceptable channels in the process of socialization via child-rearing. Man's acquisition of a set of secondary motives—loyalty, patriotism, self-sacrifice, altruism, etc.—is a fabric constructed of the primary threads of love and hate. While we might prefer a more "moral" source for what we judge to be the best and most noble in man and for what we rank to be among the most socially enriching of man's contributions to our culture, we are, if Freud is right, forced to accept a much more base and unspiritual wellspring for human endeavor. Whether Freud's vision is a true or false appraisal of the nature of man only time and scientific progress can determine. For our purposes it is sufficient to observe that the lofty statue of man may have feet of clay—a fact that should disturb us no more than the observation that each of us has an alimentary canal. We are what we are and seek only an honest appraisal of our nature. The question remains: "Where shall we seek the truth?"

Why men seek or avoid stress is as complex a question as can be asked about man's nature, and it is not one that is answerable by any single-factor approach. We need a multifaceted solution to the problem, and the analysis to be presented here is an attempt to focus attention on one aspect of the total problem. I am concerned primarily with the importance of exploring effective and defective ego-functioning in man as it relates to stress-seeking and avoidance in the decision-makers of the world.

The theoretical construction called the ego was chosen as a promising tool for the understanding of stress-seeking and avoidance because this concept of man's psychological structure was devised originally to explain why man does not live like an impulse-ridden animal. The ego is a cultural acquisition that suggests that if we can learn to control the learning process we can predict and eventually control man's behavior. Then too, the structure of the ego and the behavior that emanates from it are not immutable and unchangeable facets of existence. There is no firm evidence that learned ego functions are incapable of alteration and change at any age in an individual given the proper social or therapeutic pressures.

We need to extend our understanding of the psychological nature of man in order to improve our capacity to predict who among us will seek stress with a high degree of intensity even if that pursuit proves to be detrimental to the welfare of the rest of us. Men seek stress in one form or another and in differing degree since they cannot survive and mature while curled up forever in a fetal position. The diagnostic task mankind faces is to learn to put stress-seekers into categories in terms of the positive or negative contribution they are likely to make to our own and the planet's survival. Our capacity to diagnose others is essential to the prediction of their behavior, and with increasingly accurate prediction we expand our ability to make moves that will increase the degree of control we can exercise over the violent qualities in humankind that so often accompany the seeking of stress. It is a question of balance, really. How can we continue to produce stress-seekers yet escape the sometimes harmful or even fatal consequences of their existence? We need some device, however crude, to describe or analyze something of the psychological makeup of the typical stress-seeker as a first step in discriminating those needed by society from those too expensive for any society to afford.

The targets of our stress analysis need not include the entire populace, since the immediately crucial events in man's relation to his fellowman are international ones that threaten to engulf mankind in holocaust. To understand these international confrontations demands, I feel, a study of the ego structure of our leaders and decision-makers, a vital piece of scholarship that we have overlooked in our efforts to influence the course of world affairs.

It is not as if this suggestion were a new or alien one. Speculation about the psychological nature of our leaders has been a preoccupation of mankind ever since we banded together in crude groups and relinquished a part of our individual power for the sake of security for the total group. Armchair speculation and psychological postmortems of the decision-makers has always been a losing game, however, since the basic information necessary for such constructions has been either secondhand or filtered through a set of political or economic biases on the part of the observer. For those who feel the character of the typical members of a society forms a "national character" that has an important influence on the decisions leaders make, the literature of the social sciences is replete with broad generalizations about human nature. Some fairly recent analyses of the American character, for example, make fascinating reading even if the points of view they promulgate are not fully congruent one with the other (Fromm, 1947; Potter, 1954; Riesman, 1950; and Wolfenstein, 1951). Studies of national character in cultures distant from our own also exist, but these necessarily have incorporated fewer "facts" and more speculation.

PSYCHOLOGISTS, STRESS, AND THE NATURE OF MAN

It is not that psychologists turned in bewilderment one day to discover that men making international decisions were human and subject to the human psychological frailty. The history of psychological concern with the problem of man plus bomb has been a vigorous if somewhat disarranged state of affairs.

Psychologists have long been concerned, for example, with the why and how of the immersion of man's identity in the nation-state so that he is ready at less than an instant's notice to sacrifice his existence in the stress of warfare. There must be a quality of individual and group readiness to account for such an incredible phenomenon, and our suspicion is that this state of readiness has its reflection in the comportment of the decision-makers of the world.

Psychologists have long attempted to contain the stress-seekers who use war as an outlet, but their weapon—the peace movement—has proved to be an ineffectual tool since it is most often against things as they are, has its ranks filled with persons seeking peace for highly personal and sometimes irrational reasons, and because it achieves its most vigorous state at the very moment that cultural forces and convictions are driving hard in the opposite direction. The peace movement has only had as weapons in its "fight" the unity of a negative purpose and a great sense of moral superiority, and these have regularly proved to be inadequate to the task at hand.

Finding common cause with the peace-lovers of this planet was a convenient instrument of expression for psychologists since few of the pronouncements of social and behavioral science were destined to reach the ears of our decision-makers and even less of the content was to be heeded by them. Producing knowledge did not guarantee that it would be used (Marquis and Allen, 1966); insight and application have never been a match.

Attempts of great variety have been made to break down stress-seeking to its component parts. McClelland (1961) tried to analyze societies in terms of the influence of need for achievement; McNeil (1965) tried to assess the theoretical contributions of social science to the nature of human conflict; Adorno, Frenkel-Brunswick, Levinson, and Sanford (1950) interpreted the nature of the authoritarian personality; Bronfenbrenner (1961) tried to fathom the puzzle of why the Soviet response to us has so much in common with our response to them; and Jerome Frank (1961) searched out the emotional and motivational aspects of the disarmament problem. Computer simulation of international problems was undertaken by Harold Guetzkow (1962); the psychological basis of trust and suspicion was explored by Morton Deutsch (1960); sociopsychological analyses were applied to international behavior by Herbert Kelman (1965); and while Otto Klineberg (1965) investigated the human dimension in international relations, Konrad Lorenz (1966) sought the answer to aggression in the patterned behaviors of animals.

Ranging across the years, Pillsbury (1919) wrote of the psychology of nationality and internationalism, Richardson (1960) did a brilliant analysis of the statistics of what he termed "deadly quarrels," while Sherif and others (1961) tackled the topic of intergroup conflict and cooperation, and Stagner (1961) drove to the heart of the issue with his analysis of the relation of personality dynamics to social conflict. Finally, to make sure that all bases were touched and no war ignored, Ralph White (1966) examined the issue of misperception and the war in Vietnam.

We have tried to study whole nations (Feierabend and Feierabend, 1966); we have tried to reduce conflict and stress to its common denominators (Rapoport, 1960), and we have assessed conflict and stress in its economic as well as psychological guises. Where have we failed to learn, to communicate, or to become credible? The unfortunate answer is that social and behavioral scientists have spawned a credibility gap that staggers the imagination. While we have remained convinced that stress-seeking in man can only become coherent via the study of man, we have failed to persuade almost everybody—lay person and professional alike.

The social and behavioral sciences have emerged from their attempt to communicate about stress and the nature of man badly scarred and bleeding from the multiple wounds of misunderstanding. As a representative of this point of view I am fully aware that I am about to enter a hostile and alien arena to once more do combat as the social agent devoted to stress-seeking with the powerful enemy of "what everyone knows to be true." Every man is his own champion in this realm and with the analysis to follow I hope to readmit psychology to the study of "man empowered to decide the fate of others." What is he like, what moves him, and, at crucial moments, how does he finally sort right from wrong, reasonable from unreasonable, and short-term gain from long-term concern with the fate of the human species?

THE GRAPHIC EGO AND STRESS

Since we have chosen the structure of the ego or self as a possible avenue to approach the understanding of the internal makeup of various kinds of stress-seekers, let us turn our attention for a moment to a schematic presentation of a possible relationship between ego functioning and stress-seeking in man.

THE INTERRELATIONSHIP OF EGO AND STRESS-SEEKING/ AVOIDING[1]

Figure 1, portraying the relationship of stress-seeking/ avoiding and effective-defective ego functioning, can be used speculatively to plot various classes of human beings

FIGURE 1

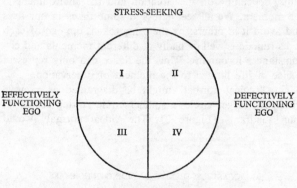

STRESS-SEEKING

EFFECTIVELY
FUNCTIONING
EGO

DEFECTIVELY
FUNCTIONING
EGO

I II

III IV

STRESS-AVOIDING

into and across respective quadrants of the diagram. The legendary "normal" person in our culture, for example, might range freely along the continuum of stress-seeking/ avoiding, and is only declared abnormal when he approaches either extreme on the scale or when his behavior becomes socially unacceptable. A business tycoon totally immersed in proxy fights for control of an industry, an astronaut riding in the nose of a missile into outer space, a

[1] Figure 1, plotting the relationship of stress to ego functioning, is designed to be suggestive only, and it will be useful to the degree it stimulates us to think seriously about other possible models of relationship. Like all diagrams, it is grossly oversimplified and highly speculative. It is a device designed to stimulate its own improvement.

professional boxer, a thoroughgoing pacifist, or a recluse philosopher might be equally applauded by various elements of our society. The avoidance of seeking of stress does not determine much of the social acceptance or rejection the individual will experience. We most often judge those persons we can place in quadrants I and III as normal, since our cultural model calls for an effectively functioning ego.

In actuality, normal, for most of us, includes a substantial number of individuals whose ego functions defectively. In addition, it is obvious that the most normal of us are in continuous movement in and out of the various quadrants, depending on the situation and the environment at the moment. We all seek stress at some times in our lives and avoid it at others; by the same token, the ego of each of us functions well or badly at different moments and circumstances in our life. Thus the figure can only represent a slice of life limited to the moment of observation.

The "typical normal" might be diagramed as a circle within the larger circle—a smaller circle cutting across all four quadrants (Figure 2). The "ideal normal" would

FIGURE 2

EGO AND STRESS-SEEKING/AVOIDING IN NORMALS

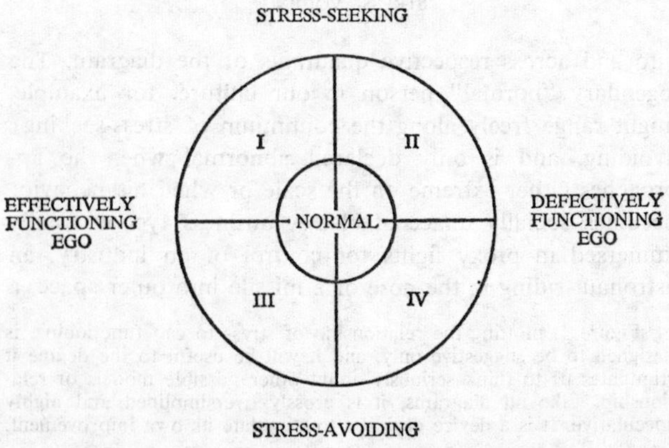

STRESS-SEEKING

EFFECTIVELY FUNCTIONING EGO

NORMAL

DEFECTIVELY FUNCTIONING EGO

I   II   III   IV

STRESS-AVOIDING

hopefully have the shape of his life contained primarily on the side of effective ego functioning and would maintain an approximately equal distribution of stress-seeking and avoiding. Normal is such an elusive concept that any attempt to represent it diagramatically must be taken with a grain of salt. You could with equal conviction argue that confines of normality ought to be expanded considerably or shrunk to a much more limited scope. You could with ease demand that the shape of normality should be more lopsided in any of the four possible directions. Another approach would be to note that "normal" would assume different configurations depending on whether it were defined in terms of one's intentions rather than one's actual behavior, or if tempered by an awareness of time, place, and social surroundings of the individual. The diagram that would successfully represent our hypothetically normal person would have to be as multidimensional and complex as each of us knows himself to be. Let us add some dimensions, one by one, and explore this model further by examining age as a variable.

If we plot a hypothetical typical person by age we might expect young persons (Figure 3) to be distributed dispro-

FIGURE 3

YOUTH, EGO, AND STRESS-SEEKING/AVOIDING

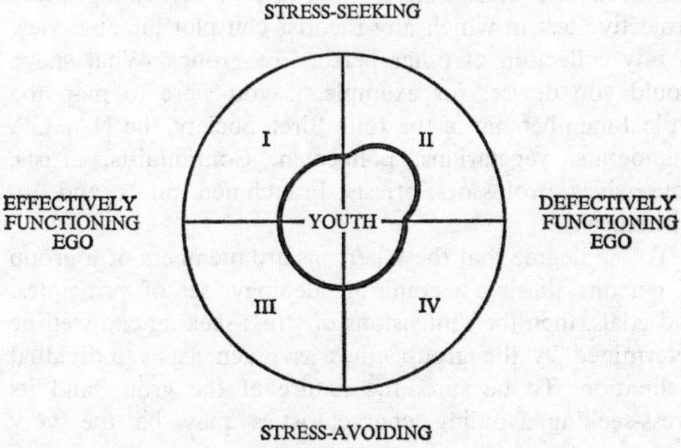

portionately in quadrant II, combining stress-seeking and a defectively functioning ego—depending on the age and experience of the young person. Older persons might reverse this model and appear more often to have effectively functioning egos, coupled with a greater emphasis on stress-avoiding (Figure 4).

FIGURE 4

AGE, EGO, AND STRESS-SEEKING/AVOIDING

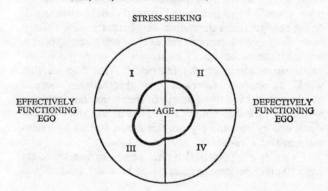

This is, of course, a highly speculative representation of the facts. The stress diagram can also be something like a projective test in which any theorist can plot his own view of any collection of other persons or groups. What shape would you devise, for example, if you were to map the typical membership of the John Birch Society, the NAACP, Democrats, vegetarians, policemen, Communists, artists, housewives, professors, priests, Frenchmen, pilots, and numismatists?

To the degree that these persons are members of a group of persons sharing a common ideology, set of principles, and goals, then the dimensions of stress-seeking can well be determined by the group ethos as much as by individual inclination. To be sure, the nature of the group and its stress-seeking/avoiding characteristics may be the very

qualities most attractive to potential members and may
serve to provide the membership with an unmistakable
group image. In most instances it is unlikely that the effectively or defectively functioning ego status of a group would
be a visible prime mover to its membership. A gangster
mob, the French Foreign Legion, the Neo-Nazi Party, or
similar avowedly radical or perceptively violent groups
might, however, "advertise" to the general public that they
sanction some forms of ego functioning that would be
judged defective by the majority of us.

This is not to say that there need be a meaningful or
dependable correlation between an ideology and the dimension of effective-defective ego functioning. By the
same token, this is not meant to deny the possibility that
such congruence can readily exist. It perhaps takes the
long reach of time and the cooling of ardent passions to
make a judgment of this sort and put it into proper perspective.

The stress diagram makes at least one fundamental observation. It indicates that simply by crisscrossing just the
two dimensions of effective-defective ego function and
stress-seeking/avoiding, one produces a host of possible
combinations and permutations. With the addition of other
dimensions of psychological, social, cultural, and historical
pressures, the variety of ways one can skin the cat of stress-
seeking and avoiding becomes astronomical. At the same
moment, the theoretical limitations of such simplistic descriptive diagraming are abundantly apparent and the possible extrapolations of it best left to the curious and
inventive. But we can at least add a set of related observations.

THE EGO AND LEADERSHIP

For the past ten years I have lived on intimate terms
with a number of groups of insurgents whose seeming sole
aim is a continuing war against the current social distribution of power. These insurgents have been antisocial delinquents selected from the ranks of the American disaffected,

deprived, and disenfranchised. Disaffected because the culture that surrounds them has made life a thing of more pain than pleasure; deprived on social, economic, and educational grounds; and disenfranchised in terms of political power by their status as a member of an impotent minority group. My insurgents have been young, without political power, and without the benefit of a guiding ideology—insurgents who have had to contend with a powerful, organized, hostile majority of members of the culture in which they reside. Their internal war is one of aimless personal attrition; it has proceeded for centuries; it has no hope of succeeding.

Experience in managing a community of aggressive delinquents would seem an unlikely breeding ground for the germination of ideas or insights regarding leadership in this or other cultures, yet strange plants are often nourished in alien soils. It is from the ranks of such disaffected, disenchanted, and discontented that the leaders, the lieutenants, and the rank and file of social movements are drawn. It is in the chemistry of the lives of such as these that grassroots movements evolve into a *carte blanche* for decision-makers that before long becomes a massive mandate. These children, when they become adults, constitute the roar of the crowd, the recruiting pool of bullyboys, and the cohorts who have an almost instinctive awareness that "one must break eggs to make omelets."

As I alluded before, the seeking of guidelines for insurgency and revolution in the internal workings of delinquents is a painful stretch of theoretical credibility. From what I know of political revolutionaries it appears they are often drawn from segments of the population not identical to that of delinquents, the quality of the revolutionary response is somewhat different from that of the delinquent, and the degree of emotional stability and rational ideology of the serious revolutionary certainly sets him apart from the blind antiactions of what I suggest might be his emotional counterpart.

Despite these disclaimers regarding the exact identity of these two groups—lest I offend all past, present, and future revolutionaries—the basic emotional and cognitive similarities between the two groups are too striking to dismiss easily. While differing in purpose and intent, the methods, techniques, and psychological view of what is right and necessary in life may link delinquents and political leaders and insurgents in a variety of important but unexpected ways.

I have been a participant-observer in the aggressive struggle for power of more than one thousand emotionally disturbed, delinquent boys in the last decade. My task has been to diagnose the dimensions of this conflict within society, to determine policies calculated to reduce, alter, direct, and fashion it into a more acceptable form, and to determine the means by which this aggressive energy can be converted into the social equivalent of noninsurgence. Finally, my labors have been directed particularly to training persons in a variety of disciplines to understand, manage, and alter the course of violent human behavior as an offshoot of stress-seeking as a way of life.

From the careful observational and experimental exploration of this peculiar process of insurgence I have reached conclusions, or convictions, really, that may have some relevance to the study of stress-seeking and avoiding. While these convictions are drawn from events far removed from the reality of developing nations flung across the face of the globe, it must be kept in mind that almost all of our psychological studies of international events are either secondhand or based on models that do not correspond exactly to world events. In contemplating the nature of stress-seeking and avoiding my primary concern is that we not lose sight of the nature of leadership. In this era's emphasis on group and social psychology, the individual within the culture has not been accorded a proper place.

What intrigued me most about the role of personality in international affairs was that as I reviewed the ideas of pioneer thinkers I became aware that on a smaller scale I was witnessing what seemed to be a similar phenomenon in the many power struggles among the delinquent gangs of boys with whom I worked closely. Living with hard-core delinquents months at a time provided an unparalleled opportunity to observe the evolution of gang leadership and the structuring of power based on aggression and violence. In addition, my typical delinquent has organized his perception of the world and of his status in it along the dimensions of toughness, fierceness, fearlessness, and ability to resist the influence of others. Inevitably, these boys express this self-image by engaging in a militant probing of the relative strength and weakness of one another in order to establish a scale of group dominance and submission. The methods of communicating threat between aggressive, power-oriented young people follow a highly predictable sequence that is suggestive of and resembles national and international methods of interaction. For example, while emerging leaders of delinquent gangs are still subject to influence by their followers, their following does little to alter the functioning of their fundamental personality structure. In times of crisis violent leaders are liable to act on impulses fully sanctioned by the subordinates with whom they have surrounded themselves—subordinates who share an orientation to raw power as a means to an end.

In our democratic society we see leadership as a magic event in which a reluctant citizen has power thrust upon him by an enthusiastic electorate, and we tend to view with suspicion any avowed desire on the part of the candidate to seek power for its own sake. There is something of a charade involved in ascending to power in America, and other nations may find it difficult to understand the discrepancy between the fact of exercise of power and our perception of its proper use.

Admittedly the social mechanisms used by the aspirants to power and political influence in our culture are ones regularly taken skeptically by the populace. The most casual perusal of the content of cartoons by the humorous political critics in our midst would indicate the tongue-in-national-cheek with which most of us view the conventional ways of denying an urge to leadership at the same moment that the desire for it is ardently affirmed. Our ritual power dances fit sensibly with the patterns of behavior we value most highly, even if they contain a quality of conscious self-deception. We need to be cautious about generalizing our cultural patterns to societies that only remotely resemble our own, however. Cultural blindness of this sort can lead us into errors of perception that are too costly to afford when man has at his command such an excess of control over the power of nature.

Leaders of other countries emerge from social conditions so unlike our own that we err greatly in assessing them and predicting their reactions by using the frame of reference of our own style of leadership. In this respect, the delinquent leader and his unabashed quest for personal power might be a more fitting model for judging the personality structure of leaders of other cultures. In such leaders, power may not corrupt solely in the classic sense of converting good to evil. A leader's use of power for personal glory and aggrandizement is more likely to have been the original motivation in his rise to power, and this may not seem reprehensible to members of his own culture who support his efforts and hope to share in the material and psychological loot he promises them.

Some leadership is a function of a lifelong self-image constructed on notions of personal destiny, the mysticism of being chosen to lead, and the equating of power and leadership. For such a leader the exercise of power is a way of life, and if he is highly sensitized to the perception of threat and ready to act violently and to ignore counsel when his emotions are sufficiently aroused, he becomes a person who can easily override rational considerations of history, economics, military preparedness, or the opinion of others and seek stress as an outlet for his personal needs. Personal qualities of an emotional and dramatic sort have always puzzled the members of more "civilized and refined" cultures. The hours-long harangues of a Castro, the dramatic stylizing of a Lumumba, the martyr-like posturing of a Gandhi, and the invective of a Mao Tse-Tung take one aback and seem inflammatory at worst and in bad taste at best. The premise of leadership in other cultures is not the same as our own, just as the standards, values, and expected behaviors of middle-class persons in our society are incompatible with the way of life of those less favored economically within our own borders. When a segment of the culture, such as delinquents, is openly defiant of the conventions established by the ruling majority, we have a situation analogous to the revolutionary group and its leaders. The question to be explored has reference to the ego structure of the delinquent and to the degree to which it can be applied to the ego structure of the leader of nations with which we must have congress.

I think we can examine with some profit a few of the characteristics of the functioning or malfunctioning of the delinquent ego. The implication of the speculative analysis will be that in the ego functioning of the avowed delinquent we have a hint of the psychic characteristics of the aggressive leader and that from these suggestions it might be possible to lay bare some of the forces that shape the form of human interaction at a personal, national, and international level. Redl and Wineman (1957) outlined the components of faulty ego function in aggressive young people and I have drawn heavily from their observations in this analysis.

What are the ego difficulties aggressive delinquents present?

A LOW FRUSTRATION TOLERANCE

Most humans learn to delay gratification when necessary, but the aggressive delinquent insists on gratification at the moment he desires it, whatever the cost may be. There is a capricious and impulse-ridden flavor to his response to life. Some frustrations are, of course, inevitable, and when frustration occurs, the emotions that accompany it are uncomfortable and unpleasant to experience. Toleration of frustration is trying for such a person, and when it is coupled with the emotional pileup of the effects of frustration, the ego is rendered less and less capable of making rational, objective judgments.

There is a continuing—and scientifically unsupported—myth that some delinquents plan in a rational, cool, and intellectually sound manner. The movie model of the syndicated mobster-business man may exist in real life but I have been unable in the last decade to discover that talent pool from which such executives are drawn. Any close clinical appraisal of a true delinquent makes it clear that he succeeds despite himself and his impulsive inability to live with conflict and tolerate frustration. He is not capable of mature and objectively weighed judgment.

INABILITY TO COPE WITH INSECURITY AND ANXIETY

The "pauperized" ego of the aggressive delinquent is particularly subject to erosion when it is exposed to continued insecurity and anxiety. When the usual mechanisms for dealing with such psychic pains are absent, the response of the victim may be "flight and avoidance" or "ferocious attack and diffuse destruction." Such persons should not be threatened, since their reaction to threat is neither appetizing nor constructive. The social device of humoring the hysterical individual having a temper tantrum or making a breast-beating demand for justice has some relevance here. Attempts to make such persons "face reality" only increase the degree of insecurity and anxiety they must contend with and provoke an escalation of the dramatic and sometimes violent behavior. It is why trapped rats fight so desperately and viciously.

LITTLE TEMPTATION RESISTANCE

An ego functioning on too few cylinders cannot resist the temptation to seek gratification for impulses that would normally lead to danger and provoke powerful guilt. Irresistible impulses can make legitimate half-thought-through actions that wiser heads would resist. Such persons are subject to temptation. The normally watchful ego that weighs psychological profit and loss to protect the individual is trampled by the sudden rush of impulse and ceases to function effectively. There is excitement and group intoxication that destroys rational judgment, making the risky seem safe. Such leaders can be swayed by events and by the impulsiveness of their advisers.

In such situations the appraisal of risk undergoes a subtle transformation. What would seem rationally to be risky and fraught with unpleasant consequences begins to assume a new and less threatening shape, just as any frightening form can have its outline softened by focusing on the possible good and beautiful rather than the bad and ugly. With the compelling rise of temptation one can still call out clearly the characteristics of the risk involved yet dismiss them as the calculated cost of the quest for power and authority.

The list of characteristics assembled from clinical observation of young aggressive leaders would stretch beyond a reasonable length. It ranges through an inability to control the floodgates of past experience and emotion, disorganization when faced with the rare experience of guilt, an inability to perceive their own contribution in a causal chain of events that leads to catastrophe, a continuing war with time in the form of impatience for gratification, an inability to make realistic adaptations to rules and regulations imposed from without, a distorted conception of social reality, and an unusual reaction to failure, success, and mistakes. This is not a complete list but it is sufficiently long to paint a picture of an ego functioning in ways alien to our conception of how the average person is put together psychologically. How these kinds of ego structures are formed by the interpersonal environment of the emerging leader is too massive a topic to tackle here. That they occur in leaders who are prone to the use of direct, violent action has been clear to us for some time.

Assume for a moment that leadership is achieved by a human being possessing part or all of such an ego structure. (You will note that I speak of ego structure with little reference to the mysteries of the unconscious or related psychological structures.) In such a circumstance it would seem probable that the quality of the thousands of leadership decisions he must make would eventually lead him to the brink of destructive adventuring with the fate of man.

> The leaders of people do not issue from the common mold of man; they tend, rather, to be drawn from among those deviates from the average whose personal charisma matches closely the needs and spirit of the time. Leaders with the unique ability to draw the human race willingly down the path of its eventual destruction must—in

this view of humanity—have assembled a collection of personal characteristics and ways of behaving that fit the temper of the times and match the age in which they live. The nature of their developing years is a critical factor in understanding their response to the state of the world (McNeil, 1966; p. 156).

We have always tended to glamorize leaders in direct proportion to the length of time they have been dead and to the degree that little factual evidence of the nature of their real personalities is available. Time is a great romanticizer and it acts very capably to fulfill our need for a set of untarnished heroes. We like our leaders and heroes to be the epitome of what we wish ideally for ourselves, and we treat them very much with the reverence Asians have for the massive and expensively ornate temples that stud the poverty-stricken land. The assumption that the great leaders of antiquity were somehow better-adjusted human beings whose egos were on the side of the angels and effective function is to attribute, *post hoc,* qualities that *ought* to exist even if they never did. The reasoning is that a man who accomplished—or conquered—so much had to have predominantly stable psychological qualities. There is no evidence that these two aspects of leadership are both required for success.

When stress-seeking has violence as its handmaiden—as it so often has had in man's history—it is frightening to all of us and becomes our principal concern. In the ego model I have outlined there is an implicit plea for greater attention to the psychology of man in world affairs. Our failure to comprehend our own species is discouraging but an insufficient reason for abandoning renewed attempts to gain insight into what makes the stress-seekers tick. In this respect one more observation is worth reporting here.

The complexity of the human psyche has made it so forbidding an area of exploration that modern theorists have discounted human personality as an important influence in the affairs of mankind. It is, indeed, an alien concoction and one not easily digested by the politico-economic-sociological theorists of this generation. Yet, denying that the psychological nature of man has relevance in understanding human violence has produced only a bankrupt and barren vision of the future of humanity. Man's psychic nature cannot remain an unknown in the equation of violence or we will find ourselves presiding over the dissolution of the human race.

In the course of development of the hostile human being destined for leadership, we see an organism fashioned to perceive a world composed primarily of threatening elements—threatening to him as a person and threatening to his conception of the way things ought to be in the world. The threat so visible to such a person is reacted to rapidly, intensely, and violently. Thus, his violent response happens easily, it happens often, and it needs little provocation. Faced with threat, the aggressive leader has few alternative forms of response at his command and, being incapable of tolerating stress, he falls back rapidly on the only response that has served him faithfully in the past. Cornered, he is incapable of a rational judgment free of the urge to aggrandizement or the impulse to strike out and destroy those he perceives as plaguing him with anxiety (McNeil, 1966; p. 157).

This analysis has ranged somewhat widely but it contains a sequence of thinking that needs to be readmitted to our consideration of international events. The premises here are fairly straightforward. Individuals learn to be the kind of adults they become, and the control of violence must explore the process of development with a critical eye if we are to solve the riddle of aggressive stress-seeking. The fate of our planet still rests in the hands of the chosen few who must eventually make the decisions that will plunge us either into peace or war.

I have suggested that the qualities of aggressive leadership are not nearly as alien as we might at first suppose and that the characteristics of aggressive, delinquent youth in our society might be an appropriate model for the examination of the decision-making process of national leaders. I am certain that the more complex the society, the less relevance this analysis will have, but I am equally convinced that we live in an era in which the small emerging nations will have an increasing impact on the course of world affairs. It is paradoxical that a nation as mighty as America cannot, as a consequence of its very might, take aggressive action against Cuba, that Russia is helpless in the face of the defection of Albania, and that Red China cannot dismantle Quemoy, Matsu, or Taiwan.

Leaders still make decisions, and their view of the world remains an important, if neglected, aspect of the proper study of mankind. A Charles de Gaulle, an L.B.J., a Mao Tse-Tung, and a Ho Chi-Minh may be the critical factors in planetary survival. At any rate, man proposes and the gods still dispose. If we cannot study the gods we can yet examine man and learn of his contribution to the course of history.

BIBLIOGRAPHY

Adorno, T. W.; Frenkel-Brunswick, E.; Levinson, D. J.; and Sanford, R. Nevitt. *The Authoritarian Personality* (New York: Harper & Brothers, 1950).

Boulding, Kenneth. *Conflict and Defense* (New York: Harper Torchbooks, 1962).

Bronfenbrenner, Urie. "The Mirror-Image in Soviet-American Relations: A Social Psychologist's Report," *Journal of Social Issues,* Vol. 17, No. 3 (1961), pp. 45–56.

Deutsch, Morton. "The Effect of Motivational Orientation Upon Trust and Suspicion," *Human Relations,* Vol. 13 (1960), pp. 123–39.

Feierabend, Ivo K. and Rosalind L. "Aggressive Behaviors Within Polities, 1948–1962: A Cross-National Study," *Journal of Conflict Resolution,* Vol. 10 (1966), pp. 249–71.

Frank, Jerome D. "Emotional and Motivational Aspects of the Disarmament Problem," *Journal of Social Issues,* Vol. 17, No. 3 (1961), pp. 20–27.

Fromm, E. *Man For Himself* (New York: Rinehart & Company, Inc., 1947).

Guetzkow, Harold. "A Use of Simulation in the Study of International Relations," in Harold Guetzkow (ed.), *Simulation in Social Science: Readings* (Englewood Cliffs, N.J.: Prentice-Hall, Inc., 1962).

Kelman, Herbert C. (ed.). *International Behavior: A Social-Psychological Analysis* (New York: Holt, Rinehart & Winston, Inc., 1965).

Klineberg, Otto. *The Human Dimension in International Relations* (New York: Holt, Rinehart & Winston, Inc., 1965).

Lorenz, Konrad. *On Aggression* (New York: Harcourt, Brace & World, Inc., 1966).

Marquis, Donald Q., and Allen, T. J. "Communication Patterns in Applied Technology," *American Psychologist,* Vol. 21 (1966), pp. 1052–60.

McClelland, David C. *The Achieving Society* (Princeton, N.J.: D. Van Nostrand Company, Inc., 1961).

McNeil, Elton B. (ed.). *The Nature of Human Conflict* (Englewood Cliffs, N.J.: Prentice-Hall, Inc., 1965).

———. "Violence and Human Development," *The Annals of the American Academy of Political and Social Science*, Vol. 364 (1966), pp. 149–57.

Pillsbury, W. B. *The Psychology of Nationality and Internationalism* (New York: D. Appleton and Company, 1919).

Potter, D. M. *People of Plenty* (Chicago: The University of Chicago Press, 1954).

Rapoport, Anatol. *Fights, Games, and Debates* (Ann Arbor: University of Michigan Press, 1960).

Redl, F., and Wineman, D. *The Aggressive Child* (Glencoe, Ill.: The Free Press, 1957).

Richardson, Lewis F. *Statistics of Deadly Quarrels* (Chicago: Quadrangle Books, Inc., 1960).

Riesman, D. *The Lonely Crowd* (New Haven: Yale University Press, 1950).

Sherif, Muzafer, and others. *Intergroup Conflict and Cooperation* (Norman, Okla.: University of Oklahoma Press, 1961).

Stagner, Ross. "Personality Dynamics and Social Conflict," *Journal of Social Issues*, Vol. 17, No. 3 (1961), pp. 28–44.

White, Ralph K. "Misperception and the Vietnam War," *Journal of Social Issues*, Vol. 22, No. 3 (1966).

Wolfenstein, Martha. "The Emergence of Fun Morality," *Journal of Social Issues*, Vol. 7 (1951), pp. 15–25.

E. Paul Torrance

E. Paul Torrance has been constructing a bridge between the psychology of creativity and education for creativity. In *Guiding Creative Talent*, directed to educators, he reviewed the history of creativity tests and introduced one of his own—the Torrance Tests of Creative Thinking. These tests require a child to formulate hypotheses, to describe behavior of persons in pictures, to suppose something quite improbable—for example, that sunshine is solid—and then talk about it, and to improve some toys that children commonly play with.

Traditionally, the theory of learning has dominated the border between psychology and education. In his *Education and the Creative Potential*, Paul Torrance suggests shifting the emphasis to the theory of thinking. He complains that certain aspects of culture block creative development. The block derives from the dichotomy between work and play, the tendency to equate divergent with abnormal behavior, and a tendency to sanction negatively those asking new questions. With sociometric evidence, Paul Torrance records the eventual isolation of a creative child from other children in a class who consider his ideas rather wild.

For the broader intellectual community, Paul Torrance has summed up our knowledge about creativity in his article "Scientific Views of Creativity and Its Development." Creativity means sensitivity to problems and disharmonies, responding to deficiencies in knowledge, reaching out for solutions, making guesses, testing and retesting hypotheses, and then communicating the results. Thus creativity involves an application of the scientific method. In *Gifted Children in the Classroom* he offers the classroom teacher a double-barreled challenge: the teacher of the gifted child must invent teaching methods and these inventions must be unique.

His most recent book, *Constructive Behavior: Stress, Personality and Mental Health,* is a critique of personality theories which have relied on notions of adaptation and adjustment. He further presses his point about substituting a psychology of thinking for a psychology of learning by emphasizing the role of cognitive abilities in creative thinking. Personality breakdowns occur when the demands of the stresses exceed the personality and mental resources available for constructive response.

The stress-seeker Paul Torrance describes for this symposium is one who steps out into the unknown, is prepared to be different, test his limits, attempt the difficult, and respond to challenge. Stress-seekers may be typed according to whether they seek stress in response to a threat or in response to inner forces, or in arduous ways or through a pleasant thrill. These types of stress-seekers, as well as stress-avoiders, are differently distributed in various cultural *milieux*. This is demonstrated through an analysis of fanciful stories written by children from several cultures. Children in Minnesota seek stress, if at all, in response to challenge. In Toronto, the typical stress-seeking is in response to threat. Puerto Rican children proved to be more spontaneously stress-seeking than any other group he studied. German children are more accurately described as stress-encountering than as stress-seeking; difficulties just seem to find them, and they conceive their task as persisting toward a solution. Greek children seek stress more in response to internal forces.

E. Paul Torrance's findings are related directly to McClelland's work on societal achievement values. A high-achieving culture requires a reasonably high number of stress-seeking persons. They must have a reasonable expectation of success. The environment must be highly responsive, supplying both supportive and oppositional reactions to their stress-seeking.

COMPARATIVE STUDIES OF STRESS-SEEKING IN THE IMAGINATIVE STORIES OF PREADOLESCENTS IN TWELVE DIFFERENT SUBCULTURES

In this paper, I have assumed that stress-seeking is an individual difference, existing to some extent in all men but varying greatly in degree within a given culture, from culture to culture, and from subculture to subculture. I have also assumed that this individual difference is the product of hereditary and environmental forces but that the behaviors encouraged and discouraged in a child play an important role in the determination of its strength and nature. From my studies of behavior in emergencies and extreme conditions, the lives of persons of outstanding achievement, the correlates of creative behavior, and high-achieving children, it seems clear that the stress variable is important in predicting level of achievement and differentiating methods of instruction for different children within a given culture.

I shall review briefly some of the evidence that has caused me to conclude that stress-seeking is related to achievement and preferred or optimal ways of learning. I shall then describe an original investigation in which I have attempted to explore the hypothesis that the stress-seeking behavior of preadolescents is related to different levels of school achievement and that this behavior varies from one subculture to another, depending upon the kinds of behavior encouraged and discouraged by the subculture.

STRESS-SEEKING AND ACHIEVEMENT

An analysis of what is required in outstanding achievement, especially creative achievement, suggests that we should expect a positive relationship between stress-seeking and achievement. Outstanding creative achievement in-

volves a step into the unknown, getting away from the
obvious and the safe. It involves being different, testing
known limits, attempting difficult jobs, making honest mistakes, and responding to challenge. All of these behaviors
are a part of my definition of stress-seeking.

Studies of the lives of eminent people and of the personality and mental characteristics of people of outstanding
achievement suggest that one of the truly important factors
in high achievement is a strong tendency to stress-seeking.
Instead of just adapting or adjusting to their environment
they deliberately expose themselves to stressful conditions
and commit themselves to goals that require sustained ex-
penditures of intellectual and physical energy and continued
changes in behavior. This tendency abounds in studies of
eminent people (Cox, 1926; Goertzel and Goertzel, 1962).
It also emerges as an important distinguishing characteristic
in personality studies of people recognized as high achievers contrasted with unselected or low-achieving peers (Mac-
Kinnon, 1961; Torrance, Rush, Kohn and Doughty, 1957).

Since psychologists have given little attention to the measurement of individual differences that might be labeled
"stress-seeking," it is necessary to synthesize results concerning a complex of variables involved in stress-seeking.
MacKinnon's (1961) eminent architects described themselves as imaginative, active, inventive, independent, individualistic, and progressive. The psychologists described
them as enterprising, independent, assertive, energetic, and
individualistic. All of them expressed a desire to be adventurous and 80 per cent or more of them said that they
would like to be courageous, daring, enterprising, and energetic. Their early life histories, compared with those of
their lower-achieving peers, are characterized by greater
freedom of exploration, more frequent changes, and self-
assertive independence.

Psychometric studies of highly creative or original people
emphasize the importance of the stress-seeking variable.
For example, Barron (1954), in one of his early studies
of the relationship between originality and personality style,
found relationships of a low order of magnitude between
originality and (1) impulsivity, (2) skepticism, (3) daring,

and (4) expressive as opposed to suppressive dispositions in the personality. In a study recently reported by Torrance and Dauw (1966), individuals identified psychometrically as highly creative were differentiated from similar, unselected individuals by characteristics that appear to be associated with stress-seeking. The highly creative subjects were 115 high-school seniors identified psychometrically from a population of 712 seniors in a single metropolitan high school. These 115 creatively gifted seniors were compared with a sample of 100 unselected subjects with similar demographic characteristics on the Runner Studies of Attitude Patterns. The creative seniors far more frequently than the comparison group had high patterns on the Experimental, Intuitive, and Resistance to Social Pressure scales and less frequently had high patterns on Rules and Tradition, Structure and Plans, and Passive Conformity. An examination of the items indicates that there is an element of stress-seeking in the ones composing the Experimental, Intuitive, and Resistance to Social Pressure scales and an avoidance of stress in Rules and Tradition, Structure and Plans, and Passive Conformity. Using the clusters determined by factor analysis (Runner, 1965), the high creatives also more frequently had high Freedom, Achievement, and Recognition orientations and less frequently had Control orientations than the comparison sample.

The American jet ace study (Torrance, Rush, Kohn, and Doughty, 1957) deals rather directly with the stress-seeking variable. Compared with fellow jet pilots of similar rank, age, experience, and training, the jet aces reported enjoying and participating in a larger number of everyday activities involving risk and strategy. They reported that as boys they exhibited more testing-the-limits and "trouble-making" behavior and that they received more early independence training. Just before a combat mission, the aces would be anxious "to get going" and could hardly wait. They felt that they were more efficient in both intellectual and physical functioning under stress than under ordinary conditions. What tenseness they experienced before a mission faded away as soon as action started. The nonaces more frequently either felt no emotional reaction prior to combat missions and described no symptoms of being keyed up or they were tense and experienced disruption of performance under stress. The aces loved competition, while their lower-achieving peers either had a lukewarm attitude about competition or actively disliked it. Almost all of the nonaces reported that they had been assigned to jet fighter aircraft through routine personnel procedures, while almost all of the aces had found it necessary to make special attempts and employ a variety of maneuvers in order to obtain such an assignment. The nonaces welcomed and enjoyed "rest and recuperation" leave, while the aces frequently refused such leave. Most of the aces were anxious for a second combat tour, while few of the nonaces expressed such a desire.

STRESS-SEEKING AND METHOD OF LEARNING

In other sources (Torrance 1965c, 1966), I have attempted to synthesize a considerable body of knowledge that seems to indicate that different children learn in different ways and that changing methods of instruction makes a big difference in who become the high and low achievers in a given class. I shall cite here an example of a recent experiment that suggests that stress-seeking is a personality and intellectual variable about which instruction might be differentiated. The subjects were students in two of my classes in Group Dynamics, totaling one hundred and five students working in groups of five. Scores on the Runner scales were used as the measure of stress-seeking (high scores on Experimental, Intuitive, and Resistance to Social Pressure and low scores on Rules and Tradition, Structure and Plans, and Passive Conformity). Subjects were divided at the median into a high stress-seeking and a low stress-seeking group. The subjects were then assigned randomly to five-person groups and to two different conditions. In one condition, the groups, following a practice exercise, were given instructions in conducting an evaluative feedback session preceding a test period requiring the production of original ideas. Groups assigned to the other condition were instructed in the conduct of what I have called "creative feedback" (no criticism or evaluation, looking at and enjoying the practice production, talking about how they thought of their ideas, and the like).

The problem task for both the practice and test sessions was Simpson's Dot-Squares Test (1922), which can evaluate for originality according to a previously developed scoring guide (Torrance 1965d). There was a practice period of twenty-five minutes, an instruction period of ten minutes, a feedback session of twenty-five minutes, and a test session of twenty-five minutes. The mean gains in the test session over practice performance for the two types of groups and two feedback conditions are as follows:

High Stress-seeking Groups under Evaluative Feedback	19.1
Low Stress-seeking Groups under Evaluative Feedback	87.0
High Stress-seeking Groups under Creative Feedback	110.4
Low Stress-seeking Groups under Creative Feedback	53.5

The analysis of variance indicated no statistically significant effect due either to degree of stress-seeking ($F = .006$) or type of feedback ($F = 2.29$) but the interaction effect was significant at about the .02 level of confidence ($F = 8.22$). The high stress-seekers profit more from creative than evaluative feedback, and the low stress-seekers, more from evaluative than creative feedback.

CULTURAL DIFFERENCES IN STRESS-SEEKING

A great deal of evidence suggests that cultures and subcultures differ in the nature and degree of their stress-seeking and that these in turn are related to the dominant child-rearing procedures of the culture and the behaviors encouraged and discouraged therein. McClelland (1961) developed a procedure for quantifying the achievement motivations of different societies on the basis of their literature. He found interesting differences among societies in

such characteristics as risk-taking, energy and/or novel instrumental activity, long-range planning, restless expressive
movements, child-rearing practices, and the like.

In my own comparative studies of the concept of teachers of the ideal child, there emerged wide differences in
what behaviors are encouraged and punished from one culture to another (Torrance, 1965ab). Large numbers of
teachers in a variety of cultures and subcultures were asked
to describe their ideal personality by indicating the extent
to which they would encourage or discourage each of a
set of sixty-six behaviors. By assigning weights on a four-
point scale to the varying degrees of encouragement and
discouragement and combining them for all of the members
of a sample, it is possible to rank the characteristics. Detailed information about the construction of the instrument,
selection of samples, and complete rankings for selected
groups is reported elsewhere (Torrance, 1965ab). The following are examples of the comparative rankings of some
of the characteristics associated with stress-seeking (rank of
1 is most encouraged and rank of 66 is most discouraged):

Characteristic	U.S.	Greece	Germany	India	Samoa	Philippines
Adventurous	19	52	10	25	30	25
Attempting the difficult	20	21	5	15	18	22
Desires to excel	21	35	55	29	12	36
Independent in judgment	16	17	6	31	32	23
Willing to take risks	29	45	21	40	51	29

PROCEDURES

During the past five years, the author has collected approximately fifty thousand imaginative stories by preadolescents in about thirty different subcultures. These imaginative stories have been written about animals and people
displaying divergent behavior presumably involving stress-
seeking (The Flying Monkey, The Lion That Won't Roar,
The Cat That Won't Scratch, etc.). In the school selected
as representative of a culture or subculture, all of the pu-

pils in all fourth, fifth, and sixth grades wrote stories; in several school systems, all fourth-, fifth-, and sixth-grade pupils participated. In the present study, samples were drawn from the stories available from four dominant American subcultures, four minority subcultures in the United States, and four European subcultures. In addition, the stories of a sample of high-achieving and a sample of low-achieving pupils were analyzed.

While it cannot be claimed that the samples analyzed fully represent the total groups from which they were drawn, and while in some cases the number of stories is smaller than I would have liked, I believe that the samples reflect their cultures reasonably well. In most cases, the stories were drawn randomly from the stories available. In some cases, I was limited to the number of stories that had been translated. Very briefly, the samples studied are as follows:

1. Two hundred children in the public schools of Minneapolis, Minnesota, and its suburbs. In general, these children represent the dominant culture of this area.
2. One hundred children in the public white schools of Glynn County (Brunswick, Georgia).
3. One hundred and five children in the public schools of Toronto, Canada.
4. Two hundred and nine children in San Juan, Puerto Rico, largely from upper-middle-class neighborhoods.
5. One hundred and twelve Rimrock Navajo children in New Mexico.
6. Sixty Rimrock Zuñi children in New Mexico.
7. Ninety-eight Chippewa children from the Red Lake Reservation in Minnesota.
8. One hundred and twenty-six Mexican-American children in Texas and California.
9. One hundred and eighty-eight children from Paris and Roanne, France.
10. One hundred and sixty-five children from Milan and Turin, Italy.

11. One hundred and sixty-three children from Berlin, Germany.
12. Sixty-four children from Athens, Greece.
13. One hundred and seventy-one high-achieving sixth graders in a Minneapolis suburban school (achieving at about ninth- or tenth-grade level with Stanford-Binet Intelligence Quotients of above 130, and selected from the entire school system).
14. Seventy children in a Minneapolis school selected by their teachers as most likely to drop out of school, all achieving well below grade level on standardized tests.

The imaginative stories were in all cases written under nonthreatening, nonevaluative conditions during a twenty-minute period. Emphasis was placed upon the creation of an interesting, imaginative, and exciting story rather than upon correctness. In no case were the stories corrected or graded. The topics involved animals or people possessing some divergent characteristic that would serve as the basis of stress-seeking or stress-avoiding.

Each story was classified as to the nature of the stress-seeking of the main character of the story. The following categories were used:

1. *Spontaneous stress-seeking stemming from the nature of the animal or person.* The stress-seeking is in response to challenge, the goals and commitments of the animal or person, etc.
2. *Provoked or stimulated stress-seeking stemming from environmental pressure.* The stress-seeking is in response to threat, force, or compulsion from some external source.
3. *Unsuccessful attempt to avoid stress.* Stress is not sought and active attempts are made to avoid it, but somehow conditions preclude avoidance.
4. *No stress-seeking or successful avoidance.* Stress is successfully avoided or there is no expressed awareness of opportunities for stress-seeking.

Each story was also rated for the degree of success of the central character of the story, using the following scale:

(1) very successful, (2) moderately but not outstandingly successful, (3) unsuccessful but survived, and (4) death or destruction. An analysis was also made of the responsiveness of the environment to the central character of each story. If the central character was supported by his environment in his stress-seeking or avoidance of stress, the support category was scored. If the central character experienced opposition, hostility, ridicule, rejection, etc., the opposition category was scored. Some characters experienced both support and opposition, while others experienced neither. For this reason, a single story might be checked for both categories.

RESULTS

The results of the analysis of the imaginative stories will be presented first for the twelve different subcultures. Then, in order to establish a base line upon which to interpret these results, the analyses will be presented for the high achievers and potential dropouts. In all of these analyses it has been assumed that, when asked to write imaginative stories about flying monkeys, roarless lions, swimming cats, and the like, preadolescent children will project through fantasies the ideals and values of their cultures and subcultures as well as their unique concepts, perceptions, and psychological characteristics. Psychologically unsophisticated readers of imaginative stories almost instantly recognize wide individual differences within each culture and at the same time sense a commonness within each culture. Almost no one misses the imprint of Roman and Greek mythology on the stories of the Italian and Greek children, the light fantasy of the French stories, the magic and superstition of the stories by American Indians, the German fairy tale influence on the German stories, and the rigid social standards in the Canadian stories. From the results presented in Tables 1 to 4, an attempt will be made to identify some of the quantifiable similarities and differences.

Data for all of the analyses are presented in a single

Table 1

Summary of Classification of Imaginative Stories by Preadolescents in Four Dominant American Subcultures

Category	Spontaneous Seek.				Provoked Seek.				Unsuccessful Avoid.				Non-Stress-Seeking			
	Minn.	Ga.	Can.	P.R.	Minn.	Ga.	Can.	P.R.	Minn.	Ga.	Can.	P.R.	Minn.	Ga.	Can.	P.R.
Very successful	41	16	4	41	11	5	12	1	8	1	0	0	4	0	6	18
Moderately successful	24	28	9	34	11	3	9	2	7	1	9	2	2	4	8	21
Neither successful nor unsuccessful	22	2	1	18	3	2	4	1	0	0	1	1	6	4	7	5
Unsuccessful but survived	29	14	12	35	5	0	13	3	4	1	2	1	5	0	0	1
Killed, destroyed	16	11	1	24	0	3	0	0	1	2	0	0	1	0	1	3
Supportive environment	47	18	7	81	13	3	12	3	5	2	3	2	7	1	7	36
Oppositional environment.	36	18	10	53	4	12	9	3	4	2	5	2	4	2	4	4
Return to an earlier, less stressful state	26	22	5	47	9	9	2	0	5	1	2	2	3	0	1	5

Sample Sizes: Minnesota, 200; Georgia, 100; Canada, 105; Puerto Rico, 209 table for four dominant American subcultures to conserve space and to maintain simplicity in data presentation. Similar tables are presented for four minority subcultures in the United States, four European subcultures, and groups representing three achievement levels in a single metropolitan area. Unfortunately, this means that the reader must pull out the data for himself as the results for each set of variables are discussed. When differences are identified, chi-square analysis has been used.

NATURE OF STRESS-SEEKING EFFORTS

Table 1 contains the data for four dominant American subcultures. In analyzing the data on the nature of stress-seeking manifested in the stories, one is impressed by the unusually close similarity between the Minnesota and Georgia samples, suggesting that the instrument may be tapping something characteristic of the dominant culture of the United States.

The Minnesota, Georgia, and Puerto Rico subcultures generally emphasized the self-acting nature of man with definite majorities projecting an image of spontaneous stress-seeking in response to one's nature, to internal rather than external forces, to challenge rather than external threat. The Canadian subjects differed markedly from the other three dominant subcultures in this respect. The Canadian stories reflected greater emphasis on receptivity and response to social and other external pressures rather than on the self-acting nature of their heroes. This finding is in harmony with Karoussos' (1961) finding that Canadian children are motivated more strongly by social pressures than are children in the United States and Greece.

The Canadian and Puerto Rican groups are similar to one another and differ from the Minnesota and Georgia subjects in their higher proportion of non-stress-seeking behavior. Further examination of the stories categorized as non-stress-seeking, however, suggests that the Puerto Rican stories emphasize an active, pleasure-seeking orientation not leading to stress, while the Canadian stories describe a more affectless kind of stress avoidance.

Table 2

Summary of Classification of Imaginative Stories by Preadolescents in Four Minority Subcultures in the United States

Category	Spontaneous Seek.				Provoked Seek.				Unsuccessful Avoid.				Non-Stress-Seeking			
	Nav.	Zuñi	Chip.	Mex.	Nav.	Zuñi	Chip.	Mex.	Nav.	Zuñi	Chip.	Mex.	Nav.	Zuñi	Chip.	Mex.
Very successful	12	7	5	33	3	5	4	7	0	0	0	0	9	0	3	0
Moderately successful	5	16	18	21	7	1	5	8	0	0	1	2	7	0	3	4
Neither successful nor unsuccessful	2	4	12	14	3	0	2	4	0	0	1	0	31	0	10	5
Unsuccessful but survived	7	13	16	10	2	1	4	4	1	0	4	1	0	1	8	3
Killed, destroyed	1	9	1	6	1	3	1	2	0	0	0	1	1	0	0	1
Supportive environment	11	14	11	33	5	5	1	5	0	0	2	2	9	0	8	3
Oppositional environment	8	25	23	26	7	6	8	14	0	0	2	1	1	0	3	4
Return to an earlier, less stressful state	2	5	13	17	1	0	5	6	0	0	0	0	0	0	7	0

Sample Sizes: Navajo, 112; Zuñi, 60; Chippewas, 98; Mexican-Americans, 126

Data concerning the nature of stress-seeking efforts are presented in Table 2 for the four minority subcultures in the United States. There is much diversity in the patterns reflected by these results. The Navajos are characterized by strong tendencies in the direction of stress avoidance and lack of striving. One obtains the impression that they would even deny the presence of forces in the direction of change. The Zuñis are characterized by an unusually strong tendency in the direction of stress-seeking in response to internal forces and a keen awareness of the presence of stress and forces in the direction of change. The Chippewas present no such clear-cut pattern as the Navajos and Zuñis. Next to the Navajos, they are characterized by the greatest tendency to stress avoidance; a bare majority reflects a tendency to stress-seeking in response to internal forces. The pattern of the Mexican-Americans is rather similar to that of the Zuñis; they are somewhat more prone to stress avoidance and less prone to stress-seeking in response to challenge and internal forces.

The data for the four European subcultures are shown in Table 3. The stories of the French and Italian children are characterized by non-stress-seeking. The non-stress-seeking French stories are quite different from the Italian ones, however. The French children revel in fantasy, gaiety, and non-stressful pleasure-seeking. The Italian stories, however, reflect a strong tendency to suppress fantasy and avoid playing with the possibility that a monkey can fly or that a lion would not roar. At the same time, a large percentage (42.5) of the Italian stories involve spontaneous response to stress. The German and Greek stories tend more in the direction of response to challenge than do the others. The German stories also have a rather heavy emphasis on response to stress, force, and coercion (as seen by their high proportions in the second and third categories).

DEGREE OF SUCCESS OF THE HERO

It will be observed from Table 1 that the distributions of ratings of success in the stories from the four dominant

Table 3

Summary of Classification of Imaginative Stories by Preadolescents in Four European Subcultural Groups

Category	Spontaneous Seek.				Provoked Seek.				Unsuccessful Avoid.				Non-Stress-Seeking			
	Fr.	Ital.	Ger.	Greece	Fr.	Ital.	Ger.	Greece	Fr.	Ital.	Ger.	Greece	Fr.	Ital.	Ger.	Greece
Very successful	10	13	32	16	11	0	7	1	0	0	1	1	52	3	2	6
Moderately successful	6	20	18	11	21	1	6	4	3	2	4	2	36	7	5	3
Neither successful nor unsuccessful	0	10	8	3	1	0	14	2	0	0	2	2	4	21	7	4
Unsuccessful but survived	4	20	21	4	9	4	12	1	8	4	8	0	11	48	8	0
Killed, destroyed	0	7	4	3	3	0	1	0	1	1	2	2	8	4	1	1
Supportive environment	4	33	55	16	5	1	22	2	5	3	10	2	18	24	17	4
Oppositional environment	10	24	38	13	33	2	25	5	6	4	9	4	49	12	5	1
Return to an earlier, less stressful state	2	16	23	3	3	0	12	1	0	1	2	3	8	2	5	4

Sample Sizes: France, 188; Italy, 165; Germany, 163; Greece, 64

American groups are remarkably similar, especially if the two success categories are collapsed into one category and the two failure categories are combined to form another. Doing this compensates for the definitely conservative trend of the Canadian stories. About 23 per cent of the Canadian stories fell in the highest and lowest success categories, compared with 41, 40 and 41.6 per cent for the Minnesota, Georgia, and Puerto Rican groups.

In the data for the four minority subcultures in Table 2, the Navajos appear to be characterized by the neutral neither successful nor unsuccessful category. Again, this is in contrast to the Zuñis, who tended strongly to avoid the neutral category, about one half describing their heroes as successful and the other half describing theirs as unsuccessful. A larger proportion of the Zuñi heroes than any other group's met with death or destruction. The Chippewas are the conservatives among the minority subcultures, with only 14.2 per cent of their stories describing either a high level of success or failure. The Mexican-American heroes more frequently than the heroes of the other three minority groups achieved outstanding success.

The degree of success attributed to their heroes by the French, Italian, German, and Greek authors is shown in Table 3. The French heroes tended to be successful more frequently than those of any of the other eleven subcultures, with the Greek heroes coming second. The French children are also characterized by their rather extreme avoidance of the neutral category. The Italian heroes have a greater proclivity for failure with survival than those of any of the others. The German heroes also met failure rather frequently but about one half of them still achieved success, whereas only about 28 per cent of the Italian heroes achieved any degree of success. The Greek heroes encountered failure or death more frequently than those of any of the other eleven subcultures.

ENVIRONMENTAL RESPONSE

From Table 1, it would appear that the Puerto Rican heroes received the most support from their environment, with the Minnesota heroes ranking second and the Georgia heroes the lowest. The Canadian heroes tended to encounter opposition more frequently than the heroes of any of the other dominant subcultures.

As will be seen from the data in Table 2, the Navajo stories are characterized by the lowest level of general responsiveness (supportive plus oppositional) and the Zuñis by the highest level. Much of the responsiveness described by the Zuñi authors, however, is oppositional in nature. The Mexican-American authors also described a relatively high level of general responsiveness.

As seen in Table 3, the German stories are characterized by a higher level of general responsiveness than those of any of the other eleven groups. The Greek children also encountered a generally high level of responsiveness, both supportive and oppositional. The French and German heroes encountered opposition with about the same degree of frequency, almost 50 per cent in both cases.

REVERSION TO LOW STRESS LEVEL

Some educators working with disadvantaged groups such as the Chippewas, Zuñis, Navajos, and Mexican-Americans have complained that even those who have high levels of aspirations and achieve a relatively high degree of success give up successful careers in the cities to return to a low-key existence on the reservation or in the home community. The comparative data for the occurrence of a reversion to a lower level of stress reported in the stories from each of the twelve subcultures are contained in Tables 1 through 3. The Puerto Rican, Chippewa, and German stories rate a high overall level of reversion to a low-key existence and the French, Navajo, and Zuñi accounts rate a low level of such reversion. These results must be interpreted with reference to the cross tabulations. Few of the French heroes reverted to a low level of stress because so few of them encountered stress. The French culture appears to have a high level of tolerance for divergency and being different tends not to be perceived as stressful by the French authors. The Navajo heroes avoided stress and were perceived as neither successful nor unsuccessful. The Zuñis, however, have quite different patterns. The Zuñi heroes tended to be self-acting and frequently encountered both opposition and support. Each of the three subcultures having a high level of reversion to a low-key existence are characterized by stories reflecting high levels of opposition, rejection, ridicule, and hostility.

HIGH ACHIEVERS AND POTENTIAL DROPOUTS

The data concerning the nature of the stress-seeking efforts of the main characters in the stories of the high achievers, potential dropouts, and unselected children from a single urban area (Minneapolis, Minnesota) are shown in Table 4. Chi-square analysis indicates that the differences among the three groups are statistically significant at better than the .01 level. The high achievers more frequently than either of the other two groups reported stress-seeking efforts that are spontaneous and in response to internal forces or challenge. All three groups are at about the same level in frequency of provoked stress-seeking in response to threat or other external pressures. The really striking difference, however, is in the extremely high frequency of non-stress-seeking among the low achievers, the potential dropouts.

The results of the chi-square analysis of the degree of success of the main character indicate that the differences among the three groups are significant at better than the .01 level of confidence. The differences are especially striking on the "very successful" and "unsuccessful but survived" categories, the high achievers anticipating the most success and least failure and the low achievers anticipating less high-level success and the most failure.

The results of the analysis concerning the responsiveness of the environment indicate that the differences are statistically significant at better than the .01 level. It will be noted that the high achievers, compared with the low achievers and unselected subjects, perceived more supportive and more oppositional response from the environment. While the results concerning the supportive response are stronger

Table 4

Summary of Classifications of Imaginative Stories by High-Achieving, Low-Achieving, and Unselected Preadolescents in Minneapolis, Minnesota, Area

Category	Spontaneous Seek.			Provoked Seek.			Unsuccessful Avoid.			Non-Stress-Seeking		
	High	Low	Unsel.	High	Low	Unsel.	High	Low	Unsel.	High	Low	Unsel.
Very successful	97	6	41	15	1	11	0	0	8	4	1	4
Moderately successful	12	6	34	1	2	11	1	0	7	2	5	2
Neither successful nor unsuccessful	5	3	18	2	0	3	0	0	0	0	5	6
Unsuccessful but survived	16	6	29	4	1	5	1	5	4	1	21	5
Killed, destroyed	10	1	16	0	3	0	0	5	1	0	2	1
Supportive environment	96	9	47	11	3	13	2	1	5	2	2	7
Oppositional environment	53	5	36	11	4	4	1	5	4	0	2	4
Return to an earlier, less stressful state	25	5	26	15	1	9	0	0	5	4	2	3

Sample Sizes: High Achievers, 171; Low Achievers (Potential Dropouts), 70; Unselected, 200 than those for the oppositional response, the latter results are statistically significant.

DISCUSSION

The results related to different levels of achievement support the hypothesis that stress-seeking tendencies are involved in high achievement and that non-stress-seeking is characteristic of low achievers. These results can now be used as a backdrop in searching for meaning in the results obtained for each of the twelve subcultures.

THE DOMINANT UNITED STATES CULTURE

The results obtained from the analysis of the Minneapolis, Minnesota, and the Brunswick, Georgia, samples are in most respects similar and might well be pooled to derive a set of results that could be assumed to represent the dominant culture of the United States. This culture emerges as high-stress-seeking, among the highest of those studied. Its dominant ideal seems to emphasize the self-acting nature of the organism. Anticipations of success are also relatively high, but this culture does not emerge quite as the success-oriented culture many analysts have maintained. About one third of the stories described some kind of failure for the hero. This may be due, however, to the fact that their heroes manifested divergent behavior and did not conform to social expectations or norms. At least the Minnesota environment comes off as a moderately responsive and supportive subculture. The Georgia subculture, however, ranks as one of the least responsive of those studied. This is interesting in the light of the strong tendency to make heroes self-acting and responsive to internal forces and challenge.

TORONTO, A CANADIAN SUBCULTURE

Although the Toronto stories are in many ways similar to those of the Minnesota and Georgia ones, they display some characteristic differences that suggest somewhat dif-

ferent behaviors are encouraged and discouraged. The Toronto subculture emerged as only moderately stress-seeking
and largely in response to threat and other external pressures. The self-acting nature of the hero was not greatly
emphasized. This subculture is unusually conservative and
seems to abhor extremes insofar as success and failure are
concerned. It is a moderately responsive subculture with
somewhat more opposition than supportiveness. There is
relatively little return to a lower level of stress, perhaps
because of the dominant conservatism of not ever having
gone to an extreme.

This picture agrees rather well with other studies of this
subculture (Seeley, Sim, and Loosley, 1956; Karoussos,
1961). As one reads a study such as *Crestwood Heights,* an
examination of a Toronto suburb, he gains the impression
that he might be reading about some Minneapolis suburb
or another suburban area in the United States. Everywhere,
however, there seems to be a great concern about social
standards, the avoidance of extremes, and conservatism
about the adoption of innovations. The author and other
innovative educators have been invited frequently to Toronto to present their educational ideas to educational leaders. They have been heard with much respect and treated
with hospitality, but it is my impression that there has been
little experimentation with these ideas. One fellow psychologist, when I initiated my cross-cultural studies of creative
development, volunteered to administer tests of creative
thinking ability to a sample of children in the Crestwood
Heights schools from grades one through six, and to collect
other supporting data. All testing materials were shipped to
the psychologist but he never gained acceptance of the testing and he has used the materials only in his own clinical
work with individual children or small groups. On a visit
some years later to Toronto schools, I was told by a high-
school official that they had been interested but they did
not think that they had had enough experience with the
tests of creative thinking to justify their use.

The authors of *Crestwood Heights* describe high-school
students there as "exhibiting a fear of anything serious or
controversial coming up in class and value above all cau-

tious good manners and the cool approach." The authors also show how both parents look to the school to mediate in their own struggles and to compensate for their own ambivalences. The authors report that even the nursery schools seek to help the child take his cues from the group rather than from his own predilections and inclinations. Thus we see the stories of preadolescents rather lacking in self-acting heroes who respond to internal forces and challenge.

UPPER-MIDDLE-CLASS PUERTO RICAN SUBCULTURE

Just as the Toronto subculture emerged as one of the most conservative in stress-seeking, the Puerto Rican emerged as one of the most extreme. It ranks among the highest in spontaneous stress-seeking in response to challenge and internal forces but also ranks among the highest in successful stress avoidance. The dominant orientation is one of success but is well tempered with expectations of failure. The environment is pictured as being quite responsive and predominantly supportive.

Again, this picture seems to fit rather well recent cross-cultural studies involving upper-middle-class Puerto Ricans. Green (1960), for example, reported that when they migrate they take with them their major areas of strength and conflict and that they are strong in the continuities of encouragement, their extensive social relationships, and their ideals of fatalism and acceptance. Field, Maldonade, Wallace, Bodarky, and Coelho (1962) reported that although previous studies had shown that Puerto Ricans compared with United States subjects are less autonomous, independent, and self-directed, recent forces have changed this direction. They point out that certain forces have been upsetting both the Puerto Rican dependency and the United States independence or autonomy.

RIMROCK NAVAJO SUBCULTURE

The stories of the Rimrock Navajo children paint this subculture as exceptionally low in stress-seeking and reflect a strong belief in the receptiveness of the organism. The heroes in the Navajo stories tended to be neither successful nor unsuccessful and experienced little responsiveness from their environment, either supportive or oppositional. There was little reversion to a low-key existence because there had been little stress-seeking.

The Rimrock Navajos have been studied rather thoroughly by anthropologists, one of the more thorough and recent studies being one by Kluckhohn and Strodtbeck published in 1961 at about the time the imaginative stories were written. The history of the Rimrock Navajo is one of failure to achieve success. They have gradually been pushed back onto extremely unproductive land. Their ceremonials are predominantly curing ceremonials and otherwise have to do with the day-to-day problems of warding off disaster. The fact that they are extremely concrete-minded in thought and expression may explain some of their reluctance to engage in fantasies about flying monkeys and roarless lions. A rather large proportion of the Navajo stories could not be included in this study because they simply said that there could be no flying monkeys or roarless lions. The lack of responsiveness in the environment is reflected in the Kluckhohn and Strodtbeck finding that the most unfavorable judgment that one Navajo can pass on another is to say, "He acts as if he didn't have any relatives." Kluckhohn and Strodtbeck describe much in the Rimrock Navajo subculture that conspires against change and stress-seeking. It remains to be seen how this subculture will change in response to programs initiated during recent years.

ZUÑI SUBCULTURE

The analyses of the stories of the Zuñi children present a very different picture from those of the Rimrock Navajos. Their heroes are pictured as rather stress-seeking and self-acting but somewhat failure-prone. In about 48 per cent of their stories, the hero achieved some degree of success. The environment was depicted as a rather responsive one; they expected opposition about twice as frequently as a supportive response, however.

The Zuñi, like the Rimrock Navajo, have been the object of considerable study. The very fact that recent studies such as those of Kluckhohn and Strodtbeck (1961) are at variance in some respects to earlier studies indicates that they have been changing, and this is in harmony with the picture of the Zuñi heroes as stress-seeking and self-acting. Beneath what Ruth Benedict (1934) has called the Apollonian culture of the Zuñis, recent investigators find a considerable amount of strife and friction. Marriages are easily and often dissolved. Their cultural isolation continues and investigators find it difficult to establish rapport with them. Their surface friendliness seems to mask a strong and stubborn rejection. The Zuñis have long lived in a hostile natural and social environment, so it is natural that the stories of their children would be characterized by a relatively high degree of opposition, rejection, and ridicule and a relatively high level of failure expectations. In fact, it is remarkable that their heroes are as stress-seeking and self-acting as they are. This, too, is in harmony with other findings; their culture has been steadily augmented by diverse cultural elements through the operation of amalgamation, diffusion, and acculturation. They are also described as having an activity orientation (Kluckhohn and Strodtbeck, 1961, p. 306). An important underlying theme of the Zuñi is that life can be hard, but their harmony-with-nature and subjugation-to-nature orientations seem to be changing. Today they listen to radios, attend movies, send their young men to the military services, and educate their children in modern schools.

MINNESOTA CHIPPEWA SUBCULTURE

The Minnesota Chippewa subculture emerged as about midway between the Rimrock Navajo and Zuñi subcultures both in stress-seeking and responsiveness. They ranked, however, as one of the most conservative groups, expecting neither a high degree of success nor an extreme degree of failure, and ranked high on reversion to a low level of stress.

This characterization of the Chippewa subculture is in

harmony with those of anthropologists (Barnouw, 1950; Hilger, 1951). Barnouw characterized them as suspicious of others, spiritually isolated, fearful, and undemonstrative in affection. Divergent behavior is strongly discouraged and there seem to be few problems of delinquency and non-conformity, according to Dunning (1959). In view of the large number of taboos and restrictions on behavior, the conservatism of the Chippewa children's heroes is to be expected. They also have attitudes and practices that discourage children from outstanding achievement ("becoming something special"). According to Hilger (1951), Chippewa education emphasizes conformity to conventional tribal standards, the mental content of the tribal cultural pattern, and customs and beliefs concerning religion, health, politics, economics, and social life.

MEXICAN-AMERICAN SUBCULTURE

The Mexican-American pattern of responses is surprisingly similar to that of the two dominant United States subcultures. Their heroes are predominantly self-acting and stress-seeking, responding to challenge and internal forces. Their success orientation is rather strong and the environment is described as responsive, providing both support and opposition with almost equal frequency. Their heroes experienced only a moderate degree of reversion to a lower level of stress.

It is interesting that the immigrant Mexican-American group is more similar to the dominant United States pattern than are the native minority groups. It may be that the Mexican migrants, like the dominant groups that settled the United States, in immigrating are rather stress-seeking, self-acting, and success-oriented.

FRENCH SUBCULTURE

In this study the French subculture emerged as pleasure-seeking (eustress rather than dys-stress). Just as the French children had no difficulty in playing with the idea of a flying monkey or a roarless lion, their heroes successfully avoided distress and found pleasure. Their success orientation is the highest of the twelve subcultures examined. This is especially remarkable in the light of their high degree of stress avoidance and the high frequency with which their heroes experience opposition.

While France may have declined in military strength, economic position, and political position, it is generally recognized that there has been no decline in French ideas (Park, 1954). French cultural ideas seem to be as original and challenging as ever. The Frenchman's passion for individual rights, respect for human equality, and critical spirit are well known. Although the French literature of defeat is enormous, there is almost boundless idealism, nervous energy, independence of thought, and originality. There seems to be much diversity in French education. According to Park (1954), the elementary student wastes no time in getting down to fundamentals. This is reflected in their stories in this study; there were no wasted explanations that there could be no flying monkey or roarless lion. The theoretical seems to take precedence over the empirical and experimental. This intellectual trend is reflected in their stories in the ease with which they do suppositional thinking.

ITALIAN SUBCULTURE

The main characters of the Italian stories proved to be among the least stress-seeking of the subcultures in this study. Their characters, however, seemed to be self-acting, either seeking stress or successfully avoiding it. Their heroes were often unsuccessful but managed to survive; very few of them were killed and few of them achieved great success. Their environment was perceived as moderately responsive and somewhat more supportive than oppositional.

This portrait is in most respects in harmony with the one derived by others. In an independent analysis of the imaginative stories used in the present study, Panzica (1965) compared the concepts concerning divergent behavior of the Italian stories with a Boston, Massachusetts, sample. He found the Italian stories to be characterized by reluctance of self-expression, avoidance of suppositional thinking, and expression of hostility as a form of pressure against divergency, as well as skeptical of the value of divergent behavior and rather concerned about the causes of divergency.

Barzini's (1964) popular characterization of Italians attempts to debunk some of the commonly held concepts of them, and his characterizations seem to be more in harmony with those derived from the imaginative stories than do commonly held ideas. He maintains that Italians are not individualistic but that they serve loyally their own organizations and conform to the behavioral norms of their families. Barzini maintains that Italians find it easy to weave in and out of political parties, conceal their thoughts, accept and repeat the current official ideas, because they want to avoid risk. He sees these as survival skills in all insecure societies. Mastrocinque (1964) calls attention to the fact that although Italian boys are "waited on hand and foot" by their mothers and can do nothing for themselves, they often get along better than their counterparts in other cultures, who are always battling reality (seeking stress). He maintains that these youths manage all their lives to latch onto someone who will take the place of the solicitous mama.

BERLIN, GERMANY, SUBCULTURE

If not stress-seeking, the heroes of the German stories were certainly stress-encountering, much more so than any of the other European groups. They were rarely able to avoid stress. They are divided, however, between the self-acting and receptive nature of their heroes. About 35 per cent of their heroes encountered external stress and 51 per cent were pictured as self-acting. They are also about equally divided between success and failure orientations. The environment emerged as the most responsive of the twelve subcultures studied, being both highly supportive and highly oppositional. The German hero is frequently seen as returning to a lower level of stress.

In a study of German national character, Métraux (1955a) concluded that one of the major purposes of early-childhood education in Germany is "to armor the child to face the battle of life." Another purpose is to prepare him to fulfill his life tasks. Parents are urged to prepare the child to meet the challenges of life. One theme that permeates German child-rearing literature is that the child must learn to obey so that he can be trusted to be alone without endangering himself and master the tasks set by life. A second theme is that the child must learn autonomy in order to face life independently of others and enter into relationships with them. Another theme is that the child must be loved and protected from danger, but must not be spoiled or weakened by overprotection—thus, the unusually high supportiveness and opposition of the environment suggested in the German stories.

This picture of child-rearing practices is supported by my own study (Torrance, 1963) of creative development among Berlin children. During the first three grades the Berlin children lagged well behind their United States comparison group in originality. In the fourth grade, the Berlin children began an upward surge at a time when their United States counterparts showed a decrease. In the fifth grade, the Berlin children forged ahead of their United States counterparts.

According to Métraux's study (1955a), the German child is trained to expect difficulties, pain, failure, and opposition. Much emphasis is placed upon stages of development and strict sequences of learning tasks. In German child-care literature (Métraux, 1955b), parents are repeatedly told that every misdeed must be followed by punishment and that punishment should be appropriate to the misdeed.

Responses from ninety-three Berlin teachers to the Ideal Pupil Checklist (Torrance, 1965a) indicate strongest encouragement for attempting difficult tasks, curiosity, independence in judgment, independence in thinking, industriousness, self-confidence, sense of humor, sincerity, adventurousness, and promptness. They discourage most strongly such characteristics as disturbing classroom organization and procedures, expressing strong emotion, fault-finding, haughtiness, negativism, occasional regression, stubbornness, talkativeness, and timidity.

ATHENS, GREECE, SUBCULTURE

Of the European subcultures, the Athenians came out as the most stress-seeking in response to internal forces and challenge. At the same time, there was a moderate frequency of successful stress avoidance. The big difference between the stories of the Athenians and those of the Berliners is that the former were far less concerned with threat, external pressure, and abortive attempts to avoid stress. About 35 per cent of the Berlin, compared with 20 per cent of the Athens stories, used this theme. The Greek heroes were pictured as being quite successful. The responsiveness of the environment was also described as being high, divided about equally between supportiveness and opposition.

Anthropologists (Benedict, 1934; Kluckhohn and Strodtbeck, 1961) have referred to both Greek and Zuñi cultures as Apollonian, and it is interesting to note that these two cultures emerged as similar in many ways. Both pictured their heroes as self-acting and stress-seeking. The Greek heroes, however, failed less frequently than did the Zuñi heroes. Both encountered responsive environments, but the Zuñi heroes encountered a predominance of opposition, while the Greek heroes enjoyed a slight predominance of supportiveness, and there was less of the "do or die" element in the Greek stories. Benedict (1934) pointed out that Apollonian institutions had been carried out much further in the Zuñi pueblos than in Greece. According to her, the Greeks did not ever carry out the distrust of individualism that the Apollonian way of life implies.

Modern observers of Greek culture (MacVeagh, 1955; Theotokas, 1955; Reifenberg, 1957) refer frequently to the camaraderie, love of life, confidence in and respect for human dignity, generosity, helpfulness, and individuality of the Greek personality. Rodocanachi (1955) points out that education in Greece was never a question of merely learning facts. Disputation, thought and the expression of thought, argument and gesticulation are everywhere. The Greek is pictured as having a passion for truth but as not being fanatic.

The classical Greek spirit, according to Theotokas (1955), acknowledged man's ignorance and limitations. Nature was seen as being in harmony with man and as yielding the center of the universe to him. The Greek was described as easily capable of heroism and self-sacrifice when fighting for freedom, but he wants to know for what he is fighting and convince himself that the cause is just. Carey (1962) comments that Athens remains the symbol of the academic man and stands for reason, analysis, objectivity, and the truth of research and experiment.

LIMITATIONS OF THE STUDY

The limitations of this study are freely acknowledged. The data rest their claims for validity on the projective hypothesis and consistency checks against what is known about the subcultures under study. The review of what is known is incomplete, sketchy, and more superficial than the author would like. The samples leave much to be desired in both size and representativeness. In most cases, however, the samples were drawn randomly from larger samples of stories. It is believed, however, that the stories in our samples catch the spirit of their respective cultures. One would be more concerned if he were striving for precision. Since rather gross phenomena are examined, however, this limitation is not quite so serious.

CONCLUSION

There seems to be justification for the assumption that stress-seeking is an individual difference, varying in degree and nature within a given culture or subculture and from one culture or subculture to another. From the data presented, a high-achieving culture or subculture requires a reasonably high number of self-acting, stress-seeking persons who have reasonable expectations of success and a

highly responsive environment that supplies both supportive and oppositional reactions to stress-seeking.

REFERENCES

Barnouw, V. "Acculturation and Personality among the Wisconsin Chippewa," *American Anthropologist,* Vol. 52 (1950),
pp. 19–27.

Barron, F. "Some Relationships between Originality and Style
of Personality," *American Psychologist,* Vol. 9 (1954),
p. 326.

Barzini, L. *The Italians* (New York: Atheneum Publishers,
1964).

Benedict, R. *Patterns of Culture* (Boston: Houghton Mifflin
Company, 1934).

Carey, J. J. "Jerusalem and Athens: The Religious Worker on
the College Campus," *Personnel and Guidance Journal,* Vol.
40 (1962), pp. 426–31.

Cox, C. M. *Genetic Studies of Genius: Vol. II, The Early Mental
Traits of Three Hundred Geniuses* (Stanford, Calif.: Stanford
University Press, 1926).

Dunning, R. W. *Social and Economic Change among the
Northern Ojibwa* (Toronto: University of Toronto Press,
1959).

Field, P. B.; Maldonade, E. D.; Wallace, S. E.; Bodarky, C. J.;
and Coelho, G. V. "An Other-Directed Fantasy in a Puerto
Rican," *Journal of Social Psychology,* Vol. 58 (1962), pp.
43–60.

Goertzel, V. and M. G. *Cradles of Eminence* (Boston: Little,
Brown & Company, 1962).

Green, H. B. "Comparison of Nurturance and Independence
Training in Jamaica and Puerto Rico, with Consideration of
Resulting Personality Structure and Transplanted Social Patterns," *Journal of Social Psychology,* Vol. 51 (1960), pp.
27–63.

Hilger, Sister M. I. *Chippewa Child Life and Its Cultural Background* (Smithsonian Institution Bureau of American Ethnol-
ogy Bulletin 146; Washington, D.C.: Government Printing
Office, 1951).

Jahoda, G. "Child Animism: I. A Critical Survey of Cross-
Cultural Research," *Journal of Social Psychology,* Vol. 47
(1958), pp. 197–212.

Karoussos, J. "A Comparative Study of Originality of Thinking
and Concepts of Divergency in Imaginative Stories by Greek,
Toronto, and Twin Cities Children" (Master's research paper,
University of Minnesota, Minneapolis, 1961).

Kluckhohn, F., and Strodtbeck, F. *Variations in Value Orientations* (New York: Harper & Row, 1961).

McClelland, D. C. *The Achieving Society* (Princeton, N.J.: D. Van Nostrand Company, Inc., 1961).

MacKinnon, D. W. (ed.). *The Creative Person* (Berkeley, Calif.: University of California, University Extension, (1961).

MacVeagh, L. "Introduction to Perspectives of Greece," *Atlantic Monthly,* Vol. 195 (June 1955), p. 100.

Mastrocinque, S. "Life in a Matriarchy," *Atlas,* Vol. 7 (March 1964), pp. 170–71.

Mead, M., and Wolfenstein, M. (eds.). *Childhood in Contemporary Cultures* (Chicago: The University of Chicago Press, 1955).

Métraux, R. "Parents and Children: An Analysis of Contemporary German Child-Care and Youth-Guidance Literature," in M. Mead and M. Wolfenstein (eds.), *Childhood in Contemporary Cultures* (Chicago: The University of Chicago Press, 1955a), pp. 204–28.

———. "The Consequences of Wrongdoing: An Analysis of Story Completions by German Children," in M. Mead and M. Wolfenstein (eds.), *Childhood in Contemporary Cultures* (Chicago: The University of Chicago Press, 1955b), pp. 306–23.

Panzica, A. L. "A Comparative Study of Perception of Divergency in Imaginative Stories of Preadolescent Children in Italy and Massachusetts" (Master's research paper, University of Minnesota, Minneapolis, 1965).

Park, J. (ed.). *The Culture of France in Our Time* (Ithaca: Cornell University Press, 1954).

Reifenberg, B. "The New Generation," *Atlantic Monthly,* Vol. 199 (March 1957), pp. 174–78.

Rodocanachi, C. P. "Eternal Athens," *Atlantic Monthly,* Vol. 195 (June 1955), pp. 120–25.

Runner, K. and H. *Manual for the Runner Studies of Attitude Patterns* (Golden, Colo.: Runner Associates, 1965).

Seeley, J. R.; Sim, R. A.; and Loosley, E. W. *Crestwood Heights* (New York: Basic Books, Inc., 1956).

Simpson, R. M. "Creative Imagination," *American Journal of Psychology,* Vol. 33 (1922), pp. 234–43.

Theotokas, G. "The Modern Greeks," *Atlantic Monthly,* Vol. 195 (June 1955), pp. 101–5.

Torrance, E. P. *Education and the Creative Potential* (Minneapolis: University of Minnesota Press, 1963).

———. *Role of Evaluation in Creative Thinking* (Minneapolis: Bureau of Educational Research, University of Minnesota, 1964).

———. *Rewarding Creative Behavior* (Englewood Cliffs, N.J.: Prentice-Hall, Inc., 1965a).

———. *Gifted Children in the Classroom* (New York: The Macmillan Co., 1965b).

Torrance, E. P. "Different Ways of Learning for Different Kinds of Children," in E. P. Torrance and R. D. Strom (eds.), *Mental Health and Achievement* (New York: John Wiley & Sons, Inc., 1965c), pp. 253–62.

———. *Preliminary Guide for Scoring Dot-Squares Test for Originality* (Minneapolis: Minnesota Studies of Creative Behavior, University of Minnesota, 1965d), mimeographed.

———. "History of the Concept 'Guided Learning' and Its Applications in Teaching for Creative Development," in R. H. Ojemann and K. Pritchett (eds.), *Giving Emphasis to Guided Learning* (Cleveland: Educational Research Council of Greater Cleveland, 1966), pp. 6–37.

———, and Dauw, D. C. "Attitude Patterns of Creatively Gifted High School Seniors," *Gifted Child Quarterly*, Vol. 10 (1966), pp. 53–57.

———; Rush, C. H., Jr.; Kohn, H. B.; and Doughty, J. M. *Factors in Fighter-Interceptor Pilot Combat Effectiveness* (Lackland Air Force Base, Tex.: Air Force Personnel and Training Research Center, 1957).

APPENDIX
ILLUSTRATIVE STORIES AND SCORING

Canadian (Toronto)
THE HORSE THAT WOULD NOT RUN

Once upon a time (as all good stories begin) there was a horse. He was a white horse and his master's name was Tom. Tom was a very good master and he liked his horse very much. One day Tom went to ride his horse. He saddled it and got on, slapped the horse on the back and said, "Giddp" but the horse did not go. He wondered what to do but if the horse did not go he said to himself, "I might as well not make him." He went in the house and got some oatmeal then he went out and sprinkled some on the barn floor. The chicks and ducks ran for the oatmeal and when it was finished all the ducks left except one little duck who did not get any. He started to cry. The horse who was lying down said, "Why do you cry, little duck?" The duck said, "I cry because (sniff) all the bigger ducks get to the oatmeal before I do then I do not get any."

"Well," said the horse, "Your're not the only one who has troubles. I do not like to tell anybody but I (sniff, sniff) I have rheumatism," and he burst out crying, "and I don't like it, it hurts."

That night when Tom came to comb the horse the horse said, "You know that little duck in the yard." "Yes.", said Tom, "I know him."

"Well, he isn't getting enough to eat."

"Well, it looks like I'll have to feed him separate from the other," and he did.

The duck (being a wise, nice, duck) told about the horse's rheumatism and, as all good stories end, they lived happily ever after.

Scoring: A. Avoidance of stress-seeking; B. Very successful, constructive; C. Supportive.

Chippewas (Red Lake, Minnesota, Reservation)

THE FLYING MONKEY

This is a story about a monkey that wanted to fly. He seen birds fly by and thought, "How nice it would be to fly." He kept wishing and finally his wish came true. He loved to fly after he had wings.

Other animals wondered how he got wings and asked, "How did you get wings." He said, "Wish and you will see." But one day he got tired of flying. He wished he wouldn't have got wings. He wished and wished and finally he didn't have wings. And never wished for anything again.

Scoring: A. Spontaneous, response to inner forces; B. Moderate success, constructive; C. Return to low-key, supportive environment.

Dropouts, Potential (Minneapolis, Minnesota)

THE DOG THAT WON'T FIGHT

The dog won't fight because he is chicken, so I took him to the doctor and he said he won't fight because he don't have a wife. So they got him a wife and every time he seen a cat or a dog he would fight them. And then one day he had a fight with a wolf and the wolf killed him and now he won't ever fight any more.

Scoring: A. Provoked, response to external forces; B. Death; C. Supportive and oppositional.

France (*Paris and Roanne*)

THE FLYING MONKEY

The flying monkey had two small wings covered with beautiful blue fur. He belonged to a little girl whose name was Mimi.

During lunch he used to fly very near the ceiling.

One day he was tired of flying and plop! There he was right in Mimi's chair. All of the thick soup was stuck to his tail. Then, he jumped all over and the next day, there wasn't a corner that wasn't covered with soup. Then Mimi gives him a good swift kick in the behind and he went back, sitting on the clock.

But Mimi caught him and caressed him. Then she put a nightcap on him. Which could be quite amusing.

Scoring: A. Spontaneous, response to inner forces; B. Moderately successful; C. Supportive and oppositional.

Georgia (*Brunswick*)

THE FLYING MONKEY

Once there was a monkey; his name is Jimmy. Jimmy lives in a New York zoo. His mother was a big one. The man in the zoo brought him a toy airplane. He said, "It flys." The little monkey wanted to fly. So the man built him a little airplane for him to learn to fly. Jimmy liked the airplane so he named it the Big Red, White and Blue Bird. He liked to fly. But mother said, "You will have to go to school sometime."

Scoring: A. Spontaneous, response to challenge; B. Very successful; C. Supportive.

Germany (*Berlin*)

THE FLYING MONKEY

Once when I was in a zoo, I was very surprised to see a monkey flying back and forth in his cage. The attendant came to see what was going on. But when he opened the door of the cage, the monkey flew out. The attendant was beside himself and called and called. But the monkey just flew about and did tricks. He flew up into a tree. The attendant got a ladder and then climbed up the tree. The monkey moved the ladder and threw the attendant to the ground; then he flew away.

The guard was determined to catch the monkey and ran after him. But the monkey thought to himself, "Since I'm free now, I'm going to stay that way."

But the attendant had other ideas and still ran along on the ground below. The monkey flew back to his cage. The guard thought he was inside and ran in. But the monkey, who had stayed outside, slammed the door. Then he flew away.

The warder was caught, and when he was finally let out an hour later the monkey was long gone over the mountains. After a couple of years, he felt he was safe at last.

Scoring: A. Spontaneous, response to challenge; B. Very successful; C. Oppositional.

Greece (*Athens*)

THE FLYING MONKEY

We are in a forest where different animals—squirrels, rabbits, deer, etc., but not beasts—are living. Among them is a monkey. It is surprising how he was found here, because all the monkeys live in jungles. These animals talked to one another and they wanted to have a newspaper, as men have, in order to learn the news of the forest. They assigned the monkey as their reporter but he could not get the job done. He got an assistant who didn't help him very much, so he thought he would buy a couple of wings and he fastened them on his body by wax like Daedalus and Icarus did in the olden times. He really solved his problem and he did his job very well. One time the animals read in the newspaper that a witch was around the forest and they were all terrified, so they stayed close in their dens. The monkey was hidden on a tree looking for the witch. When she appeared he jumped on her and hurt her, but the witch finally killed him and disappeared. The other animals buried him and put on his tomb the following sign: "Here is buried the flying monkey."

Scoring: A. Spontaneous, response to challenge; B. Death; C. Supportive.

High Achievers (*Minneapolis, Minnesota*)

THE FLYING MONKEY

Once there was a winged monkey. He was very smart. He invented a jet propelled rocket cylinder. He gave other winged monkeys the same thing. They built air fields all over the world. They built control towers and installed miniature radios, so they could talk to other airfields. They built their own big society.

Scoring: A. Spontaneous, response to inner forces; B. Very successful; C. Supportive response from environment.

Italy (*Milan and Turin*)

THE FLYING MONKEY

Once upon a time in the time of the Gods there was a monkey and a hawk and one day Jove the king of the gods held a meeting in his palace for the animals in order to obtain a wish. At that meeting there were animals of all sizes. After more than three hours it was the turn of a monkey and she said she was tired of walking and asked him if instead of hands he could make her a pair of wings, and Jove consented and pronounced a magic word, and suddenly instead of hands there appeared two fine wings, the monkey thanked him and flew away.

After many animals came the turn of a hawk who complained about his wings so Jove instead of wings give him a pair of legs. After two or three years the monkey began to complain because she didn't have any hands and couldn't eat bananas. And the hawk was complaining because he felt homesick for the fine mountaintops. When Jove heard those laments he summoned the monkey and the hawk who explained their repentance, the one explained that he couldn't eat bananas anymore and the other could not go on the mountaintops. So Jove gave the hawk back his wings and as soon as he saw that he was able to fly he flew off without even thanking, and to the monkey made the wings disappear and a pair of hands return, but the monkey told him that with hands alone she could leap between one tree and another, as if she was flying, and Jove gave her a prehensile tail, so with that tail she could hang onto the trees. In fact monkeys can still jump from one tree to another.

Scoring: A. Spontaneous, in response to inner forces; B. Failure but survived; C. Supportive; return to lower key.

Mexican-Americans (*California and Texas*)
THE MONKEY WHO COULD FLY

Once upon a time there lived in a jungle a baby monkey. This was no ordinary monkey. This monkey could really truly fly. You see his father was captured by some Americans. The Americans took him to a zoo. There he met a very beautiful bird. This bird was called a peacock. Well, one day the monkey got homesick. So the peacock gave the monkey one of the feathers. The peacock said that the feather was magic and that anyone who touched the feather could fly. So the monkey touched the feather and flew away. After some time the monkey came home. The monkey's wife had a baby. The father took very good care of this baby. Then the baby monkey grew very fast. The father told his story to his little son. The father took the feather to touch his son with it. Then the baby started to fly.

Scoring: A. Provoked, response to threat; B. Very successful; C. Supportive and oppositional.

Minnesota (*Minneapolis and Suburbs*)
A DOG WHO WOULDN'T FIGHT

Once there was a dog who wouldn't fight with cats. All he did was have tea parties. Until one day they decided to fight because it was no fun being friends. So the next day they would fight all day. At the end of the day they were so sore from fighting they promised never to fight again, and they didn't.

Scoring: A. Spontaneous, response to inner forces; B. Neither successful nor unsuccessful; C. Return to low key.

Navajos (*New Mexico*)
THE FLYING MONKEY

There was once a monkey who lived in Africa. He was a monkey that would fly around ever where he went. This all started when an old monkey came to visit him.

The old monkey ask him to make one wish. So the monkey thought and thought about what he wanted so finally he decided to wish to fly.

Her wish came true. So off he went flying through the jungle. All the other animals were afraid of him. They called him the Flying Monkey. He like to fly around. He soon did not have any more friends because they all were afraid of him. He felt very lonely. So he wish to get rid of flying around. He wanted all his friends back. So the old monkey visit him again. He told him that he wanted to be like the other monkeys. So he got to be himself again. His friends all came back. He was very glad about it. So he never wished to fly again.

Scoring: A. Spontaneous, response to challenge; B. Very successful; C. Supportive and oppositional; return to low key.

Puerto Rico (San Juan, Upper and Upper-Middle Class)
THE FLYING MONKEY

Once upon a time in Africa there were many species of monkeys. One day a monkey was seated on a rock crying. All of a sudden a beautiful fairy appeared out of the darkness. "Why are you crying, monkey?" "I want to have wings." "I will give them to you because you are well behaved." "Give them to me, lovely fairy." The monkey went out into space with his wings. On the way he met another fairy and she said to him, "How happy you look; ask a wish of me." "I asked for a princess, a palace, chickens, dogs." The fairy shrieked loudly. The fairy went away and punished the monkey, leaving him to live on the earth. Poor monkey. He was very sad.

Scoring: A. Spontaneous, response to internal forces; B. Failed but survived; C. Supportive and oppositional.

Zuñis (New Mexico)
THE FLYING MONKEY

One day the monkey got out of the zoo, and came to a place where they help sick people. Then the monkey came in and took some pills. The monkey jumped up and down. The next morning the monkey was sick. He ate some bananas but he wasn't feeling better. Then he took some pills out of the red box where the pills were. He started to jump and then the monkey flew. They shot the monkey but the monkey was flying faster and faster. The monkey didn't know how to stop. He came to a building; he went right through the building. He was taking more pills; then he came bigger and bigger. His wings were small. Then he fell down. The monkey died because he fell down three miles from the sky.

Scoring: A. Spontaneous, response to inner forces; B. Died; C. Supportive.

Stress-seeking and the Legal Order

Richard A. Falk

In "The Relations of Law to Culture, Power, and Justice," Richard A. Falk complained that legal theorists were spending too much time on problems presented by clients. These are by and large straightforward, mundane problems arising out of existing legislation—problems of antitrust law, or problems arising from the economics of competition. Lawyers are not spending enough time in judicial creativity. They should be concerned more deeply with law in relation to societal fulfillment, law as an instrument in promoting social justice. This article pointed out such a direction by exploring the relationship between law and culture, the growth of law through formalization of norms, the tendency of legal systems to reinforce the prevailing power structure, and the ability of a legal system in a given cultural setting to promote the ideals of justice.

Law, Morality, and War in the Contemporary World put this concern into practice with respect to the law of nations. Richard Falk proposed some rules of thumb for discriminating between legitimate and nonlegitimate bases for resorting to international violence. A direct threat to the territory of a nation would, for instance, be considered a legitimate basis for armed defense and limited intervention by its allies.

Ultimately, he anticipates an international legal order that will reduce the force of national sovereignty. National sovereignty eventually may be limited through strengthening international courts and by extending the power of domestic courts to international relations. "The Complexity of Sabbatino" describes litigation in a domestic court in the United States between an American whose sugar had been expropriated in Cuba and the Banco Nacional de Cuba. The Supreme Court ruled that a domestic court may not deal with the expropriation of property within the territory of another nation. Richard Falk argues for the extension of the jurisdiction of a domestic court to cases of this type. In *The Role of Domestic Courts in*

the International Legal Order, he asks that domestic
courts give international law precedence over the foreign policy of the nation in which they are located. A
domestic court would thus have a dual function, both
as a national institution and as an agent of an emerging international legal order.

More recently, his activity with the World Law
Fund has led to the publication of a four-volume work,
The Strategy of World Order, jointly edited and written with Saul Mendlovitz. The volumes seek to explore
the problems of transition from a world of sovereign
states to a condition of limited world government.

In his contribution to the present symposium, Richard Falk treats the collective actor—the national society
—as a stress-seeker. From the societal point of view,
stress-seeking is a basic energy resource with no intrinsic social utility or disutility. It can be beneficial or
destructive. Law has the task of distinguishing between
these outcomes and establishing the framework for
beneficial expression of stress-seeking. A narrow interpretation that conceives of autonomous law as separated from politics cannot accomplish this. A more
sociological jurisprudence is needed in which law participates in the ongoing social and political process.
Domestically, such a framework for stress-seeking,
and its guidance toward beneficial ends, is provided
through regulatory techniques such as those contained
in antitrust legislation. In democratic societies, discontented groups may express grievances, and laws establish rules of the game which cite limits of permissible
stressful behavior. Law has been employed to channel
stress-seeking in international society. For it to be successful, conflicting parties would have to respect legal
norms, accept a principle of reciprocity, and accept the
legitimacy of international competition for dominance.
Within this framework, states may receive tacit authorization to employ violence to carry out such legislative or revisionist programs as have already been
accorded international sanction. This authorization
would be granted under rules of the game which limit
the type and scope of interventions and counterinter-
ventions. The institutionalization of such rules Richard
A. Falk terms "routinization of authorized coercion."

STRESS-SEEKING AND THE LEGAL ORDER:
SOME POSITIVE CORRELATIONS

This inquiry is directed at the role of law in maintaining the distinction between socially beneficial and socially destructive forms of stress-seeking behavior in various political systems. In particular, inquiry is directed toward characteristic differences between legal responses in relatively "open" political systems—those that tolerate the marketplace of ideas and provide procedures for peaceful change—and in relatively "closed" political systems—those that suppress political opposition.

Furthermore, attention is given to the legal responses to stress-seeking behavior in the context of relatively centralized political systems that exist in leading nation-states and in the context of the relatively decentralized political system that operates in international society. The purpose of these analytic distinctions is to emphasize the extent to which the role of law is dependent upon the political values and social structure that dominate its various arenas of action.

One other introductory point needs to be made. The ideal of social harmony is found throughout utopian literature, reflecting the belief that evidences of stress are disclosures of human and social inadequacy. Such a view denies any permanently beneficial role for stress-seeking behavior, and thereby appears to distort the subject. If stress-seeking is an integral aspect of human nature, then the serious line of nonutopian inquiry concerns not prospects for the elimination of stress-seeking, but the potentialities for increasing its socially beneficial expression.

I. The Relevance of Stress-seeking to the Operation of the Formal Legal System: An Illustration

On June 18, 1966, the International Court of Justice in
The Hague rendered a judgment in *The South West Africa
Cases* that appears to bear significantly on the relevance of
law as a social technique to the phenomenon of stress and
stress-seeking. By a closely divided vote of 8–7, the World
Court decided, after a remarkably lengthy proceeding, that
Ethiopia and Liberia did not possess the kind of legal
interest in the enforcement of the terms of the mandate
over the territory of South West Africa to challenge the
major policies pursued by South Africa in its role as the
administering authority.[1] Ethiopia and Liberia were interested especially in reestablishing the administrative supervision of the organized international community that South
Africa contended had lapsed with the dissolution of the
League of Nations, and in obtaining from the World Court
a finding that the imposition of *apartheid* on the life of the
territory was in direct violation of South Africa's basic
obligation under the mandate agreement to "promote to
the utmost the material and moral well-being and the social progress of the inhabitants."[2]

The judicial controversy revolved around a very technical question of interpretation, the determination of whether
the mandates system as originally set up in 1920 contemplated the sort of judicial enforcement being attempted by
Ethiopia and Liberia.[3] However, underlying this technical
controversy was a tense dispute concerning the racial poli-

[1] For a more detailed account of the legal proceeding see Richard
Falk, *South West African Cases: A Preliminary Cost-Accounting, In-
ternational Organization*, The Netherlands, 's Gravenhage: Sijthoff,
N. V., 1967.

[2] Article 2 (2) of the mandate agreement.

[3] Article 7 (2) of the mandate agreement requires that the manda-
tory (South Africa) submit disputes with other members of the
league concerning compliance with the mandate to the Permanent
Court of International Justice in the event that these disputes cannot
be settled by negotiation. Cf. also *South West Africa Cases* (*Preliminary Objections*), ICJ Rep. (1962), p. 319.

cies of the South African government that had been going on since shortly after World War II. The international community, especially as reflected in the General Assembly of the United Nations, was demanding that South Africa abandon the policies and practices associated with *apartheid*, whereas South Africa responded that its racial policies were matters exclusively within domestic concern and that in any event it was unwilling to change them.[4] The recourse to the International Court of Justice was part of an effort to increase the legal basis for eventual coercive action against South Africa; there was no widespread belief on the part of the advocates of the litigation that South Africa would voluntarily comply with an adverse judgment, nor that further efforts by the United Nations at persuasion would succeed in influencing the government in Praetoria. The African group at the United Nations had grown convinced that superior force alone could satisfy their demands *vis-à-vis* South Africa, and the judgment of the Court was being sought to strengthen their campaign to organize international sanctions, especially by putting pressure on the United States and the United Kingdom to take whatever action was needed to implement the Court's decision.[5] Without the active support of these two powerful states there was no prospect for effective sanctions against South Africa, and without an enforceable legal judgment in a limited setting—that is, restricted to the mandated territory of South West Africa—there was no hope of persuading the United States and the United Kingdom to move beyond the verbal denunciation of *apartheid* in the direction of taking the more costly steps that would exert influence on a behavioral level. The assumption here, one evidently encouraged by diplomats from the United States and the United Kingdom, was that inducing compliance with judicially declared positive law would create a much more favorable atmosphere for the eventual employment against

[4] For general background see W. A. Nielsen, *African Battleline*, (New York: Harper & Row, Publishers, 1965), pp. 110–26; David W. Wainhouse, *Remnants of Empire* (New York: Harper & Row, Publishers, 1964), pp. 48–60.

[5] As provided for by Article 94 of the United Nations Charter.

South Africa of various forms of coercion. It should be noted that the moral, social, and political posture of the dispute about *apartheid* was not in issue in the *South West Africa* litigation; the quest for a judgment was part of a quest for political influence arising from the authoritative status of a judicial determination and, especially, from an interest in making use of legal institutions to prepare the way for legitimated coercion. There is, then, at work here the implicit notion that the violent resolution of an inter-group dispute becomes more acceptable to the relevant community if undertaken on the basis of legal authority.[6] It is the same logic that distinguishes the legalized homicide that a state inflicts upon a defendant convicted of murder and sentenced in accordance with legal procedures from the action taken by a lynch mob against a murder suspect.[7] The legal order provides a procedure of inquiry that is supposed to provide an authoritative basis for the use of force.

The role of legal forms in the establishment of legitimacy is a complex and largely neglected subject. We know that the attitudes of those affected by the outcome of the legal procedures depend upon the acceptance of the underlying justice of the particular legal regime. In a totalitarian state where legal institutions merely ratify the desires of the governing elite, there is little additional legitimacy, if any, that derives from the reliance upon a legal proceeding to vindicate a coercive punishment. In contrast, in a society where there is confidence in the independence and impartiality of legal proceedings, there is a tendency—on occasion an excessive tendency—to presuppose that whatever has been decreed by the legal proceeding is legitimate and beyond serious question. In such a situation the demands of justice

---

[6] In general, the idea of peaceful change under the authority of law is central to the establishment and existence of an ordered political community. In essence, the search in international society is to find substitute procedures for the legislative functions discharged in the past by the "institution" of war.

[7] Hans Kelsen regards the capacity of a legal order to classify any use of force as either a sanction or a delict as the essential distinguishing attribute of law. Kelsen, *Principles of International Law* edited by Tucker, revised 2nd edition, Vol. 17 (New York: Holt, Rinehart & Winston, Inc., 1966).

are satisfied by the use of the procedures of law, even if these procedures may be biased or inaccurate in their determination on any given occasion. There are many attempts in literature to demonstrate the moral complacency involved in a mechanical assumption that what is legal is legitimate. Kafka's *The Trial,* Camus' *The Stranger,* and Stendhal's *The Red and the Black* are prominent illustrations of fictional attempts to depict the potentiality for illegitimacy that arises precisely because there exists a prevailing public attitude that what is legal is also legitimate.

In *The South West Africa Cases* it is difficult to assess the degree to which attitudes of legitimacy would support a judicial outcome that decreed the use of force against South Africa. It is certainly true that the willingness of the litigants to submit to the jurisdiction of the International Court of Justice does not imply a willingness to acquiesce in the legitimacy of the relief awarded by an adverse decision. In fact, it would seem reasonable to suppose that if the majority of the Court had ordered South Africa "to cease and desist forthwith" the practice of *apartheid* in South West Africa, such a determination would have been perceived as illegitimate—reflecting bias and pressure—by the governing groups in South Africa. Furthermore, the legitimacy that attaches to *apartheid* would have almost certainly given moral support to the South African government in the likely event that it would have repudiated such a decision. Therefore, the legitimacy that attaches to a legal determination is dependent upon relevant attitudes toward both the justice of the process and the justice of the outcome.

The outcome of the *South West Africa* litigation came as a great surprise to most observers and has aroused great hostility to the procedures of law and to the Court as a legal institution throughout international society.[8] World public opinion appeared stunned that an anti-South Africa litigant

[8] Cf. *The New York Times,* June 19, 1966, p. 1; see also *The New York Times,* Oct. 11, 1966, p. 25, for account of 40–27–13 vote in the Administrative and Budgetary Committee of the General Assembly to withhold $72,500 from the ICJ, previously approved and spent for clerical and salary expenses; the move was sponsored by Guinea and represented a gesture of retaliation.

would suffer a legal defeat when appearing before the judicial organ of the United Nations after a succession of victories achieved through recourse to the political organs of the organization; most dramatically, given the overwhelming and repeated denunciations by the General Assembly over the past decade of *apartheid* as a violation of the Charter of the United Nations, which is an international treaty binding upon members of the organization, including even South Africa, it was difficult to envisage the International Court of Justice doing anything other than affirming the illegality of *apartheid*.

The division among the judges in the World Court reflects a direct confrontation between two major jurisprudential conceptions of the relation of law to social conflict. The prevailing majority emphasized a narrow conception of judicial function that is conditioned by a sharp separation between law and morals and between law and politics. Unless there exists a legally well-established legal ground, and in international society this requires for the jurisprudential conservative strong evidence of consent by the sovereign state that is to be bound, there is no basis for a judicial challenge; the fact that South Africa's racial policies violate world community sentiments is of no legal consequence.[9] This attitude, still influential in European legal thinking, emphasizes the "scientific" character of legal science and the autonomy of the legal order with regard to social and political tendencies. The judge is expected to apply the law as he finds it without regard to its moral, social, or political implications.[10]

Several of the dissenting judges in the *South West Africa* decision adhere to a more sociological variant of jurisprudence. Namely, these judges regard law as essentially part of an ongoing social and political process, the essence of which is to incorporate changing standards of moral well-being; the consequence of this attitude is to emphasize the openness of legal order to infusions of morality and to

[9] This is the legal position best exemplified by the views of Judges Sir Percy Spender and Sir Gerald Fitzmaurice.
[10] See Samuel I. Shuman, *Legal Positivism* (Detroit: Wayne State University Press, 1963).

acknowledge the relevance of politics to the discharge of judicial function. As Judge Tanaka of Japan suggests, "The principle of the protection of human rights is derived from the concept of man as a *person,* and his relationship with society cannot be separated from universal human nature. The existence of human rights does not depend on the will of a State. . . ."[11]

In one sense it is natural to expect the International Court of Justice to reflect the social outlook of those nation-states that took the principal role in its creation. Attitudes toward law are dependent on the overall normative context and therefore the Eurocentric jurisprudence of the International Court of Justice is to be expected, given its locus, its origin, its traditions, and its personnel. In fact, the dependence of legal institutions upon their relevant social and political setting gives some assurance that the legal decisions reached will be received as legitimate. The *South West Africa* decision suggests that the relevant context of the Court needed to be expanded to take fuller account of the expansion of international society to include the participation of the ex-colonial countries of Asia and Africa. Critics of the decision are better advised to direct their efforts at finding ways to overcome the Eurocentric setting rather than to castigate the Court for acting as a court by treating the controversy in light of the Eurocentric setting that continued to prevail, if ever so slightly (as evident by the close vote and the cultural perspectives of the two factions).[12]

This introductory section argues that the mode of legal thought adopted by a judge reflects the influence of his overall social context, including the values associated with

[11] Quoted from p. 313 (temporary text of 1966 judgment).
[12] The actual vote was 7–7, with the tie being broken by Sir Percy Spender, who, as President of the Court, was given a second or "casting" vote. The voting was as follows: for South Africa—Spender (Australia), Gros (France), Winiarski (Poland), Spiropoulos (Greece), Fitzmaurice (United Kingdom), Morelli (Italy), Van Wyk (South Africa); for Ethiopia and Liberia—Jessup (United States), Koretsky (Soviet Union), Koo (China-Taiwan), Forster (Senegal), Mbanefo (Nigeria), Tanaka (Japan), Padilla Nervo (Mexico). This voting pattern discloses the Eurocentric character of the pro-South African majority.

the relations between law and politics and between law and morals. The *South West Africa* litigation illustrates the clash of two very distinct jurisprudential orientations, each of which has a very different bearing on the relevance of law to stress-seeking in man. The conservative jurisprudence regards law as a regime of order established by definite procedures and incorporating a general disposition favorable to a sharp separation between the legal order and social conflict, whereas sociological jurisprudence emphasizes that law is a social process that must be constantly and creatively responsive to challenges posed by a changing social and political environment. The crystallized moral preferences and political demands of the United Nations *vis-à-vis* South Africa condition the entire legal inquiry, rather than being discounted as irrelevant to it. The conservative jurisprudence, in contrast, relies on the stabilizing influence of law as an autonomous source of authority in human affairs that stands aside from moral and political pressures and by this autonomy engenders respect.

Respect for law is achieved by restricting law to a very passive role whenever a political system grows unstable. This passivity is accented in international society by the tradition of deferring to sovereign states and by the absence of a legislative organ able to take account of changing community preferences.

II. The Assumed Opposition between Stress-seeking Behavior and the Objectives of the Legal Order

Conservative jurisprudence has long dominated the legal imagination and as a consequence has inhibited lawyers and jurists from recognizing the dynamic interrelation between legal order and stress-seeking. By and large, legal thought has accepted the ideals of social harmony, images of community and solidarity, and a utilitarian conception of human nature. There has been little inclination on the part of jurists to be explicit about the role of law in providing a framework for socially useful forms of conflict. This lack of consideration is especially surprising in relation to the sort of capitalist ethos prevailing in the United States; a major function assigned to law has been the maintenance of competition through antitrust regulation. The policy underlying this regulation has assumed that the establishment of certain forms of harmony among producers of the same line of products was more dangerous to the public interest than was stressful competition, including price wars that eliminated—"killed"—the less efficient competitors. European regulation of business has assumed, on the contrary, that a greater level of cooperation than is permitted in the United States is in the public interest.[13] Using regulatory techniques to attain the level of beneficial competition is a use of law to sustain socially desirable forms of stress. The comparison of United States and European definitions of "beneficial" in the setting of economic competition suggests the need for comparative inquiry and confirms the assertion that the legal order is a quasi-dependent social variable.

Marxist legal theory, of course, emphasizes the beneficial necessity of class struggle, a struggle enacting the historical drama of the unfolding of higher forms of political order through the stress-induced stimulus of revolutionary action. Marxist thought contends that law reflects the ideology of the dominant class and necessarily functions as a weapon in the class war wielded by the reactionary or oppressive side in any non-Communist society. If law is an instrument of social struggle, its beneficial or detrimental character depends, in theory, on which social class is in power. The international consequence of such an attitude toward the legal order is quite dramatic in a world composed of social systems with different dominant classes. The early Soviet view was that the inherited system of international law was altogether decadent, merely projecting the international interests of the bourgeois class. Increasingly, however, Soviet jurists have emphasized the need for a reformulation of international law in terms of peaceful coexistence, a reformulation that would stress such shared goals as the avoidance of war and the reaffirmation of

[13] See, e.g., *British Nylon Spinners, Ltd. v. Imperial Chemical Industries, Ltd.*, [1952] 2 *All England Law Reports* 780; [1954] *All England Law Reports* 88.

national sovereignty. Although doctrinaire Marxism has vanished as Communist countries have discovered that a convenient and predictable legal framework is essential for their external relations with both Communist and non-Communist countries, there is reason to believe that Communist elites do not respect the law as such, but continue to adopt an instrumental view of the claims of law to regulate behavior, manipulating its rules to serve their interests. Such manipulation is also frequently observed in the international dealings of non-Communist countries as well, and is in certain respects inevitable in view of the discretionary character of many sectors of international law. There is a degree of openness or indefiniteness that invites actors in controversy to pursue their distinctive or exclusive interests whether or not those interests are in harmony.[14]

III. REMARKS ON STRESS-SEEKING WITHIN THE DOMESTIC POLITICAL SYSTEM

The real distinction is not between *pure* ideal-less politics and *impure* ideal-oriented politics, but between a war-like view of politics and a legalitarian view of politics.

Giovanni Sartori
DEMOCRATIC THEORY 35 (1962)

In general terms, the reality of stress-seeking leads to the formulation of individual and group demands that are not normally satisfied by persuasive techniques of assertion. Every political system must take into account the reality of stressful behavior, but the terms of this account are heavily influenced by the characteristics of each particular political system. The remarks below illustrate this influence in light of the distinction between relatively democratic and relatively autocratic political systems.

In a relatively democratic society there is an effort made

---

[14] An example of interests that are in harmony would be conservation of the resources of the high seas or adequacy of international postal service.

to legitimate the expression of certain forms of stressful behavior. The process of legitimation is in part expressive of the dependence of such a government, in myth if not in fact, upon the consent of the governed. In particular, political stability results from giving discontented group interests an opportunity, or at least an apparent opportunity, to express their grievances, and some means to rectify them.

ORGANIZED LABOR: THE LEGITIMATION OF LIMITED COERCION

The history of labor-management relations in the United States illustrates this process. The stormy battle to legalize unions and the strike as modes of self-assertion by working men was a way of introducing some bargaining equality into relationships between labor and management. The idea of a strike was based upon the social utility of legitimating a limited right of coercion. Management often responded by hiring squads of goons, occasionally abetted by the local police, and by relying upon subtler methods of coercion such as union lockouts. As union power grew strong enough to coordinate the strength of labor on an industry-wide basis, an effort was made by pro-business groups to limit the activities of labor. The regulation of labor activities, legislative restrictions on the right to strike, and the emergence of laws on the state level permitting workers to hold jobs without joining a union are indicative of an antilabor backlash. The consequence of this history of action and reaction has been the evolution of a dynamic framework within which the natural conflict of interest between labor —maximum wages—and management—maximum profits— can be reconciled in a manner that acknowledges both the positive function of stressful behavior and the dangerous social consequences of a *laissez-faire* attitude toward it. As the character of the society changes, adaptations take place with respect to the content given to this distinction between the positive and negative effects of stressful behavior. Essentially, the interplay of domestic pressures produces a kind of balancing mechanism that affirms the right to rely upon stress-seeking dispositions as a technique of competition and denies this right to the extent that it results in violence or causes major social dislocations.

CIVIL-RIGHTS MOVEMENT

The effort of the civil-rights movement to awaken in Negroes a consciousness of their deprived status has generated a similar set of responses. Recourse to legal institutions by the civil-rights groups, especially to courts, was useful at one stage in the campaign to make effective the assertion of demands for social reform, giving publicity and endowing with legitimacy the objectives of the movement. The legitimation of these social demands through their formal legal ratification helped to build public support for the assertion of nonlegal pressure by civil-rights groups in those parts of the United States where the relevant legal standards were rejected. Sit-ins, boycotts of discriminatory facilities, marches, and demonstrations became acceptable means of communicating certain claims for equal treatment and dramatizing demands for reform which, if left unsatisfied, would lead eventually to violence. There seems to be considerable reason to suppose that the efforts of the Federal government to promote civil rights during the last decade resulted from the successful political utilization of stressful behavior on behalf of the Negro minority. An acquiescent Negro community would not have aroused the moral indignation of the society.

In the last few years a countertendency associated with a white backlash can be detected. The Negro leadership has grown more radical, in part because of a redefinition of its goals in more comprehensive terms requiring correspondingly more coercive means. As a consequence, the spirit of accommodation that set the dominant mood of white America until 1965 is increasingly giving way to the drive to exert further control over unauthorized coercion. Therefore, it seems likely that antiriot laws will be enacted and enforced, that the civil-rights movement will be either blunted or escalated, and that challenges directed by the impatient new leadership of the civil-rights movement at the repressive capabilities of the community will be unsuccessful. The outcome of the referendum on the November 1966 ballot in New York City repudiating a Civilian Review Board competent to receive complaints about police activities provides some evidence of a reaction against the drift of the civil-rights movement. No one event is decisive. Patterns emerge in response to changing balances of domestic forces.

The important conclusion is that in a relatively democratic society the legal process is constantly adapting the rules of the game with regard to the limits of permissible stressful behavior. There is a general willingness to tolerate stress-seeking within certain limits as an effective political instrumentality, but the legal order reinforces such limits in a manner responsive to the dominant mood.

OTHER EXAMPLES OF THE USE OF LAW TO REGULATE STRESSFUL BEHAVIOR

Any political system tends to increase the extent of social control whenever the ends proposed by stress-seeking behavior endanger the identity or survival of the system, even if the means relied upon do not involve a very high degree of coercion. The regulation of the domestic Communist Party in the United States and the punishment of treason everywhere are illustrative cases for studying this aspect of the relationship between law and stress-seeking. More dramatic, if more special, cases are those involving the "crucifixion" of the false savior or those arising from the failure to solve the royal murder. The story of Christ illustrates the former category and the continuing debate about the assassination of President Kennedy illustrates the latter one. In both situations the legal order plays a crucial role in terms of vindicating the official ideology and legitimating the claims of the governing elite. Shakespeare was fascinated by this problem, posing again and again the questionable legitimacy of a claim to govern so long as the controversy surrounding a royal murder continued. The fate of the Warren Commission, arising from its assigned role to restore confidence and its partial failure to do so, can be explained by its inability to provide an official version of the assassination that was sufficiently convincing to put doubts finally to rest; within the United States the authoritativeness of the report was temporarily able to put an end to controversy, but with the passage of time and under the pressure of independent scrutiny, the controversy has been revived to a point where there is now more public controversy about the assassination than at any time since its occurrence.

The point here is that the most fundamental varieties of stressful behavior seek to promote or to prevent drastic change in the nature of the political system. The legal process, as an institutionalized aspect of the existing system, emphasizes system maintenance, which may include an encouragement of certain moderate proposals for system reform. In a democratic society the ideology of the ruling classes regards a capacity to absorb system reform as the best strategy to achieve system maintenance.

An autocratic society tends to disallow system reform through popular initiative. The legal system does not tolerate any pressure directed at demanding social and political change, the institution of the purge is often an essential aspect of rulership, and the legal system tends to uphold orthodoxy and to proscribe as heresy any unwanted modification of it. Whatever change is allowed to take place is introduced by those administering the government, and disguised as a mere continuation. The legal system is regulative, devoted to system maintenance in a political environment hostile to any challenge directed at either the legitimacy or adequacy of existing social and political arrangements. The legal system helps to sustain the rigidity by suppressing the assertion in any effective form of demands for social change.

The government of South Africa in the last decade has moved in the direction of orthodoxy and suppression in running its own domestic society. A political vacuum is likely to result. The possibility of accommodating antagonistic group interests is increasingly ruled out. Those who oppose *apartheid* in any of its principal dimensions must choose between suppression and tacit acquiescence. The effect is to eliminate the middle ground between the *status quo* and revolutionary violence. In such a political system there is, contrary to the facts, a pretension of political solidarity that does not exist. This pretension is an aspect of a larger illusion of solidarity that is sustained by heavy sanctions imposed on any conduct inconsistent with this illusion.

If an authoritarian regime seizes control of the state, there is a tendency to use the apparatus of law to vindicate its claims to govern. The leaders of the old system are prosecuted and executed, as was done in Cuba after Castro came to power; normally, later in its career, such a regime invokes the legal system to purge members of its own elite alleged to be engaged in counterrevolutionary activity. Such trials dramatize the ethos of submission and operate to communicate throughout the society a warning to anyone who might be tempted to act in opposition to the wishes of the prevailing government. These trials make it plain that if such a government is unwilling to spare even its own elite, then there is no prospect for mercy toward the general public. The role of law is to intimidate, to internalize anti-regime stress-seeking in such a way as to produce fear and hatred, and to encourage pro-regime stress-seeking by means of militarism, repressive practices, and by offering citizens of the dominant groups bureaucratic rationalizations and sublimations for direct or indirect expressions of intergroup hatred. The Frankfurt trials of the administrators of the Auschwitz death camp illustrate this phenomenon in extreme form.

The moderation of a highly authoritarian regime, as has been the general drift in the Soviet Union since the death of Stalin in 1953, usually is accompanied by a reduction of drastic repression. In particular, the cost of dissent is no longer to be measured in terms of prolonged imprisonment or death. At least within the realm of words, a framework emerges that protects the critic of existing policies. The illusion of solidarity is shattered and pressures for reform from below are generated.

If the regime has been based upon the suppression of a

distinct group or class, especially if this group or class is in the majority, then the prospects decline for an accommodation through gradual adjustment of differences. The suppression generates hatred, and a situation of struggle is predicated in which the outcome will involve some form of domination by the winning side. The situation in Algeria between 1954 and 1962 took on some of these dimensions as the anticolonial war against the French persisted in an unresolved state; the war for control of South Vietnam, and the future of South Africa illustrate instances in which the challenge directed at a repressive regime will probably eventuate in either the restoration of the old pattern of domination or the substitution of some new but equivalent pattern.

IV. Remarks on Stress-seeking and Law within the International Political System

The challenges of the nuclear age have accentuated the search of centuries for a solution to the problem of war. Most proposals emphasize the desirability of strengthening the capacity of international institutions to maintain world peace and usually involve plans whereby nations divest themselves of their right to maintain national military establishments. Constitutional revisions of international society are unlikely to come about except as a consequence of a peace settlement after a third world war or as a result of a successful world conquest by a nation or an aligned group of nations. Without such a coercive transition from a condition of decentralization to one of centralization no very significant change in the structure of international society can be anticipated.

The previous paragraph suggests only that the transfer of significant military capability from the national level to the supranational level is unlikely to result and has not in the past resulted except as a reaction to an international catastrophe. It may be that, in time, a certain degree of supranationalization of the security function will occur by voluntary action on the regional level. Certain hesitant moves in this direction can be discussed in the inter-American system. Also, there are partly successful efforts at supranational integration with regard to nonmilitary subject matter, most notably the progress toward European economic integration that has taken place since World War II. But such integrative phenomena on the regional level are not necessarily relevant to the prospects for integration on a global level. In the global setting there is no "other," the existence of which provides part of the basis for regional integration. At this stage in international society it is almost impossible to assess the strength and significance of regionalism to the ordering of international relations on a world level.

International law is quasi-dependent upon the decentralized structure of international society. This degree of dependence results in the conferring of a dominant role on the principal nation-states that remain the centers of power, and hence authority, in the system. To understand the limited role of international law it is essential to accept its decentralized operation, and to subordinate international institutions to a secondary position. In this regard, the main role of international law is to provide a framework for the conduct of international relations within agreed limits, the exceeding of which limits is likely to lead to destabilizing and dangerous responses.

The basic conception of international legal order since the Peace of Westphalia (1648) has been to coordinate the activities of national units each supreme within its territorial sphere. The competitive pursuit of territory, wealth, and prestige has generated conflict involving violence. Until after World War I, war was a legal form of competitive behavior. The antiwar effort of international law was confined to moderating its scope—laws of neutrality—and mitigating its cruelty—laws of war. As with economic competition in capitalist countries, international warfare was tolerated as a medium of adjustment. International law legitimated the fruits of conquest by validating the new rights and duties created in a peace treaty dictated by the victor. War has shocked the conscience of mankind from the dawn of human history, but the persistence of war as the main legislative energy in international history is undeniable.

Since after World War I recourse to war has been legally prohibited. However, the legal prohibition has not been accompanied by any comparable restructuring of international society nor by any important transformation of national attitudes. The extent of international peace rests much more upon the stalemate occurring in the exchange of mutual threats between antagonistic power groupings than upon any confidence in the solidarity of world support in the United Nations and elsewhere for a global system that implements the legal prohibition upon force by siding against an aggressor or violator of the peace. Decentralization persists and the legal prohibitions upon force are upheld by the military posture of potential enemies. The precariousness of such a system has aroused forebodings of catastrophe since the atomic explosions over Hiroshima and Nagasaki. There are various indications that individuals and groups are dissatisfied with the decentralized ordering capabilities of the international system, regarding these capabilities as woefully insufficient to cope with the dangers of the contemporary international environment. One relevant inference is that the socially destructive tendencies of stressful behavior among states can no longer be held in sufficient check by the mere unregulated interplay of competitive forces. It is this situation that has led worried individuals to sound alarm bells and warn that mankind is doomed unless there is soon an acceptance of world government. Against this background of appraisal and skepticism, it remains possible to identify some rather characteristic attempts of law as a social technique to constrain and channel stress within international society as presently constituted.

THE MANAGEMENT OF INTERNATIONAL CRISES

International law facilitates precise communication of claims and counterclaims by rival powers in periods of crisis. Such precision discourages overreaction and facilitates acquiescence by one side to the claims of the other.

The Cuban missile crisis of 1962 offers a paradigm.[15] The legal adviser to the Secretary of State played an important role, not in determining the policy to interdict the emplacement of Soviet missiles on Cuban soil, but in executing this policy in such a way as to minimize friction. Departure from the relevant legal standards applicable to the freedom of the seas and to the use of force was minimized. The regional community gave its formal approval to the unilateral claim of the United States, thereby giving a cover of legitimation to the undertaking. A pledge by the United States to refrain from invading Cuba injected an element of mutuality into the transaction and indicated a willingness by the United States to acquiesce, in form, at least, to part of the Soviet counterclaim. The structuring of this crisis in terms of respecting, to the extent possible, legal norms, seeking the support of the organized regional community, and basing settlement on a semblance of reciprocity is illustrative of the manner in which international law can help solve the complex tasks of crisis management.[16]

POLITICAL MOBILIZATION

Respect for enacted law exerts some independent influence upon national behavior even with regard to problems of war and peace. The failure to respond to a violation of clearly established legal restraints leads to their obsolescence. In the Suez crisis of 1956 the United States opposed its closest allies, in part at least, to indicate that its support for the legal norms of restraint on the use of force took precedence over diplomatic alignments. The breaking of a clear legal boundary helps to mobilize the kind of political energies that are required to make a response effective. This mobilization process also followed the attack upon South Korea in 1950 by North Korea, again a clear challenge at the primary claim of law—

[15] For analysis along these lines see Albert and Roberta Wohlstetter, "Controlling the Risks in Cuba," *Adelphi Papers* (London), No. 17 (April 1965).

[16] Cf. Abram Chayes, "Law and the Quarantine of Cuba," *Foreign Affairs*, Vol. 41 (1962), p. 552.

namely, the settlement of international disputes by recourse to overt and massive military aggression across an acknowledged frontier.

The ineffective response by the United States in Vietnam has been, in part, a consequence of the ambiguous facts surrounding the allegation of aggression by North Vietnam, and the larger ambiguity arising from the absence of a clear boundary between civil and international warfare. The conduct of North Vietnam, unlike that of North Korea in 1950, appears to be conduct in a borderland area of behavior inhabited by various forms of coercive intervention in the internal affairs of foreign states. The interventionary nature of world politics in the present era makes formal prohibition a rather meaningless ritual.[17] The facts do not establish a clear violation and the attempt to undertake a neutralizing response is likely to be tentative and controversial even within the country acting on behalf of the alleged victim.

Legal events are relevant to political mobilization in a quite different way. The African countries are eager to persuade the United Nations to take coercive action in Southern Africa. The members of the organization with the requisite military capabilities, especially the United States and the United Kingdom, possess conflicting economic and political interests, and as a consequence are reluctant to implement their verbal support for the African demands with significant sanctions. One way to mobilize support for sanctions is to establish clear legal boundaries that will be violated by the state that is to become the target of sanctions.

International law, then, can be used by states that lack capabilities for independent action to find support for their claims through a process of political mobilization. This process might be regarded as a partial substitute for traditional forms of coercive settlement. Revisionist states increasingly seek to organize centralized uses of force under

---

[17] Cf. M. Halpern, "The Morality and Politics of Intervention," and Falk, "Janus Tormented: The International Law of Internal War," in J. N. Rosenau, ed., *International Aspects of Civil Strife* (Princeton: Princeton University Press, 1964).

the auspices of the United Nations—authorized coercion might begin to take the place of war as an ultimate form of international legislation. It is the routinization of authorized coercion that we associate with the operations of an effective law government in domestic society.

SOCIAL AND POLITICAL CHANGE

Closely related to the mobilization of the international system is the jurisprudential, controversial process whereby states receive tacit authorization to employ violence to carry out legislative or revisionist programs. The role of international law in this setting is to legitimate the legislative objective, thereby creating an atmosphere supportive of the means used to attain it. For instance, the condemnation of colonialism that has taken place over and over again in the General Assembly alters the legal status and community response to anticolonial uses of force. The extent of alteration of legal status to be attributed to action by the General Assembly is presently a subject of heated debate among international lawyers.

India's conquest of Goa in 1961 or the overt support given by African states in recent years to the rebellions in Angola and Mozambique illustrate extreme forms of this function of law. These anticolonialist efforts take on a role that is functionally similar to the actual authorization of force or to the explicit organization of sanctions directly under the auspices of the United Nations. The stress-seeking energy challenges the *status quo* and provides the legislative basis for initiating changes despite the absence of a legislative organ in international life.

RULES OF THE GAME

The reality of international conflict is undisputed. Increasingly, however, the costs and dangers of military conflict among the leading states are perceived as creating the need for an effective system of minimum order, or—as the Soviet Union and their allies prefer to call it—a law of peaceful coexistence.[18] Such a regime of legal order attempts to specify certain mutually desirable limits on stressful behavior in international society, including especially a renunciation of all intention to wage war or to intervene forcibly to coerce a change in regime in a foreign country.

These rules of the game establish a constitutive structure as the basis of international relations and are constantly being adapted by the players to the exigencies and vagaries of new situations. The main arena of uncertainty—that is, as to agreed-upon limits on coercive competition among states—presently involves the relation of third states to a condition of civil strife, the outcome of which is likely to alter the international or regional balance of power. There are some basic rules of restraint that act to moderate the consequences of this competition without altogether forbidding its occurrence.[19]

1. No use of nuclear weapons;
2. No objection to nonmilitary forms of adverse intervention;
3. No counterintervention in the immediate sphere of influence of the rival superpower;
4. No military intervention, except in an emergency, without some indication of multilateral support;
5. No military counterintervention outside the national boundaries of the territory wherein the struggle is going on.

These illustrative rules set limits on the content of permissible behavior. These limits remain tacit so as, in part, to avoid any appearance of incompatibility with the Charter system of norms that are premised on false assumptions of social solidarity and presuppose a nonexistent commitment to noncoercive procedures of political change. The rules of the game posit a framework for international com-

---

[18] E.g., Myres S. McDougal and Florentino P. Feliciano, *Law and Minimum World Public Order* (New Haven: Yale University Press, 1961).

[19] This section is based on a presentation by Roger Fisher and myself to a conference on Peaceful Revolution sponsored by the Stanley Foundation in Washington, D.C., on October 14–15, 1966.

petition for dominance that seeks above all to avoid the sort of competition—general warfare—that would be mutually destructive. The "third world" offers the testing ground of these rules of the game by providing arenas wherein competition can be carried on without substantial risk to the great powers. The war in Vietnam illustrates both the process and the strain upon its limits. The unprecedented scale and duration of United States counter-intervention, as well as the sustained violation of the fifth rule, indicate that the framework may not be able to contain the conflict within tolerable limits. There are two main problems created by violations of the rules of the game. First, the ceiling placed upon maximum competition shows signs of giving way as the intensity, duration, and scope of violence escalate. Second, a precedent is established that makes less authoritative the more moderate prior framework, and thus makes it harder to contain a subsequent conflict of a sort similar to Vietnam (e.g., Thailand) within the rules of the game.

The role of international law is to set forth rules of the game that serve the interests of the dominant actors. These rules of the game are quite inconsistent with the Charter of the United Nations precisely because the Charter does not allow for stress-seeking in terms that are realistic, given the present conditions and structure of international relations. At the same time the ordering effort of these rules is similar to that of the Charter rules—limitations on state discretion to avoid socially destructive conduct.

SUPRANATIONAL TRENDS

Stress-seeking may serve to promote the integration of international society or, more likely, sectors of it. The realistic projection of a common enemy is a unifying energy, calling for sacrifices of identity and independence. The science-fiction solution to problems of world order usually is by way of meeting the threat of extraterrestrial aggression by the rapid transition to a world state. Stress provides one basis, then, for moving beyond the nation-state.

Since the earth has, as yet, no common enemy, the integrating effects of stress are seen on a subsystemic or regional scale. For instance, Israel as the common enemy in the Middle East provides the main positive energy in the efforts to promote Pan-Arab objectives. It is the common enemy that mitigates some of the competitive pressures and somewhat overcomes inertia, thereby allowing the Arab states to work within the framework of the Arab League. The success and failure of the movement toward European integration in both the security and welfare fields has been largely dependent upon the extent of the perceived external threat.

External stress may be generated or consciously manipulated to promote law and order within domestic society. Sukarno seems to have concocted the confrontation with Malaysia between 1963 and 1965 primarily to create—which it failed eventually to do—the domestic basis for stable rulership. The possible correlation between external stress-seeking and domestic legal order suggests a further example of the socially constructive uses to which stress-seeking may be put. There is a great need to study systematically the internal conditions under which external challenges or adversaries are integrative rather than disintegrative. Obviously such a study must include a consideration of different kinds of external challenges and their impact on different sorts of domestic settings at various stages. The successful manipulation of the outer enemy is partly dependent on the art of mass communication and the extent to which the risks associated with combat are perceived as desirable by the domestic populace. If the risks are not deemed worth taking or the contention that the external actor is an enemy is not generally credible, then the creation of an external challenge may be domestically disintegrative.

V. Conclusion

This survey of stress-seeking and legal order suggests the complexity of the inquiry. In particular, it is essential to clarify the causal relationship between stress-seeking and human welfare in a manner sufficiently sophisticated to take account of benefits as well as detriments. Instead of seeking ways to eliminate stress-seeking behavior it would seem desirable to search for means to lead stress-seeking in socially useful directions. Part of the point of this essay is that law has been used implicitly to carry out this re-channeling task despite the explicit myths to the contrary.[20] A further point is that it is important for social scientists to deal with stress-seeking as a basic energy resource that has no intrinsic social utility or disutility but which, like other energy resources, can be used destructively or not. It is time to plan consciously the beneficial manipulation of stress-seeking, especially in the international sphere of human relations.

[20] Groups advocating "world peace through world law" usually subscribe to the naïve view that all forms of stress-seeking are inimical to the objectives of social and legal order. A prominent, although extreme, scholarly example of this kind of thinking is to be found in B. Sohn, *World Peace Through World Law,* 3rd revised edition (Cambridge: Harvard University Press, 1966).

Selected Works of the Contributors

Bernard, Jessie. "Factors in the Distribution of Success in Marriage," *American Journal of Sociology*, Vol. 40 (July 1934), pp. 49–60.

——, with Kaplan, A. D. H., and Williams, Faith M. *Family Income and Expenditure in the Southeastern Region, 1935–1936* (Washington: U. S. Government Printing Office, 1939).

——. "Differential Influence of the Business Cycle on the Number of Marriages in Several Age Groupings," *Social Forces,* Vol. 18, No. 4 (May 1940), pp. 539–51.

——. *American Family Behavior* (New York: Harper & Brothers, 1942).

——. "Where is the Modern Sociology of Conflict?" *American Journal of Sociology*, Vol. 56, No. 1 (July 1950), pp. 11–16.

——. *Remarriage, A Study of Marriage* (New York: The Dryden Press, 1956).

——. *Academic Women* (University Park, Pa.: The Pennsylvania State University Press, 1961).

——. *American Community Behavior,* revised edition (originally published 1949) (New York: Holt, Rinehart & Winston, Inc., 1962).

——. "Some Current Conceptualizations in the Field of Conflict," *American Journal of Sociology*, Vol. 70, No. 4 (January 1965), pp. 442–54.

——. *Marriage and the Family Among Negroes* (Englewood Cliffs, N.J.: Prentice-Hall, Inc., 1966).

Burke, Kenneth. *The White Oxen and Other Stories* (New York: Albert and Charles Boni, 1924).

——. *The Grammar of Motives* (Englewood Cliffs, N.J.: Prentice-Hall, Inc., 1945).

——. *The Rhetoric of Motives* (Englewood Cliffs, N.J.: Prentice-Hall, Inc., 1950).

——. *Counter-Statement,* 2nd edition, revised (originally published 1931) (Los Altos, Calif.: Hermes Publications, 1953).

——. *Permanence and Change,* 2nd edition, revised (originally published 1935) (Los Altos, Calif.: Hermes Publications, 1954).

——. *The Philosophy of Literary Form* (New York: Vintage Books, Inc., 1957).

——. *Attitudes Toward History,* 2nd edition, revised (originally published 1937) (Los Altos, Calif.: Hermes Publications, 1959).

——. *Rhetoric of Religion* (Boston: Beacon Press, Inc., 1961).

Davis, David Brion. *Homicide in American Fiction, 1798–1860* (Ithaca: Cornell University Press, 1957).

——. "Some Ideological Functions of Prejudice in Ante-Bellum America," *American Quarterly,* Vol. 15, No. 2 (Summer 1963), pp. 115–25.

——. *The Problem of Slavery in Western Culture* (Ithaca: Cornell University Press, 1966).

Falk, Richard A. "The Relations of Law to Culture, Power, and Justice," *Ethics,* Vol. 72 (October 1961), pp. 12–27.

——. *Law, Morality, and War in the Contemporary World* (New York: Frederick A. Praeger, Inc., 1963).

——. *The Role of Domestic Courts in the International Legal Order* (Syracuse, N.Y.: Syracuse University Press, 1964).

——. "The Complexity of Sabbatino," *American Journal of International Law,* Vol. 58, No. 4 (October 1964), pp. 935–51.

——, with Mendlovitz, S. H. (eds.). *The Strategy of World Order,* 4 volumes (New York: World Law Fund, 1966).

Houston, Charles S., with Bates, Robert H., *et al. Five Miles High: The Story of an Attack on the Second Highest Mountain in the World by Members of the First American Karakoram Expedition* (New York: Dodd, Mead & Company, Inc.,1939).

——, and Bates, Robert H. *K-2, The Savage Mountain* (New York: McGraw-Hill Book Co., Inc., 1954).

Klausner, Samuel Z. "Social Class and Self-Concept," *Journal of Social Psychology,* Vol. 38 (1953), pp. 201–5.

——. "Immigrant Absorption and Social Tension in Israel: A Case Study of Iraqi Jewish Immigrants," *Middle East Journal,* Vol. 9, No. 3 (Summer 1955), pp. 281–94.

——. "Inferential Visibility and Sex Norms in the Middle East," *Journal of Social Psychology,* Vol. 63 (1964), pp. 1–29.

——. *Psychiatry and Religion* (New York: The Free Press of Glencoe, 1964).

——. "Sacred and Profane Meanings of Blood and Alcohol," *Journal of Social Psychology,* Vol. 64 (1964), pp. 27–43.

—— (ed.). *The Quest for Self-Control* (New York: The Free Press, 1965).

——. "Rationalism and Empiricism in Studies of Behavior in Stressful Situations," *Behavioral Science,* Vol. 11, No. 5 (September 1966), pp. 329–41.

Marshall, Samuel L. A. *Blitzkrieg* (New York: William Morrow & Company, Inc., 1940).

——. *Armies On Wheels* (New York: William Morrow & Company, Inc., 1941).

——. *Island Victory* (New York: Penguin Books, Inc., 1944).

——. *Pork Chop Hill* (New York: William Morrow & Company, Inc., 1956).

——. *Sinai Victory* (New York: William Morrow & Company, Inc., 1958).

——. *Men Against Fire: The Problem of Battle Command in Future War* (New York: Apollo Editions, 1961).

——. *The Officer As A Leader* (Harrisburg, Pa.: Stackpole Books, 1966).

——. *The Soldier's Load and the Mobility of a Nation*, revised edition (originally published 1950) (Quantico, Va.: Marine Corps Association, 1966).

McNeil, Elton B., and Blum, Gerald S. "Handwriting and Psychosexual Dimensions of Personality," *Journal of Projective Techniques & Personality Assessment*, Vol. 16 (1952), pp. 476–84.

—— (ed.). "Therapeutic Camping for Disturbed Youth," *Journal of Social Issues*, Vol. 13 (1957), pp. 1–64.

——. "Aggression in Fantasy and Behavior," *Journal of Consulting Psychology*, Vol. 26 (1962), pp. 232–40.

——. "The Paradox of Education for the Gifted," in Estrin, Herman A., and Goode, Delmer (eds.), *College and University Teaching* (Dubuque, Iowa: Wm. C. Brown Company, 1964).

——. *The Concept of Human Development* (Belmont, Calif.: Wadsworth Publishing Company, Inc., 1966).

Torrance, E. Paul. *Guiding Creative Talent* (Englewood Cliffs, N.J.: Prentice-Hall, Inc., 1962).

——. *Education and the Creative Potential* (Minneapolis: University of Minnesota Press, 1963).

——. *Constructive Behavior: Stress, Personality, and Mental Health* (Belmont, Calif.: Wadsworth Publishing Company, Inc., 1965).

——. *Gifted Children in the Classroom* (New York: The Macmillan Co., 1965).

——. "Scientific Views of Creativity and Its Development," *Daedalus*, Vol. 94 (Summer 1965), pp. 663–81.

ANCHOR BOOKS

ANTHROPOLOGY AND ARCHAEOLOGY